Positive Effective Parenting

Positive Effective Parenting

Carol Lynne
B.S. Psychology

Edited by: *Carol Sellinger*   Forward by: *Cathy Bice*

authorHOUSE®

AuthorHouse™
1663 Liberty Drive
Bloomington, IN 47403
www.authorhouse.com
Phone: 1-800-839-8640

Published by AuthorHouse   03/14/2012

ISBN: 978-1-4685-3723-9 (sc)
ISBN: 978-1-4685-3721-5 (e)

Library of Congress Control Number: 2011963713

POSITIVE EFFECTIVE PARENTING
P.E.P.

TABLE OF CONTENTS

Dedicated to the memory of Charles Fortmeyer

And Jon Sellinger

Two Bright Lights in My Life

ACKNOWLEDGMENTS

This work is the result of my life long passion for helping children everywhere as well as those responsible for their care and well being. It began in my heart 15 years ago while teaching parenting education classes at Interface Children, Family Services; a local human services agency in Ventura, CA. Over these years there have been numerous people who have supported my efforts in this endeavor. I only wish I could list them all. I regret I can not.

First, I would like to thank my husband, Jon Sellinger, for teaching me there is nothing I cannot do. Then to my father, Charles Fortmeyer, for making me laugh when all I wanted to do was cry.

A big thank you goes to my sister Cathy Bice for making me feel that "Positive Effecting Parenting" is worthy of being published.

Thank you to the Interface Children, Family Services' teachers and facilitators for inspiring me to write this book in the first place.

Finally the biggest thank you goes to my son and his wife, Ryan and Kim Bradshaw for always saying, "You can do it Mom" even when I thought I couldn't. Moreover, thank you Ryan and Kim for giving me the best gift ever and my biggest inspiration; my precious granddaughter, Bryanna Lynne Bradshaw.

FORWARD
By Cathy Bice

I feel honored that I have the opportunity to write the forward for this wonderful book. Carol Lynne is my older sister so I have known her my whole life. She has been, at times, my mentor, my teacher, my team mate and even a shoulder to cry on. I am proud of the work she has done for the last 15 years teaching parents techniques to raise healthy, happy and self-sufficient children.

I believe that "*Positive Effective Parenting*" will help parents and other child care-givers learn to make child rearing more efficient and pleasant. Most of those working with children, such as teachers, child therapists and more, must have special training. However, parents often get no such formalized training. In the past, families relied on imitating the same family discipline that they saw their own parents using. They lived in an autocratic society where parents used the old "do as I say" method of discipline and did not let children have any rights to their own decisions.

However we have moved into a more democratic way of doing things and this includes raising our children. Carol guides you, the reader, in this direction. She shows that children of today expect to be treated with respect and dignity. And, we must use different parenting techniques than were used in the past.

I believe that "*Positive Effecting Parenting*" is unique in that it includes not only the traditional subjects such as: discipline and behavior modification but also such topics as temperament, stress management and anger management.

I feel this is a must read for all of those who work with children. Raising children today is not an easy job but "*Positive Effecting Parenting*" can help you find ways to make it a little easier.

INTRODUCTION

"Positive Effective Parenting" aims to guide the reader on how to become an effective parent or child care giver for today's children.

In "Positive Effective Parenting" we propose that child care givers need training, especially when tasked with raising children in today's modern society. Some may say that parenting is instinctual-something that comes naturally and, therefore, cannot be learned. This book claims that although being a parent is the hardest and heaviest responsibility we have to face, it is also a task we are "poorly" prepared for.

One of the factors that affect parenting methods is society. The drastic change from society's autocratic to democratic attitude causes families to shift as well. Parents should no longer treat their children as inferior but as an equal "in terms of worth as human beings." I suggest that modern parenting methods must be based on "democratic" principles and techniques that will empower children to grow into responsible and self-regulating adults.

"Positive Effective Parenting" walks the reader along some of the positive and effective ways of parenting that are grounded on "principles of equality and mutual respect." With these two foundations, parents will be able to raise their children without taking control of their lives.

The goal is not to be perfect but to gain understanding, compassion and wisdom that will help you enjoy your child, yourself and parenting. Remember, the job of parenting is to help your children develop healthy self-esteem and the necessary skills to be effective, happy and self-regulating adults. Good luck and enjoy!

POSITIVE EFFECTIVE PARENTING
P.E.P.

CHAPTER ONE
Family Systems

CHAPTER ONE

Family Systems

TARGET POPULATION

"Positive Effective Parenting" will benefit everyone who has the responsibility for the care and well-being of children everywhere.

MAJOR GOAL OF THIS BOOK

For more than 15 years I have had the privilege of offering guidance to many families and individuals who attended my Positive Effective Parenting classes.

The major goal of this book is to give you some understanding and skills that will enable you to put some P.E.P. in your parenting STEP. It will help you to raise happy, successful, self-regulating adults by using Positive Effective Parenting skills. This parenting education workbook is designed to help you make changes in your children's attitudes and behaviors. It will give parents, and other child care providers, ways to decrease conflicts, stimulate communication and cooperation, raise self-esteem and enhance what is already working. It can also help you change the quality of adult-child relationships through specialized training geared to all who are responsible for the care and well-being of children

WHAT YOU WILL LEARN IN THIS POSITIVE EFFECTIVE PARENTING WORKBOOK

- The developmental needs of your children at different ages.
- How to express your anger in a healthy way.
- How to nurture, empower, validate, encourage and respect your children.
- How to encourage positive changes in your children's behavior and attitudes.
- How to reduce conflicts and provide effective means for conflict resolution.
- How to heighten the confidence and self-esteem of your children.
- How to engender mutual respect and cooperation.
- How to treat your children with respect and dignity.

3

- Learn about your child's temperament.
- Learn how to mange stress and anger.
- Learn how to parent a child of divorce.
- Learn how to design strategies for healthier approaches to parenting.

Your major goal as a parent is:

_____

_____

_____

_____

_____

_____

_____

PARENTING TODAY VS YESTERDAY

Why do parents need training? Isn't parenting something we just know how to do? Can't we just do it like our parents did? We turned out OK. These are questions many of you may be asking right now, and the answer is No! Raising children is one of the most difficult jobs we will face in our lifetime. Yet it is the one for which we may be the least prepared. Learning "on the job" or modeling our parents' parenting techniques can be full of pitfalls. Stanley Kruger put it well when he said, "Of all the responsibilities people are called upon to undertake in life it is hard to imagine one more perplexing and more demanding or a more rigorous test of wisdom and patience and judgment under fire than that of being a parent. Nor one for which most people are so poorly prepared." This statement is very true. Parenting is one thing we weren't taught in school; no parenting 101. For a long time, our society has demanded special training for all kinds of workers who deal with children—teachers, counselors, psychologists, social workers, and child psychiatrists. Yet the only way most of us learned to parent was from modeling our parents, and that is similar to the blind leading the blind.

The need for training parents is becoming well recognized because it is more and more evident that many child-rearing methods of the past aren't working today. The reasons for this are mainly related to social change. In recent years there has been a shift in our society from an autocratic attitude to a democratic attitude and the demand for social equality has presented challenges most people, especially parents, are not well prepared to meet.

Most of us grew up in an autocratic society where there was a "pecking" order of superiors and inferiors. In the home, the father was the highest authority, mother was subservient to him and the children were subservient to them both. Everyone knew their place and acted accordingly. However, society has made some drastic changes in a very short period of time. There are many reasons for these changes including TV, movies, computers, the decrease in two parent families and the decrease in extended family support. The important thing is that the switch from an autocratic society to a more democratic society has brought about fundamental questions about the proper basis for social order. Groups of people once thought to be in a lower position within society become tired of being treated as inferior. Examples of this are workers organizing unions to protect their rights, minorities demanding equal treatment and women who are challenging the principle of the "superior" male.

Of course children have been influenced by this change in social relationships and they have decided that they have rights too. In seeking their rights, children are no longer willing to submit to the arbitrary rules of adults. The old "Do it because I said so," rule is no longer acceptable to many children. It's becoming evident that the relationship between parents and their children has changed and that parenting styles we once thought were effective don't seem to be working any longer.

What do we do now? We must be willing to create a new relationship between adults and children. We must develop new Positive Effective Parenting techniques based on "democratic" principles and techniques that will empower children to grow into responsible, self-regulating adults. These new techniques must be based on the principles of equality and mutual respect. Equality, as it is used here, does not mean sameness. Adults and children are not the "same" physically, mentally (knowledge base), legally or economically. Equality here means that the children are recognized as being equal to the adults in terms of their worth as human beings and that they are entitled to always be treated with dignity and respect.

OUR JOB AS PARENTS

Our job as parents is not to control our children but to empower them so that they learn to control themselves. One of the most empowering things you can do for your children is to validate their feelings and thoughts. Parents need to take care of basic needs that children are not developmentally capable of taking care of themselves. We must provide an atmosphere in which they can be and feel safe to explore, learn and grow into responsible, self-regulating adults. How do we do this? We do it by setting limits within which they can explore and set some of their own boundaries. Basically, parenting is providing someone with something they need to live and grow that they can't yet give themselves and to teach them the skills necessary to eventually be self-sufficient. President John F. Kennedy put it well when he said, "A child mis-educated is a child lost."

WHAT EFFECTIVE PARENTS DO

1. Set and maintain appropriate limits based on the child's age and development.
2. Permit choice. They give children an opportunity to make their own choices within appropriate limits.
3. Hold the children accountable for their decisions without using blame.
4. Use encouragement generously.
5. Validate the children's feelings.
6. Influence and teach rather than control and dominate.
7. Empower their children.
8. Discipline rather than punish.
9. Practice mutual respect. We must give respect before we can get respect.
10. Communicate openly and positively.
11. Use natural and logical consequences rather than retaliatory ones.
12. Cut down on power struggles between parents and children.

FAMILY SYSTEMS

Parenting does not happen in a vacuum. It happens within a family system. So let's start by examining these systems.

A family is simply a structure or system made up of two or more parts or people. Each part or person is unique and at the same time part of the whole. For the whole to be strong and healthy, each of the parts must be individually strong and healthy.

A good analogy of this would be the mobile. If you bump one of the pieces not only does it move but it affects all of the other pieces as well. The other interesting and very predictable thing that will happen to the mobile is that every individual piece will eventually return to exactly the same spot that is was in before you bumped it. This is the principle of balance.

The mobile tells us a lot about the principles of systems in general, which includes the family system. Family systems have a definite structure to them. The family is more than just individual people. Each member of the family has his place. It would not be the same family if we were to change any of the individual members. Changes in one member in the family affect all of the other members but not necessarily in the same way.

A family is a whole unit with its own identity and it is defined by how all the members interact. In other words, the whole is greater than the sum of the parts. This is known as synergism.

Like other systems, family systems always try to return to their original state. They try to maintain balance.

FAMILY FUNCTIONS

Why do we need families? What function do they serve? Actually, the family serves several functions, such as:

- Maintenance functions: food, clothing, shelter.
- Safety functions: protection from harm.
- Sense of belonging: love, warmth, nurturing.
- Spirituality: not formal religion but the relationship with the universe, unexplained, etc.

Families exist then to provide a safe and nurturing environment or atmosphere in which we can best live and survive. Of course every family provides for these needs and carries out these functions differently. Just like with any system, family structures can breakdown. So, let's take a look at some of the differences between healthy and unhealthy families.

HEALTHY/ADAPTIVE FAMILIES

All families have problems and experience stress. Healthy families handle problems and stress in a healthy way. Everyone works together to find solutions to family and or individual problems. Healthy families can adjust when something interferes with the balance of the family. In healthy families members get to make mistakes. Healthy systems leave room for human error and imperfection.

In healthy families members listen to each other. Expressing wants and needs is acceptable. Emotions and feelings are validated.

In healthy families, feelings and thoughts are genuine, honest, loving and considerate. In healthy families there are no family secrets. Healthy families have clear boundaries. Clear boundaries are required for optimal functioning. Clear boundaries leave no question as to who is the parent and who is the child. Parents don't feel that they must give up or disclaim their adult power, and children don't feel that they must assume premature adult responsibilities. Children do not feel the need to fill the needs that the parents really should provide one another. If this happens, the emotionally parentified child is at risk for becoming the problem that parents polarize or unite around. When boundaries get muddied they collapse and lead to unhealthy alliances, such as Mom and child against Dad. This is basically an unsuccessful attempt to resolve conflict. The very foundation of any HEALTHY family is clear boundaries.

In healthy families boundaries are flexible; there are no rigid roles or rules. In healthy families life is relaxed. The family atmosphere is loving, nurturing and no member is more important than any other.

Healthy families allow autonomy or separateness. A healthy family will allow its members to be largely self-determining; make their own choices about their lives. Children will be allowed to find out what they like and don't like about the world, what they want to do for a living, etc. They will be allowed to have some privacy and a sense of uniqueness as well as belonging. Both parents and children will be allowed to change their minds about things like careers and roles as their needs change or as their personalities develop over time. Parents and children are allowed to love each other without having to be enmeshed and tangled up in each other's lives.

Healthy families also function to promote self-esteem or a sense of worth in each member. Each member of the family praises rather than criticizes. All use healthy skill building rather than relentless pushing and demanding for perfect performance. A healthy family will let each person find and have that sense of personal value, dignity and worth.

UNHEALTHY /DYSFUNCTIONAL FAMILIES

In unhealthy families, boundaries swing back and forth between ridged and diffuse. Roles, rules and expectations are rigidly defined and always fulfilled. The atmosphere in the home is cold, frozen, extremely polite, boring, foreboding and it abounds in secrecy. There is little evidence of friendship among family members and little joy in one another.

Family members are hopeless, helpless and lonely. They try to cover up as they endure misery or inflict misery on others. Members of the unhealthy family don't listen to each other and individuals rarely speak up when there is a problem. There is a communication breakdown.

There is little evidence of friendship among family members, little joy in one another and humor is sarcastic and cruel; adults **tell** children what to do and what not to do. The family is expected to be 100% efficient, predictable and stable. Since this is impossible, any variance from these expectations of perfection must be justified. It has to be someone's "fault."

Therefore, a child usually ends up becoming the scapegoat. And the other members of the system also develop dysfunctional roles which we will discuss later.

BOUNDARIES

What exactly are boundaries? Boundaries are invisible lines that are like a psychological fence around us and are defined by us. There are three categories of boundaries and they include psychological and social issues: 1) Individual Boundaries; 2) Family Boundaries, and; 3) Intergenerational Boundaries. Within each type, we can have three boundary states: Rigid Boundaries (too strong); 2) Diffuse Boundaries (too week); and 3) Flexible Boundaries (healthy.)

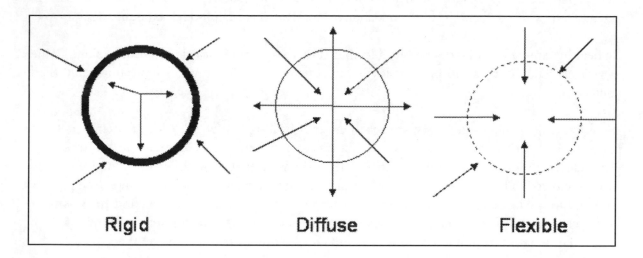

INDIVIDUAL BOUNDARIES: invisible lines, which are defined by the person themselves.

Rigid Individual Boundaries: nothing gets in and nothing gets out.

Diffuse Individual Boundaries: you are able to do what ever you want to anyone and others are able to do anything they want to you.

Flexible Boundaries: allow things in that you are comfortable with while keeping things out that you are uncomfortable with.

FAMILY BOUNDARIES: invisible lines that surround the family as a whole unit.

Rigid Family Boundaries: no talk, no compromising, rigid roles and rules.

Diffuse Family Boundaries: no sense of unity, no one seems to be in charge, no clear limits and rules.

Flexible Family Boundaries: active listening, open communication, feelings validated, sense of family unity, clear limits and rules.

INTERGENERATIONAL BOUNDARIES: invisible lines separating adults and children.

Rigid Intergenerational Boundaries: love not shown, rigid roles and rules, cold and empty feeling, little interaction between adults and children and no empathy.

Diffuse Intergenerational Boundaries: children put into adult role, adults lean on children and adults ask children to fill their emotional needs.

Flexible Intergenerational Boundaries: adult and child roles well defined, children loved and well cared for.

INDIVIDUAL BOUNDARIES

Each individual human being should have a clearly defined boundary around themselves. This individual boundary lets certain things into our lives and keeps certain things out of our lives. It says, "This is what you can do to me and this is what you can't do to me." If boundaries are too weak, you are able to do what ever you want to anyone, and others are able to do anything they want to you. If boundaries are too rigid, nothing gets in and nothing gets out. Flexible boundaries allow us to let things into our lives that we feel OK with and keep things out of our lives that we're not OK with. In dysfunctional or unhealthy families, we swing back and forth between rigid and diffuse boundary states, hoping to find some kind of balance.

FAMILY BOUNDARIES

Family boundaries are those which surround the family as a whole unit. With a closed family system where the "no talk" rule is in full force, we speak of rigid family boundaries. It's "us" against the world. Roles and rules are very ridged. There is no compromising.

If family boundaries are diffuse, the family has no sense of unity at all. People flow in and out. No one seems to be "in charge." There are no clear limits or rules. It doesn't' feel like a family at all.

Family boundaries that are flexible are those where disagreements, thoughts, feelings, etc., can be aired without reprisal. There are open lines of communication. Feelings are validated. Individual rights are honored. The family has a sense of unity, with clear limits and rules.

INTERGENERATIONAL BOUNDARIES

Intergenerational boundaries are those invisible lines between the parents or other adults in the family and the children in the family. If parents have difficulty expressing feelings towards others, if they don't know how to show love, if their own individual boundaries are too rigid, then the intergenerational boundary will be too rigid also. Children will feel alone. The parents are never there for them, never play with them, are not empathetic and do not seem to care. It will feel cold and empty in the family.

Diffuse or weak intergenerational boundaries have lines that are very unclear between adults and children. This is very common in dysfunctional families and is most blatant where incest occurs.

Whenever we put our children in an adult role, we are crossing this boundary. The adults lean on children for support, to share their deepest problems and ask the children to fill their emotional needs. We often see this kind of intergenerational, boundary invasion happening right after a divorce. This robs the children of childhood and it teaches the child to be a victim in order to get their needs met.

Flexible intergenerational boundaries have lines that are clear. Adult roles are well defined, as well as the child's role. Children feel loved and well cared for. The parents are there for the children when the children need them to be.

SIGNS OF UNHEALTHY BOUNDARIES

1. Telling all.
2. Talking at an intimate level at the first meeting.
3. Falling in love with a new acquaintance.
4. Falling in love with anyone who reaches out.
5. Being overwhelmed by a person or preoccupied.
6. Acting on the first sexual impulse.
7. Being sexual for your partner not yourself.
8. Going against personal values or rights to please others.
9. Not noticing when someone else displays inappropriate boundaries.
10. Not noticing when someone invades your boundaries.
11. Accepting food, gifts, touch or sex that you do not want.
12. Touching a person without asking.
13. Taking as much as you can get for the sake of getting.
14. Giving as much as you can give for the sake of giving
15. Allowing someone to take as much as they can from you.
16. Letting others direct your life.
17. Letting others describe your life.
18. Letting others define you.
19. Believing others can anticipate your needs.
20. Expecting others to fill your needs automatically.
21. Falling apart so someone will take care of you.
22. Self-abuse.
23. Sexual and physical abuse.

DIFFERENT TYPES OF DYSFUNCTIONAL ROLES

The Do-er: The Do-er does a lot of things. They provide most all of the maintenance functions in the family. They make sure the kids are dressed and fed. They pay the bills, iron the clothes, cook dinner and take the kids to baseball practice and violin lessons. The Do-er does a lot. The Do-er feels tired, lonely, taken advantage of, neglected and empty. However, the Do-er gets a lot of satisfaction out of being so accomplished at his or her tasks. The family encourages the Do-er either directly or indirectly. The Do-er's own unhealthy guilt and overdeveloped sense of responsibility keeps him or her going.

The Helper: The Helper provides all of the nurturance and sense of belongingness in the family. Sometimes this person is also the Do-er, and sometimes not. For the Helper, keeping everyone together, preserving the family unit at any cost (including physical violence or even death) and trying to smooth out ruffled feathers and avoid conflict is the ultimate goal. Fear of abandonment and fear that other family members cannot stand on their own two feet are what often motivates this role.

The Lost Child: The Lost Child deals with the family dysfunction by means of escape. Actually, in a sense, this child (or parent) is taking care of the family's needs for separateness and autonomy. This child stays in her room a lot or is out in the woods playing by herself. He/she is alone, but it is not a healthy aloneness. A deep loneliness pervades those who have this role.

The Hero: The Hero provides self-esteem for the family. They go to law school and become an internationally known attorney, but secretly feel awful because they have a sister in a family hospital and a brother who has died of alcoholism. They carry the family banner for the entire public to see. They make the family proud; but at a terrible price in terms of their own well-being.

The Mascot: Often one of the younger children, the Mascot provides the humor and comic relief for the family. They give the family a sense of fun or playfulness, silliness and a distorted type of joy. The cost to the Mascot is that their true feelings of pain and isolation never get expressed and they remain an emotional cripple until they get help on their own.

The Scapegoat: The Scapegoat gets to act out all of the family's dysfunction and therefore takes the blame and the heat for the family. They get drug addicted; do badly in school; get in trouble with the law. They are the "black sheep" of the family. They get into a lot of fights, act out sexually, etc. The family then gets to say, "We'd be a healthy family if the child wasn't such a delinquent." The cost to the Scapegoat is obvious.

The Little Princess/Little Man: This role is a severe form of emotional abuse. This role feels good to a child who gets to be a little spouse to one of the parents in the system. This child does not get to be a child though and is actually seduced into the role by a parent who is too afraid and too dysfunctional to get their needs met by another adult. Those in this role usually wind up getting physically or emotionally abused by others in adult relationships, because their boundaries were not respected when they were young.

The Saint/Priest/Nun/Rabbi: This is the child who expresses the family's spirituality and is expected to become a man/woman of the cloth and not become sexual. Often the expectation is never a spoken one. It is implied, and subtly reinforced and encouraged. This child is unconsciously molded into believing that he/she will only have worth if they act out the spirituality for the family. If they don't, they will have little or no worth.

PARENTING STYLES

We all want close, loving, empowering and healthy family systems. We want our children to be socially mature, self-regulating individuals. And, parenting style plays a big part in fostering this kind of healthy family system. The question most parents face is how to do this. To answer this question and, although there is no one universally accepted model, the one most widely used is that of Diana Baumrind who emphasizes three basic parenting styles. There can be more than one kind or style going on in the family and it can change back and forth, especially from authoritarian to permissive, in the same family. The three styles are:

1. Authoritarian/Autocratic.
2. Permissive: Indulgent & Indifferent.
3. Authoritative/Democratic: what we call Positive Effective Parenting or P.E.P.

AUTHORITARIAN/AUTOCRATIC PARENTING IS:
1. Punitive.
2. Restrictive. Offers few choices.
3. Little verbal give-and-take.
4. Inflexible limits and controls on the child.
5. RESULTS: Children raised in an Authoritarian/Autocratic manner can:
   - Be anxious about social comparison.
   - Fail to initiate an activity.
   - Have poor communication skills.
   - Be overly aggressive.
   - Be insecure and fearful.
   - Obey out of fear of punishment.
   - Learn to subvert or manipulate.
   - Retaliate and strike out at times.
   - Be disobedient, sneaky and strong-willed.
   - Be rebellious.
   - Be lacking in self-discipline.
   - Be socially incompetent.

PERMISSIVE (2 TYPES)
Permissive-Indifferent
   Parents uninvolved.
   Few rules and limits.
   RESULTS: Children raised in a permissive-indifferent manner tend to:
   - Be unable to handle independence well.
   - Feel parents don't love them.
   - Be disrespectful.
   - Be lacking in self-discipline and self-control.
   - Be insecure and anxious.
   - Be socially incompetent.

Permissive-Indulgent
   Parents highly involved.
   Few demands or controls.
   RESULTS: children raised in a permissive-indulgent manner can:
   - Have poor self control.

- Be spoiled, demanding, and self-centered.
- Fail to develop consideration of others.
- Always expect to get their own way.
- Be socially incompetent.

AUTHORITATIVE/POSITIVE EFFECTIVE PARENTING

1. Encourages independence.
2. Still place limits and controls on their actions.
3. Use extensive verbal give-and-take.
4. Are warm and nurturing.
5. RESULTS: children raised in an authoritative/democratic manner tend to:
   - Be respectful.
   - Be secure and responsible.
   - Be cooperative.
   - Be courageous.
   - Be team-centered.
   - Be able to focus on the needs of the group.
   - Be self-reliant.
   - Be socially competent.
   - Be socially responsible.

PARENTING STYLES QUIZ

Please circle the answer that fits your situation MOST of the time. Circle only ONE answer for each question!

1. I use physical punishment
   Most of the time (5)
   Sometimes (3)
   Rarely (1)
2. I allow my children to "get their way"
   Most of the time (5)
   Sometimes (3)
   Rarely (1)
3. I believe children need to be punished for wrong doings.
   Most of the time (5)
   Sometimes (3)
   Rarely (1)
4. I expect my children to follow my rules without question.
   Most of the time (5)
   Sometimes (3)
   Rarely (1)
5. I believe children should have some privacy.
   Most of the time (1)
   Sometimes (3)
   Rarely (5)

Add the points found in parenthesis to every answer that you circled. Scores can range from six to 35 points. If your score is over 20 you are probably an Authoritarian parent. If your score is under 10 you are probably a Permissive parent. If your score is between 10 and 20 you are probably an Authoritative parent.

Based on the above information, I feel my parenting style is:
>   Authoritarian
>   Permissive
>   Authoritative

My parent's style was:
>   Authoritarian
>   Permissive
>   Authoritative

OTHER PARENTING STYLES

Parenting styles can also fit into the following categories.

THE DEMANDING PARENT (D)

The demanding dictatorial parent gives the message, "I'm the boss and I own you." The child believes the parent is saying, "It doesn't matter what you think, it is going to be done my way." The demanding parents are parents that push. If you were pushed as a child then you will probably continue to push yourself and your child. These parents often use the word "lazy" and often fear their children will not turn out ok. Children of demanding parents say, "He never listens to me" or; "She treats me like a baby" or; "He doesn't care how I feel." These demanding parents tend to raise two types of children; doormats and liars. Doormats are the children who can be walked all over, agree with everyone and never have a conflicting opinion. Liars are the children who look right at the parent, nod and agree with the parent and when the parent is out of sight, do as they please. Some liars become so well at it and begin to lie at such a young age that they believe their own lies and no longer deal with reality. Demanding parents do not teach their children to think, reason, set goals or make choices. Living in jail is like living with a demanding parent. You are told what to do, no one wants your opinion and you have no choice.

THE CRITICAL PARENT (C)

The critical parents are demanding parents only more so. They give the message, "You don't do anything right." Critical parents often had critical parents of their own. They often put a lot of energy into keeping secrets. They are extremely self-critical. Critical parents raise critical, negative, judgmental children who need to put others down in order to feel good about themselves. Criticism is very seldom constructive. Criticism destroys self esteem and makes children angry and resentful. Children of critical parents have few positive examples. To change behavior is to risk more criticism or to risk failure again. Sometimes we can still hear, "Sit up straight, stop biting your nails, you're just like your father, why couldn't you have been thinner, you were supposed to be a boy, etc."

THE OVERPROTECTIVE PARENT (O)

The over protective parent (smothering parent) gives the child the following message, "You can't do it, at least not by yourself," the children of this parent often make the statement, "I don't want my child to do that. I wasn't permitted to do it." Overprotective parents try to give the child all the things that they themselves did not have during their own childhood, which is impossible and insane. This parent wonders why the child is not appreciative enough and grateful enough for all the things that the parent is supplying and doing. This parent needs to parent him or herself and know that they can enjoy a childhood at any age.

THE INADEQUATE PARENT (I.)

Inadequate parents are ineffectual. They are often alcoholic, drug addicted and/or abusers. They are parents who abandon their children each time they use the alcohol or drugs or act in an out of control manner. The fear level in these children is enormous. The message these parents give is, "I am not able to give you what you need; I am overwhelmed; I might explode." The children of these parents feel a need to take care of the parents and protect him/her. The child may feel caught in a trap as they feel that they should be protected, not be doing the caretaking. Inadequate parents often ask their children to assume adult roles that they are not capable of assuming such as raising younger brothers and sisters, getting dad to bed after he has passed out, calling work and lying for the parent.

THE DISENGAGING PARENT (DI)

The disengaging parent is unavailable or preoccupied. They may be too sick, too tired or too busy. They give the message, "You are not terribly important to me." The children of these parents make statements such as, "I don't like me." "I am not important." These children often spend a lot of time denying what they see and feel. Because these parents did not receive adequate love, living is hard for them. They may even make some of the following statements: "I never wanted a child in the first place," "You were an accident," "I brought you into this world, I can take you out," "I can't cope," "You children will be the death of me" or "You are driving me to my grave."

THE VALIDATING PARENT (V)

Validating parents tend to like themselves and their children. They give the message, "I like you, and you are a good person." They produce capable kids. These parents are honest with themselves and honest about what they can do. They spend enough quantity time with their children that there is some recognizable quality time. They have good communications skills, enjoy being parents and their love takes action. These parents often come from validating parents. Their statements may sound unbelievable or unrealistic since validating parents are rare.

Most parents do not "fit" into just one style but are a combination of two or three. We need to strive to validate our children as well as the child inside ourselves. This will give you a feel for how parents can influence their children in different ways. Ask yourself: "What kind of parent did I have?" By taking the following quiz you will be able to identify what kind of parenting style your parents had and what kind of parent you are today.

What I would like you to do is check off each statement in the following list that you feel is most descriptive of the things your parents said to you. Check the statements off only if they were said <u>often</u> in your home as you were growing up. Leave the ones blank that do not apply to your family.

- ☐ (D) Not right now.
- ☐ (V) I really liked the way you did that.
- ☐ (I) I don't know. Ask your dad/mom.
- ☐ (C) What were you thinking of when you did that?
- ☐ (D) Do it now!
- ☐ (I) I'm too upset to talk.
- ☐ (O) You'd better let me help you.
- ☐ (C) You dummy. Or something worse.
- ☐ (O) It is none of your business.
- ☐ (I) I hate you!!!
- ☐ (V) That shows you put a lot of work into it.
- ☐ (D) Clean up your room now!
- ☐ (I) I'll make you pay for this.
- ☐ (Di) I am too busy maybe later.
- ☐ (C) I can't believe you did that.
- ☐ (O) You do not have to worry about that
- ☐ (V) I know it must be disappointing because I know you really tried.
- ☐ (D) Because I said so.
- ☐ (Di) I can't promise you.
- ☐ (D) That is my rule, that's why.
- ☐ (C) You look terrible. Go change.
- ☐ (O) Do you think you are ready for that?
- ☐ (V) I'm so proud of you.
- ☐ (I) I can't talk to him. You do it.
- ☐ (Di) Can't you see I'm busy?
- ☐ (I) I cannot tell your dad/mom. It will upset him/her.
- ☐ (O) You'd better not move ahead without asking me first.
- ☐ (D) No, because I said so. You don't need a reason.
- ☐ (C) You never do anything right. Let me do it.
- ☐ (D) Get over here and do what I tell you.
- ☐ (V) You did that so well. Show me how to do it.
- ☐ (Di) Maybe tomorrow.
- ☐ (D) Stop it!
- ☐ (C) I can't believe you did that again when I told you not to.
- ☐ (C) Just what do you think you are doing?
- ☐ (O) I'll do that for you.
- ☐ (O) I am afraid you are going to get hurt.
- ☐ (Di) I might get to it tomorrow.
- ☐ (Di) I don't feel well. Do you mind leaving me alone right now?
- ☐ (D) I said to do it. So do it!
- ☐ (C) You really didn't want to do that, did you?
- ☐ (V) Did I ever tell you how much I love you?
- ☐ (O) I was never allowed to do that when I was your age.
- ☐ (V) I really respect your opinion.

SCORING THE QUIZ

Count your checks in each category. The one with the most checks will help you better identify the style of parenting you grew up with and the kind of parenting style you have today.

D is the Demanding Parent   _____

C is the Critical Parent   _____

O is the Overprotective Parent   _____

I is the Inadequate Parent   _____

Di if the Disengaged Parent   _____

V is the Validating Parent   _____

POSITIVE EFFECTIVE PARENTING

The authoritative, validating parent is a Positive Effective Parent and follows the 5 principles of Positive Effective Parenting. As you can see, the first letters of these five steps appropriately spell out the word NEVER, because Positive Effective Parents NEVER give up on their children.

N = Nurture: to give tender care and protection.

E = Empower: to give a sense of confidence or self-esteem.

V = Validate: to confirm ones self worth.

E = Encourage: to give hope, confidence, or courage.

R = Respect: to create a feeling or attitude of admiration and put the child's interests first.

HOW TO BE A POSITIVE EFFECTIVE PARENT

Below are some of the things that will make you a positive effective parent and I'm sure you can add some of your own to the list.

1. Influence and teach rather than control and dominate.
2. Discipline rather than punish.
3. Set and maintain appropriate limits based on the child's age and developmental stage.
4. Permit limited choice. Positive Effective Parents give children an opportunity to make their own choices within age appropriate limits. They have faith in their children so that they can come to believe in themselves.
5. Set realistic standards and expectations that are appropriate to the age and stage of the child.

6. Hold the children accountable for their decisions without using "blame."
7. Encourage open, honest, communication within the family. Family members are not afraid to express their feelings and thoughts.
8. Use natural and logical consequences rather than retaliatory ones.
9. Do not get into power struggles.
10. Encourage. They focus on what is good about the child or the situation. They look for and find the positive. Positive Effective Parents recognize improvement and effort, not just accomplishment. Sounds of encouragement are words that build feelings of adequacy, such as:
    - "I like the way you handled that."
    - "I appreciate what you did."
    - "It looks as if you worked very hard on that."
    - "You can be proud of your improvement."
11. Avoid tacking on qualifiers, such as "but," to their words of encouragement.
12. Accept their children as they are, giving unconditional love. They don't make their love and acceptance of the children dependent on their behavior.
13. Separate the behavior from the child. Saying things like, "I don't like your behavior" NOT "I don't like you when you do . . . ."
14. Practice mutual respect with all family members. To get respect we must first give respect. They treat their children the way they would want to be treated.

FROM A CHILD'S POINT OF VIEW

1. Don't spoil me. I know quite well that I ought not to have all that I ask for. I'm only testing you.
2. Don't be afraid to be firm with me. I prefer it. It makes me feel more secure.
3. Don't let me form bad habits. I have to rely on you to detect them in the early stages.
4. Don't correct me in front of others if you can help it. I'll take much more notice if you talk quietly with me in private.
5. Don't make me feel my mistakes are sins. It upsets my sense of values.
6. Don't take too much notice of my small aliments. Sometimes they get me the attention I need.
7. Don't forget that I cannot explain myself as well as I'd like.
8. Don't tax my honesty too much. I am easily frightened into telling lies. Don't make it hard for me to tell the truth.
9. Don't be inconsistent. That completely confuses me and makes me lose faith in you.
10. Don't tell me my fears are silly. They are terribly real to me and you can do much to reassure me if you try to understand them.

FAMILY SYSTEM EVALUATION

Please circle the answer that fits your situation MOST of the time. Circle only ONE answer for each question.

1. In my family problems are handled in a healthy way.
   A) Most of the time (5)
   B) Sometimes (3)
   C) Rarely (1)

2. In my family, members actively listen to one another.
    A) Most of the time (5)
    B) Sometimes (3)
    C) Rarely (1)
3. In my family privacy is allowed.
    A) Most of the time (5)
    B) Sometimes (3)
    C) Rarely (1)
4. In my family we promote self-esteem.
    A) Most of the time (5)
    B) Sometimes (3)
    C) Rarely (1)
5. In my family we use praise rather then criticism.
    A) Most of the time (5)
    B) Sometimes (3)
    C) Rarely (1)

Give yourself 5 points for every "A" answer, 3 points for every "B" answer, and 1 point for every "C" answer. Add up your score. The higher your score the more you tend to be in a HEALTHY family system. If your score is under 15 you may be in an UNHEALTHY family system.

Based on the above information, I feel that my family system is: (circle one.)

Healthy   Unhealthy

List some ways you feel that your family is healthy or unhealthy.

_____
_____
_____
_____

Regardless of the type of family system we have or our parenting style, I think we can agree that our responsibility as parents is to provide for our children's needs until they grow into self-regulating adults.

If you feel that your family system is currently unhealthy, you can use your Positive Effective Parenting skills and begin to promote self-esteem and a sense of worth in each family member. This might not happen over night but with dedication and practice you will succeed.

POSITIVE EFFECTIVE PARENTING
P.E.P.

CHAPTER TWO
Child Development

CHAPTER TWO

Child Development

CHILD DEVELOPMENT

Why is the study of child development important? One reason is that it provides practical guidance for parents, teachers, child-care providers and others who care for children. A second reason is that it enables society to support healthy growth. Understanding early brain development, for example, means that parents can provide better opportunities for intellectual examples and society can reduce or eliminate obstacles to healthy brain growth. Third, the study of child development helps therapists and educators better assist children with special needs such as those with emotional or learning difficulties.

Finally, understanding child development contributes to self-understanding. We know ourselves better by recognizing the influences that have made us into the people we are today.

Some developments in behavior and thought are very similar for all children. Around the world, most infants begin to focus their eyes, sit up and learn to walk at comparable stages. And. children begin to acquire language and develop logical reasoning skills at approximately the same time. These aspects of individual growth are highly predictable. Other aspects of development show a much wider range of individual differences. Whether a child becomes outgoing or shy, intellectually advanced or average, energetic or subdued, depends on many unique influences whose effects are difficult to predict in the child.

Learning theories provide extremely useful ways of understanding how developmental changes in behavior and thinking occur and, for some children, why behavior problems arise. These theories can be studied scientifically and practically applied. Critics point out, however, that because of their emphasis on the guidance of the social environment, learning theorists sometimes neglect to recognize the child's active role in their own understanding and development. Scholars have long debated the relative importance of nature (hereditary influences) and nurture (environmental influences) in child development. It was once assumed that these forces operated independently of each other. Today developmental scientists recognize that both influences are essential and are mutually influential. For example, how a child responds to parenting and environmental influence is partly determined by the child's temperament and other inherited characteristics. Likewise, the environment influences how hereditary characteristics develop and are expressed.

TO FULFILL THEIR UNIQUENESS WHAT DO CHILDREN NEED

Every child has fundamental needs that must be met for him or her to have an emotionally and physically healthy life and grow and develop optimally. So, now let's take a look at these needs and how we as parents can provide for them. Abraham Maslow, a pioneer in the development of humanistic psychology, has proposed that human needs can be classified into three broad levels

FUNDAMENTAL NEEDS (FOR SURVIVAL)

1. Physiological needs: to satisfy hunger, thirst, and sex drives.
2. Safety Needs: to feel secure, safe, and out of danger.

One way we can help our children feel safe and secure is to set LIMITS. Children need limits for their safety, ("Don't touch that stove, stay out of the street," etc.); their health ("No, you can't have cookies instead of your regular meals," "You have to wear a coat today", etc.); and for their security.

What are some of the physiological and safety limits you set with your children?

_____
_____
_____
_____

How have you changed the limits since your children have grown? Although your children may not want to do what you say, setting limits sends a clear message that you as the parents are watching out for them; giving them a sense of security.

_____
_____
_____
_____

PSYCHOLOGICAL NEEDS

1. Belongingness and love needs: to affiliate with others, to be accepted and belong, attention.
2. Comfort: fun, enjoyment, sensory stimulus.
3. Esteem needs: to achieve, be competent, gain approval and recognition. Children need to feel good about themselves and have a sense of self-worth/dignity. Parents are crucial in the development of their children's self-esteem.

To develop good self-esteem children need to feel good about themselves. What are some things you can do to help your children develop self-esteem? Your answers should relate to showing respect, loving your children, praising them, noticing the good things they do, etc.

_____
_____
_____
_____

What are some of the things you have done in the last week or so to reinforce your child's self-esteem?

_____
_____
_____
_____

SELF-ACTUALIZATION NEEDS

1. The need to fulfill one's unique potential.
2. Autonomy or independence.
3. Power and control of my environment.
4. Perhaps the most basic instinct and needs is the search for "self."

To meet one's self-actualization need, we must develop our "self-concept." Self-concept is my perception of "ME"; 2) my perception of my relationship with the world; and 3) the value I attach to these perceptions. Developing self-concept is crucial in a child's development. To do this, children need some CHOICES. When children can make choices, succeed, and fail, they mature, develop confidence and are able to function more independently. As parents we must take care of any basic needs that they are developmentally not capable of taking care of themselves. We teach children things everyday. Most importantly, however, we must give children choices that are age appropriate. Children need some CHOICES.

What are some choices your children are allowed to make at this time?

_____
_____
_____
_____

What are some things you do to give your child some control of their environment?

_____
_____
_____
_____

Do children need limits on the amount of control they have on their environment and why?

_____
_____
_____
_____

What are some choices your children are allowed to make at this time?

_____

_____

_____

_____

How do you think the choices your children can make will change as they grow and develop?

_____

_____

_____

_____

There are four more things that our children need.

- Courage
- Self-Esteem
- Responsibility
- Cooperation

COURAGE: We all need courage in order to be able to handle any of life's problems. Without courage children either give up easily or do not try at all.

SELF-ESTEEM: Our self-esteem is based on how we perceive ourselves and our world. Children need to have good self-esteem to succeed. They need it to have the courage to keep on trying when the going gets rough. They need to see themselves as winners rather than incapable losers. Positive self-esteem leads to positive behavior.

RESPONSIBILITY: A child must learn that what he does not only affects him but also others. He must learn that what he does carries consequences with it. As children grow up they will be faced with many difficult decisions. Therefore, they must learn to think before they do anything.

COOPERATION: Children must learn to work together with other people. A child who does not learn cooperation may have difficulty interacting with others. They must learn to respect the rights of others and that to get respect from others they must earn it.

I NEED YOU TO TEACH ME

I need you to teach me everything you can so I'll have a chance in this world when I grow up. I need your patience. I know I'm not very orderly. I cry out for things like food and attention the second I need them. I can't help it and I know it bothers you sometimes. All I can hope is that you will be patient with me until I can learn to be patient too. Above all, I need to know you love me. Even if your parents gave you no love, try to give a little to me so I can give a little to my children and they can give a little to their children. I need so much from you yet I have only one thing I can give you in return. That is my love, today and tomorrow and for as long as I live. Author Unknown

AGES & STAGES

Does childhood growth occur continuously and gradually or is it instead a series of distinct stages? People often think of childhood as a sequence of age-related stages, such as infancy, early childhood and middle childhood. Such a view recognizes that each period of growth has its own distinct changes, challenges and characteristics. But many aspects of childhood development are more gradual and continuous, such as the development of physical skills, social abilities, and emotional understanding. Even some milestones that seem to denote a new stage of growth, such as a child's first word, are actually the outcome of a more gradual developmental process. A very important thing to understand is that a child's needs change as they grow and develop. All children go through definite stages as they grow up. Remember however, that generalized descriptions of stages of development are only given as guides to the probable direction of the changes your child will go through as he or she matures. It's the order of the stages which is important for you to know. It's kind of like climbing a ladder; to get to the top safely and successfully, we must climb one step at a time. To be Positive Effective Parents we need to be aware of our child's natural development in order to know what we can expect from them. Even a child's behavior "problem" may just be one of his/her important and normal developmental tasks. Awareness of these tasks should reassure you that your child's development is normal and likely to change again soon. A behavior "problem" often lasts more than 6 months, happens in more than one place consistently and appears as a pattern. Luckily this is some kind of learned response and can be unlearned or redirected.

WHAT IS LEARNING?

Did you know that our children are in the business of learning? They attempt to store all the things that happen to them into some type of logical form. Learning is to gain knowledge, understanding or skill. This is in accordance with the great Webster. An even broader definition of learning is any permanent change in behavior that occurs because of a practice or an experience. This makes what we teach our children even more important as it has the potential to have a lasting affect in their behavior.

HOW DO CHILDREN THINK?
Children are a bundle of ideas and thoughts. If you ever really look at your child, you will see that these thought patterns are much different from that of an adult and that there are many different ways to express them.

ERIKSON'S DEVELOPMENTAL STAGES

The renowned psychologist, Erik Erikson (1902-1994), suggests that we develop in psychosocial stages and experience developmental change throughout our lives.

He feels that there are eight stages of development. Each stage consists of a unique developmental task or goal that confronts us with a crisis that must be faced. This crisis is not a catastrophe but merely a turning point in our lives. The more we resolve each crisis successfully the healthier our development will be. During childhood, it is the parent's responsibility to provide the child with the environment needed to accomplish the goal successfully. This environment must include love, encouragement, food, shelter and opportunity for growth and learning. Since each stage builds on the one before it, it is very important that the child accomplish the central task of each stage.

TRUST VERSUS MISTRUTST is Erikson's first psychosocial stage, which is experienced in the first year of life. He believes that this first year is the key time frame for the development of attachment. In order for the infant to develop a sense of trust they need a feeling of physical comfort and a minimal amount of fear and apprehension about the future. Trust in infancy sets the stage for a lifelong expectation that the world will be a good and pleasant place to live. It also gives the infant confidence to explore new circumstances. Your responsive, sensitive parenting at this time contributes to the infant's sense of trust.

AUTONOMY VERSUS SHAME AND DOUBT is Erikson's second stage of development, occurring in late infancy and toddler-hood from 1-3 years of age. After gaining trust in a caregiver, infants begin to discover that their behavior is their own and they start to assert their sense of independence or autonomy. It is important for parents to recognize that toddlers have a lot of motivation to do what they are capable of doing; they just need to do it at there own pace. When caregivers are impatient, do for the toddler what they are capable of doing themselves or if they restrain the infants too much or discipline too harshly, they are likely to develop a sense of shame and doubt. I know every parent has rushed a child from time to time. It is when they consistently overprotect toddlers or criticize accidents such as wetting, soiling, spilling or breaking, for example, that children develop an excessive sense of shame and doubt. Erikson believes that this stage has important implications for the development of independence and identity during adolescence. The development of autonomy during the toddler years gives adolescents the courage to be independent individuals who can choose and guide their own future.

INITIATIVE VERSUS GUILT is Erikson's third stage of development, occurring during the preschool years from 3-6 years of age. Preschool children encounter a widening social world. They are challenged more than when they were infants. And, active, purposeful behavior is needed for them to cope with these challenges. This is the time when children are asked to assume responsibility for their bodies, their behavior, their toys and their pets. Erikson believes that developing this sense of responsibility increases their initiative. Widespread disappointment at this stage leads to guilt, which lowers the child's self-concept. Whether children leave this stage with a sense of initiative or guilt depends in large part on how parents respond to their self-initiated activities. Children are given freedom and opportunity to initiate motor play, such as running, bike riding, tussling and wrestling have their sense of initiative supported. Initiative is also supported when parents answer their children's questions and do not belittle or inhibit fantasy or play activity. In contrast, if children are made to feel that their motor activity is bad, that their questions are a nuisance and that their play is silly and stupid then they often develop a sense of guilt over self-initiated activities. This guilt may persist through life's later stages. The good news here is that any sense of guilt a child may feel at this stage can be quickly compensated for by a sense of accomplishment. So, it is very important to praise your child now.

INDUSTRY VERSUS INFERIORITY is Erikson's fourth developmental stage, occurring approximately in the elementary school years from 7-11 years old. Children's initiative, which was learned in the previous stage, now brings them in contact with a wealth of new experiences and they begin to direct their energy toward mastering knowledge and intellectual skills. The danger in the elementary school years is the development of a sense of inferiority, of feeling incompetent and unproductive. Erikson believes that teachers have a special responsibility now for children's development of industry (energetic devotion to a task; diligence.)

IDENTITY VERSUS IDENTITY CONFUSION is Erikson's fifth developmental stage, which individuals experience during the adolescent years. Where they are going in life and what they are all about must be faced at this time. Parents need to allow adolescents to explore many different roles and different paths within a particular role for this crisis to be resolved successfully. If the adolescent explores such roles in a healthy manner and arrives at a positive path to follow in life then he will achieve a positive identity. Youth who successfully cope with conflicting identities during adolescence emerge with a new sense of self that is both refreshing and acceptable. If an identity is pushed onto the adolescent by parents, they will develop identity confusion. This confusion takes one of two courses. Either the individuals withdraw, isolating themselves from peers and family or they may lose their identity in the crowd.

INTIMACY VERSUS ISOLATION is Erikson's sixth developmental stage. This stage is experienced during the early adulthood years. At this time, individuals face the developmental task of forming intimate relationships with others. If we do not form healthy relationships, isolation will result.

GENERATIVITY VERSUS STAGNATION is the seventh developmental stage, which is experienced during middle adulthood. This is the time when adults pursue meaningful work and home lives. They are concerned with assisting the younger generation in developing and leading useful lives. This is what Erikson means by generativity. The feeling of having done nothing to help the next generation is stagnation.

INTEGRITY VERSUS DESPAIR is the eighth and final developmental stage, which is experienced during late adulthood. In the later years of life, we look back and evaluate what we have done with our lives. We try to make sense out of life. If we have been unsuccessful in resolving the earlier stages we will likely have a feeling of despair.

What stage is your child in and what are you doing to help your child to conquer the goal at this stage?

_____
_____
_____
_____

PIAGET'S COGNITIVE (INTELLECTUAL) DEVELOPMENTAL STAGES

Below you will see an overview of the development of intellectual abilities. Children are not little adults. Until they reach the age of 15 or so they are not capable of reasoning as an adult. The stages of intellectual development formulated by Jean Piaget (1896-1980), who was a Swiss developmental psychologist known for his epistemological (or theory of knowledge) studies with children, appear to be related to major developments in brain growth. The human brain is not fully developed until late adolescence or in the case of males sometimes early adulthood. We often expect children to think like adults when they are not yet capable of doing so. It is important that parents know what to expect from their child as they develop and to be sure that the expectations they may have for their child at a given age are realistic.

In addition to these developmental stages, Piaget suggests that cognitive development (the way we think and process information) goes through four stages. Each of the stages are age-related and consists of distinct ways of thinking. He stressed that children actively construct their own cognitive worlds. Information is not just poured into their minds from the environment. Piaget believed that children adapt their thinking to include new ideas because additional information furthers understanding. His four stages of cognitive development are:

The Sensorimotor Stage, which lasts from birth to about 3 years of age, is the first Piagetian stage. During this time the child's primary mode of learning occurs through the five senses. The child learns to experience the environment. The child touches things, holds, looks, listens, tastes, feels, bangs and shakes everything in sight. For this child the sense of time is now and the sense of space is here. When the child adds motor skills such as creeping, crawling and walking, watch out. His or her environment expands by leaps and bounds. The child is now exploring his environment with both senses and the ability to get around. This just doubled your job as a parent because now you need to start dealing with such things as protection and guidance. This mode of learning actually continues through the age of twelve, but becomes less acute as the years go by. In this stage, infants construct an understanding of the world by coordinating sensory experiences (such as seeing and hearing) with physical motor actions (moving the arms or legs.) At the beginning of this stage, newborns have little more than reflexive patterns with which to work. At the end of the stage, 3-year-olds have complex sensorimotor patterns.

Developmental Sensorimotor Stage & Approximate Age	Characteristic Behavior
Reflexive Stage (0-2 months)	Simple reflex activity such as grasping, sucking.
Primary Circular Reactions (2-4 months)	Reflexive behaviors occur in stereotyped repetition such as opening and closing fingers repetitively.
Secondary Circular Reactions (4-8 Months)	Repetition of change actions to reproduce interesting consequences such as kicking one's feet to move a mobile suspended over the crib.
Coordination of Secondary Reactions 8-12 months)	Responses become coordinated into more complex sequences. Actions take on an "intentional" character such as the infant reaches behind a screen to obtain a hidden object.
Tertiary Circular Reactions (12-18 months)	Discovery of new ways to produce the same consequence or obtain the same goal such as the infant may pull a pillow toward him in an attempt to get a toy resting on it.
Invention of New Means Through Mental Combination (18-24 months)	Evidence of an internal representational system. Symbolizing the problem-solving sequence before actually responding. Deferred imitation.

0-1 YEARS

- Trust of caregiver/parent.
- Forming a secure attachment now is critical for later years.
- World view is expanding.

1-3 YEARS

- Focus Oriented, can now experience outrage.
- Establish self-control and self-management.
- Impulses are out of control.
- Parallel play is normal.
- Peers are competitors or providers.
- Perspective taking is just beginning.
- Able to learn cause and effect.
- Thinking is relatively concrete.

The Preoperational Stage, which lasts from approximately 2 to 7 years of age, is the second Piagetian stage. This is the stage between ages two and seven. During this stage, the child is busy gathering information or learning and then trying to figure out ways that they can use what they have learned to begin solving problems. During this stage of his/her life your child will be thinking in specifics and will find it very difficult to generalize anything. An example would be a ball. A ball is not something that you use to play a game it is just something that you throw. This is the time when a child learns by asking questions. You will begin to think that if you hear the word "why" just one more time that you will go crazy. The child generally will not want a real answer to his question at this point. When he asks, "Why do we have grass?" he simply wants to know that it is for him to play in. No technical answers do you need to know. The child in this age group judges everything from the "me" basis. 'How does it affect me? Do I like it?' you get the idea? This child also has no ability to go back in time and reason. If you miss your opportunity to explain or discipline when it happens forget it.

PREOPERATIONAL PHASE (2-YEARS.)

Increased use of verbal representation but speech is egocentric. They have the beginnings of symbolic rather than simple motor play. Transductive reasoning is used now. They can think about something by use of language without the object being present.

INTUITIVE PHASE (4-YEARS.)

Speech becomes more social and less egocentric. The child has an intuitive grasp of logical concepts in some areas. However, there is still a tendency to focus attention on one aspect of an object while ignoring others. Concepts formed are crude and irreversible. It is now easy for them to believe in magical increase, decrease, disappearance. Their reality is not firm. Perceptions now dominate judgment.

In moral-ethical realm, the child is not able to show principles underlying best behavior. Rules of a game are not develop yet. He or she only uses simple dos and don'ts imposed by authority.

- The child begins to represent the world with words and images.
- During the first five years of life, children are egocentric; they only see their own perspective.
- Increasing ability to tolerate frustration and to delay gratification.
- Important for them to say NO; allows them to have a feeling of control.
- Normal to have focused aggression.
- Plan is critical. Imaginary friends are useful and normal.
- External to internal control begins to develop; more able to self-regulate.
- Socialization learned; learning what is socially appropriate.
- Language develops.
- Increased use of verbal representation but speech is egocentric.
- The beginning of symbolic rather than simple motor play or Transductive reasoning occurs. Can think about something without the object being present by use of language.
- Gender identity develops.

The Concrete Operational Stage appears between the ages of 7 and 11. This is a wonderful age as this is when children begin to manipulate data mentally. They take the information at hand and begin to define, compare and contrast it. They, however, still think concretely (specific, not imaginary.) If you were to ask a pre-operations child, "How does God hear prayer?" they would most likely answer that he has big ears. The concrete child would put a little more thought into it and answer something like this: "God is smart and He made some special earphones just so He could hear me." The concrete operational child is capable of logical thought. This child still learns through their senses but no longer relies on only you to teach him. He now thinks as well. A good teacher for this age group would start each lesson at a concrete level and then move toward a generalized level. Concrete, as it is used here, means solid and real, not imaginary.

An example of this would be, statement: "Joey is kind." The teacher would start out by telling about what Joey did to be kind (Concrete.) Then she would talk about how Joey went about being kind (Less concrete/more general.) A seven to ten year old is very literal in their thinking. That means he will take everything that you say, do and teach at face value. They actually and literally mean BLACK is black and WHITE is white. These children have a difficult time with symbols and figurative language.

In this stage, logical reasoning replaces intuitive thought as long as reasoning is specific or concrete examples. The child can classify objects into different sets but, for example, concrete operational thinkers cannot imagine the steps necessary to complete an algebraic equation, which is too abstract for thinking at this stage of development.

- Evidence for organized logical thought. There is the ability to perform multiple classification tasks, order objects in a logical sequences and comprehend the principle of conservation. Thinking becomes less Transductive and less egocentric. The child is capable of concrete problem-solving.
- Some reversibility now possible (quantities moved can be restored such as in arithmetic: 3+4=7 and 7-4=3, etc.)
- Class logic-finding bases to sort unlike objects into logical groups where previously it was on superficial perceived attribute such as color. Categorical labels such as "number or animal" now available.

The Formal Operational Stage, which appears between the ages of 11 and 15, is the fourth and final Piagetian stage. This period begins at about age eleven. At this time the child will break through the barrier of literalism and move on to thinking in more abstract terms. He no longer restricts thinking to time and space. This child now starts to reflect, hypothesize and theorize. He actually thinks about thinking. In the formal operation period, children need to develop cognitive abilities.

- Thought becomes more abstract incorporating the principles of formal logic. The ability to generate abstract proposition, multiple hypotheses and their possible outcomes is evident. Thinking becomes less tied to concrete reality.
- Formal logical systems can be acquired. Can handle proportions, algebraic manipulation and other purely abstract processes. If a+b=x then x=a-b.
- Prepositional logic, as-if and if-then steps are developing. They can use aids such as axioms to transcend human limits on comprehension.
- Knowledge of facts and principals. This is the direct recall of facts and principals. Examples: memorization of date, names, definition, vocabulary words.
- Comprehension: understanding of facts and ideas.
- Application: the need to know how to use rules, principles and procedures.
- Analysis: breaking down concepts into parts.
- Synthesis: putting together information or ideas.
- Evaluation: judging the value of information.
- Can logic or find bases to sort unlike objects into logical groups where previously it was on superficial perceived attribute such as color.
- Categorical labels such as "number or animal" now available.

In this stage, the adolescent moves beyond the world of actual, concrete experiences and thinks in more abstract and logical ways. Thought is more idealistic. They may think, for example, about what an ideal parent is like and compare their parents with this ideal standard. They begin to entertain possibilities for the future and are fascinated with what they can be. In solving problems, formal operational thinkers are more systematic, developing hypotheses about why something is happening the way it is and then testing these theories in a deductive fashion.

AGES 4-7 MONTHS COGNITIVE DEVELOPMENT

During your baby's first four months did you have doubts that she really understood much that was happening around her? This parental reaction is not surprising. After all, although you knew when she was comfortable and uncomfortable, she probably showed few signs of actually thinking. Now, as her memory and attention span increase, you'll start to see evidence that she's not only absorbing information but also applying it to her day-to-day activities such as:

DISCOVERING CAUSE AND EFFECT (4-7 MONTHS)

During this period, one of the most important concepts she will refine is the principle of cause and effect. She'll probably stumble upon this notion by accident somewhere between 4 and 5 months. Perhaps, while kicking her mattress, she'll notice the crib shaking. Or maybe she'll realize that her rattle makes a noise when she hits or waves it. Once she understands that she can cause these interesting reactions she'll continue to experiment with other ways to make things happen.

Your baby will quickly discover that some things, like bells and keys, make interesting sounds when moved or shaken. When she bangs certain things on the table or drops them on the floor, she will start a chain of responses from her audience, including funny faces, groans and other reactions that may lead to the reappearance or disappearance of the object. Before long, she'll begin intentionally dropping things to see you pick them up. As annoying as this may be at times it is one important way for her to learn about cause and effect and her personal ability to influence her environment.

It is important that you give your child the objects she needs for these experiments and encourage her to test her "theories." But make sure that everything you give her to play with is unbreakable, lightweight and large enough that she can't possibly swallow it. If you run out of the usual toys or she loses interest in them plastic or wooden spoons, unbreakable cups and jars or bowl lids and boxes are endlessly entertaining and inexpressive.

DISCOVERING OBJECT PERMANENCE (4-7 MONTHS)

Another major discovery that your baby will make during this period is that objects continue to exist when they are out of her sight; a principle called object permanence. During her first few months, she assumed that the world consisted only of things that she could see. When you left her room, she assumed you vanished. When you returned, you were a completely new person to her. In much the same way, when you hid a toy under a cloth or a box, she thought it was gone for good and wouldn't bother looking for it. But sometime after 4 months she'll begin to realize that the world is more permanent than she thought. You're the same person who greets her every morning. Her teddy bear on the floor is the same one that was in bed with her the night before. The block that you hid under the pillow did not actually vanish after all. By playing hiding games and observing the comings and goings of people and things around her, your baby will continue to learn about object permanence for many months to come.

HOW DOES YOUR CHILD HEAR AND TALK?

Every child is unique and has an individual rate of development. This chart represents, on average, the listed skills. Children typically do not master all items in a category until they reach the upper age in each age range. Just because your child has not accomplished one skill within an age range does not mean the child has a disorder.

HEARING AND UNDERSTANDING	TALKING
Birth-3 months	**Birth-3 months**
• Startles to loud sounds. • Quiets or smiles when spoken to. • Seems to recognize your voice and quiets if crying. • Increases or decreases sucking behavior in response to sound.	• Makes pleasure sounds (cooing, gooing.) • Cries differently for different needs. • Smiles when sees you.

4-6 Months	4-6 months
• Moves eyes in direction of sounds. • Responds to changes in tone of your voice. • Notices toys that make sounds. • Pays attention to music.	• Babbling sounds more speech like with many different sounds, including p and b. • Vocalizes excitement and displeasure. • Makes gurgling sounds when left alone and when playing with you.
7 Months to 1 year	**7 Months to 1 year**
• Enjoys games like peek-a-boo and pat-a-cake. • Turns and looks in direction of sounds. • Listens when spoken to. • Recognizes words for common items like "cup;" "shoe;" "juice." • Begins to respond to requests. "Come here" "Want more?"	Babbling has both long and short groups of sounds such as "tata, upup, bibibibi." Uses speech or non-crying sounds to get and keep attention. Imitates different speech sounds. Uses 1 or 2 word questions. "Where kitty;" "Go bye-bye;" "What's that." Although they may not be clear.
1-2 Years	**1-2 Years**
• Points to a few body parts when asked. • Follows simple commands and understands simple questions. "Roll the ball," "kiss the baby," "Where's your shoe?" • Listens to simple stories, songs, and rhymes. • Points to pictures in a book when named.	• Says more words every month. • Uses some 1-2 word questions. "Where kitty?" "Go bye-bye?" "What's that?" • Puts 2 words together. "More cookie;" "no juice;" "mommy;" "book." • Uses many different consonant sounds of the beginning of words.
2-3 Years	**2-3 Years**
• Understands differences in meaning. "go-stop;" "big-little;" "up-down." • Follows two requests. "Get the book and put it on the table."	• Has a word for almost everything. • Uses 2-3 word "sentences" to talk about and ask for things. • Speech is understood by familiar listeners most of the time. • Often asks for or directs attention to objects by naming them.
3-4 Years	**3-4 Years**
• Hears you when call from another room. • Hears television or radio at the same loudness level as other family members. • Understands simple, "who;" "what," "why" questions.	• Talks about activities at school or at friends' homes. • People outside family usually understand child's speech. • Uses a lot of sentences that have 4 or more words. • Usually talks easily without repeating syllables or words.

4-5 Years	4-5 Years
• Pays attention to a short story and answers simple questions about it. • Hears and understands most of what is said at home and in school.	• Voice sounds clear like other children's. • Uses sentences that give lots of details: "I like to read my books." • Tells stories that stick to topic. • Communicates easily with other children and adults. • Says most sounds correctly except a few like l, s, r, v, z, ch, sh, th.

WHAT IS LEARNING?

Learning is to gain knowledge, understanding or skill. An even broader definition of learning is "any permanent change in behavior that occurs as a result of a practice or an experience." This means that what we teach our children is even more important as it has the potential to have a lasting affect in their behavior.

KEY FACTORS IN LEARNING

1. A child rarely learns in isolation.
2. Learning most generally takes place in a setting of children within the same age group.
3. Some factors that affect learning are motivation, peer relationships within the group and communication between the child and the teacher.
4. Other factors are environment, physical setting, emotional atmosphere and social and cultural norms.

LEARNING, PLAY AND YOUR 8-12 MONTH OLD

At this stage you'll finally know that your baby was listening intently during all those "conversations" you had with her. She'll let you know that she understands what you said, and she'll respond with some "words" of her own.

Keep those toys and games coming and encourage your baby's exploration of the world. She is becoming more mobile and independent but she will not want to separate from you for very long.

<u>WHAT WILL MY BABY LEARN NOW? (8-12 MONTHS)</u>

Your baby will be demonstrating her understanding of what you say in several ways. She will look at objects and people when you say their names, she will crawl to toys that you ask her to find and she will do lots of pointing and gesturing in response to your words. She should already respond well to her own name and she should look up (and at least pause) when you firmly say, "NO!"

Your baby is continuing to explore the world of objects. Now that she can get around on her own, she'll find objects all over the house to pick up, shake, bang, throw and put in her mouth. Make sure the objects she finds are safe for all of these activities.

While this object exploration continues, she'll now understand the functions of some objects. She will recognize familiar objects and understand their purpose. For example, she might see a washcloth, know that it's for washing and may hold it.

Your baby's new mobility is very exciting for her, but she's still learning the principles of object and person permanence, so she probably will not let you out of her sight for long. She will play her own "peek-a-boo" type games. She will round the corner where she can no longer see you then peek around the corner to make sure you are still there. Alternatively, she'll round the corner then make a sound or do something that she knows will bring you to her.

She will know repetitive games like "patty cake" all the way through and will recognize the slightest variation. Her attention span will be short but, when you have her attention, she will be able to point to a picture of a familiar object in a book when you say the object's name.

During this period, your baby begins to understand that people are unique individuals and separate form herself. This realization usually leads to separation anxiety. You may find that your baby has a difficult time being separated for you during the day and at bedtime. This is a perfectly normal development at the age and nothing to be concerned about. Keep your exits short and sweet, and try to enjoy your baby's attachment to you while it lasts.

WHAT SHOULD I DO NOW? (8-12 MONTHS)
Your baby is getting around now and that means she is finding all sorts of things to get into. Make sure your home is a safe place for learning and play by checking your childproofing efforts around the house.

Be sure to supply your baby with toys and household objects that will develop her hand-eye coordination. As you probably know by now, just about anything is a toy to your baby. She is likely to play with egg cartons and empty cardboard boxes with the same enthusiasm she shows for large blocks, balls, stacking toys and push-pull toys. Give her squeeze toys and containers to splash around with during bath time.

Whenever you can get your busy baby to sit still for a moment, read to her from books with large colorful illustrations. Encourage her to point out people and objects in the pictures.

Some games for babies in this age group include:

PEEK-A-BOO
Cover your face with your hands and then remove your hands and say: "Peek-a-boo, I see you!" Some babies have an insatiable appetite for this game so you may be playing it repeatedly for a few months.

THIS LITTLE PIGGY, THE ITSY BITSY SPIDER, AND POP GOES THE WEASEL
Babies love to learn these nursery rhymes and anticipate the accompanying movements.

ONE, TWO, BUCKLE MY SHOE
A counting game ideally suited for climbing up and down stairs.

HIDE-AND-SEEK

This game exploits your baby's understanding of object and person permanence. Hide your baby's toys or yourself and encourage her to seek.

Don't place conditions on your baby's play by requiring her to accomplish certain tasks or meet specific goals. If play becomes instruction, your baby may become bored or, even worse; feel that your love or attention is dependent upon how well she performs the task.

LEARNING MILESTONES

By the end of this period (8-12 months), most babies can:

- Bring two cubes together.
- Put objects into a container and take them out.
- Poke with an index finger.
- Try to imitate words and gestures.

As we can see, the older our children get the more capable of learning and storing information. The older our children get the more responsible we become in helping them to fine tune their new found capabilities.

1. My child's age is: _____
2. My child's developmental state (Erikson) is: _____
3. My child's cognitive stage (Piaget) is: _____
4. As a parent how can you help your child at this stage? _____
   _____
   _____
   _____

5. What is difficult about this stage (for the child and/or parent)? _____
   _____
   _____
   _____

6. What is fun or exciting about this stage? _____
   _____
   _____
   _____

7. At this stage how can you provide for your child's fundamental needs? _____
   _____
   _____
   _____

8. At this stage, how can you provide for your child's psychological needs? _____
   _____
   _____
   _____

9. At this stage, how can you provide for your child's need for self-actualization? _____
   _____
   _____
   _____

LANGUAGE DEVELOPMENT IN CHILDREN

Some developments in behavior and thought are very similar for all children. Around the world, most infants begin to focus their eyes, sit up, and learn to walk at comparable ages, and children begin to acquire language and develop logical reasoning skills at approximately the same time. Other aspects of individual growth are highly predictable.

LANGUAGE DEVELOPMENT AGES 4-8 MONTHS

Your baby learns language in stages. From birth he receives information about language by hearing people make sounds and watching how they communicate with one another. At first he is most interested in the pitch and level of your voice. When you talk to him in a soothing way, he will stop crying because he hears that you want to comfort him. By contrast, if you shout out in anger he probably will cry because your voice is telling him something is wrong. By 4 months, he'll begin noticing not only the way you talk but the individual sounds you make. He will listen to the vowels and consonants. Moreover, begin to notice the way these combine into syllables, words and sentences.

As well as receiving sounds, your baby also has been producing them from the very beginning, first in the form or cries and then as coos. At about 4 months, he will start to babble using many of the rhythms and characteristics of his native language. Although it may sound like gibberish, if you listen closely, you'll hear him raise and drop his voice as if he were making a statement or asking a question. Encourage him by talking to him throughout the day. When he says a recognizable syllable, repeat it back to him and then say some simple words that contain that sound. For example, if his sound of the day is "bah," introduce him to bottle, box, bonnet and baa, baa back sheep.

PARTICIPATING IN LANGUAGE DEVELOPMENT

Your participation in your child's language development will become even more important after 6 or 7 months, when he begins actively imitating the sounds of speech. Up to that point, he might repeat one sound for a whole day or even days at a stretch before trying another. But now he'll become much more responsive to the sounds he hears you make and he'll try to follow your lead. So introduce him to simple syllables and words like, baby, cat, dog, go, hot, cold and walk, as well as mama and dada. Although it may be as much as a year before you can interpret any of his babbling, your baby can understand many of your words well before his first birthday

Below you will find some developmental guidelines but remember that all children development at their own pace.

6-12 MONTHS

- Vocalization with intonation.
- Responds to his name.
- Responds to human voices without visual cues by turning his head and eyes.
- Responds appropriately to friendly and angry tones.

12-18 MONTHS

- Uses one or more words with meaning. This may be a fragment of a word.

- Understands simple instructions, especially if vocal or physical cues are given.
- Practices inflection.
- Is aware of the social value of speech.

18-24 MONTHS

- Has vocabulary of approximately 5-25 words.
- Vocabulary made up chiefly of nouns.
- Some echolalia or repeating a word or phrase over and over.
- Much jargon with emotional content.
- Is able to follow simple commands.

24-36 MONTHS

- Can name a number of objects common to his surroundings.
- Is able to use at least two prepositions, usually chosen from the following: in, on, under.
- Combines words into short sentences, largely noun-verb combinations. Lengths of sentences are given as 1-2 words.
- Approximately 2/3 of what a child says should be intelligible.
- Vocabulary of approximately 150-300 words.
- Rhythm and fluency often poor.
- Volume and pitch of voice not yet well controlled.
- Can use two pronouns correctly: I, me, you, although me and I are often confused.
- My and mine are beginning to emerge.
- Responds to such commands as: "show me your eyes, nose, mouth or hair,"

36-48 MONTHS

- Use pronouns I, you, me correctly.
- Is using some plurals and past tenses.
- Knows at lest three prepositions, usually in, on, under.
- Knows chief parts of body and should be able to indicate these if not name.
- Handles three word sentences easily.
- Has in the neighborhood of 900-1000 words.
- About 90% of what child says should be intelligible.
- Verbs begin to predominate.
- Understands most simple questions dealing with his environment and activities.
- Relates his experiences so that they can be followed with reason.
- Able to reason out such questions as: what must you do when you are sleepy, hungry, cool or thirsty?
- Should be able to give his sex, name, age.
- Should not be expected to answer all questions even though he understands what is expected.

48-60 MONTHS

- Knows names of familiar animals.

- Can use at least four prepositions or can demonstrate his understanding of their meaning when given commands.
- Names common objects in picture books or magazines.
- Knows one or more colors.
- Can repeat 4 digits when they are given slowly.
- Can usually repeat words of four syllables.
- Demonstrates understanding of over and under.
- Has most vowels and diphthongs and consonants p,b,m,w,n well established.
- Often indulges in make-believe.
- Extensive verbalization as he carries out activities.
- When someone presents a contrast, he understands such concepts as longer or larger.
- Readily follows simple commands even though the stimulus objects are not in sight.
- Uses repetition of words, phrases, syllables and even sounds.

5 YEARS-6 YEARS

- Can use many descriptive words spontaneously, both adjectives and adverbs.
- Knows common opposites: big-little, hard-soft, heavy-light, etc.
- Have number concepts of 4 or more.
- Can count to ten.
- Speech should be completely intelligible, in spite of articulation problems.
- Should have all vowels and consonants learned.
- Should be able to repeat sentences as long as nine words.
- Should be able to define common objects in terms of use such as hat, shoe or chair.
- Should be able to follow three commands given without interruptions.
- Should know his age.
- Should have simple time concepts such as morning, afternoon, night, day, later, after, while.
- Should be using fairly long sentences and should use some compound and some complex sentences.
- Speech on the whole should be grammatically correct.

6 YEARS-7 YEARS

- In addition to the above consonants, the f, v, she, Hz, the or I, should be mastered.
- He should have concepts of 7.
- Speech should be completely intelligible and socially useful.
- Should be able to tell one a rather connected story about a picture, seeing relationships between objects and happenings.

7 YEARS-8 YEARS

- Should have mastered the consonants s, z, r, voiceless th, ch, wh, and the soft g as in George.
- Should handle opposite analogies easily: girl-boy, man-woman, flies-swims, blunt-sharp, short-long, sweet-sour, etc.
- Understands such terms as: alike, different, beginning, end, etc.

- Should be able to tell time to quarter hour.
- Should be able to do simple reading and to write or print many words.

8 YEARS

- Can relate rather involved accounts of events, many of which occurred at some time in the past.
- Complex and compound sentences should be used easily.
- Should have few lapses in grammatical constrictions: tense, pronouns, plural.
- All speech sounds, including consonant blends should be established.
- Should be reading with considerable ease and now writing simple compositions.
- Social amenities should be present in his speech in appropriate situations.
- Generally, control of rate, pitch and volume are established and are appropriate.
- Can carry on conversation at rather adult level.
- Follows fairly complex directions with little repetition.
- Has well developed time and number concepts.

RECOMMENDED IMMUNIZATION SCHEDULE

DTaP, to protect against diphtheria, tetanus, and pertussis (whooping cough):

- At 2 months.
- At 4 months.
- At 6 months.
- Between 15 and 18 months (can be given as early as 12 months as long as it's at least six months after the previous shot."
- Between 4 to 6 years old.
- A booster shot as 11 or 12 years of age.

Hepatitis A, to protect against hepatitis A, which can cause the liver disease hepatitis:

- Between 12 and 23 months, two shots at least six months apart.

Hepatitis B (HBV), to protect against hepatitis B, which can cause the liver disease hepatitis:

- At birth.
- Between 1 and 2 months.
- Between 6 and 18 months.

Hib, to protect against Haemophilus influenza type B, which can lead to meningitis, pneumonia, and epiglottitis:

- At 2 months.
- At 4 months.
- At 6 months (not needed if the PedvaxHIB or ComVax brand of vaccine was given at 4 months).

- Between 12 and 15 months.

HPV, to protect against human papillomavirus, the most common sexually transmitted disease in the United States and a cause of cervical cancer:

- Three doses between 11 and 12 years, for girls (one version of the HPV vaccine prevents genital warts in males, but is not on the official schedule.)

Influenza as recommended by your doctor.

Meningococcal, to protect against meningococcal disease, the leading cause of bacterial meningitis in United States children in pre-vaccine days:

- Between 11 and 12 years.

MMR, to protect against measles, mumps, and rubella (German measles):

- Between 12 and 15 months.
- Between 4 and 6 years old.

Pheumoccoccal (PCV), to protect against pheunoccoccal disease, which can lead to meningitis, pneumonia, and ear infections:

- At 2 months.
- At 4 months.
- At 6 month.
- Between 12 and 15 months.

Polio (IPV), to protect against polio:

- At 2 months.
- At 4 months.
- Between 6 and 18 months.
- Between 4 and 6 years old.

Rotavirus, to protect against rotavirus, which can cause severs diarrhea, vomiting, fever, and dehydration (given orally, not as an injection):

- At 2 months.
- At 4 months.
- At 6 months (not needed if the Rotarix brand of vaccine was given at 2 and 4 months):

Varicella, to protect against chicken pox.

- Between 12 and 15 months.
- Between 4 and 6 years.

Immunizations are designed to protect against serious illnesses ranging from polio and tetanus to measles, mumps and the seasonal flu. Many people consider them the most important part of well-child checkups.

Just remember that all children develop somewhat differently and you must let them develop at their own pace. Every thing must be age appropriate. Just take one day at a time. When your child begins to use inappropriate behavior, try to find the goal of his behavior. Sometimes it is just a phase and will go away on its own. Most of all be patient. Give them even more rewards for good behavior. Hang in there. Things will get better.

POSITIVE EFFECTIVE PARENTING
P.E.P.

CHAPTER THREE
Behavior

CHAPTER THREE

Behavior

UNDERSTANDING BEHAVIOR

Of all our many responsibilities as parents probably the most demanding is the job of teaching our children the distinction between acceptable and unacceptable behavior. To help make this job a little easier we need to understand human behavior. Parents who understand their child's behavior, acceptable or unacceptable, are in a much better position to influence their children.

DEFINE BEHAVIOR

What exactly is behavior? Webster defines behavior as, "The actions or reactions of persons or things in response to external or internal stimuli." The question is why people react differently to seemingly identical events. Every individual's behavior is different because it is part of the person's unique personality. Therefore, to further understand behavior we need to define personality. Personality is defined as the totality of qualities and traits that are peculiar to a specific person. It is the pattern of collective character, behavioral, temperamental, emotional and mental traits of a person. Down through the years several theories of personality have emerged. Some suggest that one's personality is primarily the result of heredity while others believe it is caused by environmental influences. Most recently researchers have proposed that behavior is a combination of these two factors. We know that every human being is born with certain hereditary traits including temperament. We also know that from the moment of conception, every human being experiences a unique set of environmental influences. These two factors combine to make up one's own unique personality. The Positive Effective Parenting approach to behavior is based on the belief that behavior is learned and is the outward manifestation of our personality which is a combination of heredity and environment. This is the reason no two children behave the same. Not even twins brought up in the same home.

Not only is behavior learned, it has a purpose. The purpose or goal of behavior is to communicate our needs to others and to have these needs met. Therefore, we could say that behavior is simply a TOOL. In order to teach children acceptable behavior we must teach them the appropriate TOOL to use to meet their needs. For example, if your five year old has a question and needs your attention you can teach him to politely ask for your assistance or you can teach him that the only way to get your attention is to yell, throw a tantrum or use some other form of inappropriate behavior. Too often we unwittingly do teach children to act inappropriately.

As an example of this, consider the following scene at the grocery store. Little Bobby quietly asks his mother for something but mom is busy looking over the vegetables and doesn't answer. So Bobby's voice gets louder, whinier and more insistent. Finally Mom responds! Unwittingly, she has taught Bobby that the louder his voice gets and the more unpleasantly he insists on something, the more likely he is to get his way. Without even being aware of it, his mother has followed a perfectly designed procedure for teaching her child to be obnoxious. It is as if she said to herself, "I want little Bobby to learn to be obnoxious, to ask for things in a very irritating and unpleasant way. Every time he asks for something in a nice way and a quiet voice, I will be too engrossed in some adult activity to pay attention to him. I will only reward or reinforce him with my attention if he asks for something in an obnoxious way, if he whines or pouts or demands loudly or throws a temper tantrum." So, as you can see, we must be very careful not to teach a child unwanted behavior or we may create a monster.

HOW IS BEHAVIOR LEARNED?

How do children learn behavior? There are two basic ways behavior is learned: 1) through modeling or imitation; and 2) through reinforcement, which increases behavior. The most interesting thing about reinforcement is that it does not discriminate between appropriate and inappropriate behavior. If one finds that a certain type of behavior achieves the "pay-off" they are looking for or in other words serves the purpose, the probability that such behavior will re-occur is increased. We don't seem to care if it is appropriate or inappropriate behavior as long as it gets the job done. So, the ideal situation as parents would be to model and reinforce only acceptable behavior. Of course we know that this is not always possible, we are only human after all. Therefore, it is inevitable that children will learn some unwanted behaviors. The good news is that since behavior is learned, unwanted behavior can be unlearned or redirected. We will discuss redirecting behavior a little later but first let's look at the four basic goals of behavior.

FOUR GOALS OF BEHAVIOR

Remember that it is the goal of behavior to communicate and achieve our needs. Behavior experts have classified our needs into four basic categories. These categories can also be seen as the four basic goals of behavior since the behavior achieves something for the child. You will notice that the first letter of each goal collectively spells the word **ASET**. This is a good way to remember each of them for they are an **asset** in understanding our children's needs and changing their behavior from inappropriate to appropriate. The four basic goals of behavior are:

Attention: Attention is first on the list for good reason because it is probably what a child needs most of. Most parents don't realize how big this need really is. Children will always seek attention. They need adult attention, they want adult attention and they will get adult attention one way or another. Attention can include the need for recognition, the need for assistance with a complicated task or the need to feel powerful and in control. Often when a child is trying to get the parent's attention he is really taking a "power trip." This is a normal, natural and even necessary part of a child's development. It is their way of learning how to care for themselves. It is their way of fulfilling their self-actualization need, which is the need to fulfill one's unique potential. This need for power and control of their environment is actually preparing them to be independent and self-regulating.

Sensory Stimulation: This includes, for instance, the need for play and other physical activities or hugs and kisses, etc. When there is more than one child in the home it is important to spend some one on one time with each. Maybe Janie can help you bake a cake. Maybe go for a short bike ride with Jimmy. This not only lets each child know they are special but also gives them some of the sensory stimulus they need. This time also builds special memories they will treasure for life. Many problems disappear when children experience plenty of play time. It is also a way of building good communication skills.

Extinction or non-interaction: This would include, for instance, the need for a nap, quiet time if a child had been over stimulated and even the need for privacy.

Tangibles: Tangibles include food, toys or even going to a party.

Being able to identify these goals is necessary especially when attempting to redirect unacceptable behavior. There are some specific techniques you can use to identify behavior goals.

IDENTIFYING BEHAVIOR GOALS

Sometimes it is easy to identify the goal of a behavior. At other times it can be extremely difficult. The best approach to identifying behavior goals is to look at the results of your attempts to redirect the behavior. Let's say, for example, that five-year-old Amy is with her mom at her grandmother's. She begins to cry because mom won't give her some candy. Does Amy need **A**ttention, **S**ensory Stimulation, **E**scape or **T**angibles? Mom thinks Amy wants a Tangible (the candy), so she gives her some. The candy quiets Amy for a moment but minutes later she is whining again. This is an indication that Amy's need or goal, was something other than the Tangible. It could be that she needs Escape. She may be tired and needs a nap. Amy may need Sensory Stimulation. Perhaps she had been sitting watching TV too long and needs to move around or go out and play. Or she may need mom's attention. The point is that if your action to redirect the behavior is not effective you need to change directions. Once you feel you have identified the need/goal of the child you can take appropriate steps to effectively deal with the behavior.

REDIRECTING BEHAVIOR USING MODELING AND REINFORCEMENT

There are two ways that behavior can be taught and/or redirected: 1) by increasing an acceptable behavior or; 2) by decreasing an unacceptable behavior. Although increasing acceptable behavior is infinitely easier and more effective most parents spend the major part of their time trying to decrease unacceptable behavior. This is, in large part, because problem behaviors tend to catch our attention more easily. Have you ever stopped to think about how many times you react negatively to your child in a given day? You may find that you are criticizing far more than you are complimenting. How would you react if your boss or significant other treated you with that much negative guidance? The more effective approach is to catch your child doing something right and reinforce them to the skies. Statements such as: "You did your homework without being told. That's terrific." or, "I was watching you play with your sister and you were very patient. That is very kind behavior, good job!" will do more to encourage good behavior over the long run than repeated scolding. Make a point of finding something to praise your child for EVERY DAY. Be generous with rewards when they are warranted. Your love, hugs and compliments are often the best reward you can give. Since every behavior has a "mirror image," if we find ways to increase the opposite of the unwanted behavior redirecting our children's behavior will be less demanding.

APPRECIATIVE COMMENTS

Every member of your family should receive at least two appreciative or reinforcing comments each day. A little praise goes a long way in enhancing self-esteem and encouraging positive behavior. A little praise needs to be something more than the same few phrases repeated over and over again. Here are some creative ways of saying "good for you."

That's really nice.	I appreciate your help.
Thank you very much.	You're right on track now.
That's cleaver.	That's a good observation.
I'm proud of you.	Now you've got the hang of it.
Keep it up.	That's an interesting point of view.
Much better.	I'm proud of the way you are helping.
Wow! That's terrific.	Exactly right.
Fantastic.	Good thinking.
Marvelous.	Very interesting.
You make it look easy.	Superior work.
Sharp!	I think you handled it very well.
Now you figured it out!	That's a good point.
You are really listening.	That's coming along nicely.
You are doing a good job.	That's exceptional.

So let's take a closer look at modeling and reinforcement.

MODELING/IMITATION

Children learn much of what they know simply by observing others. Children are all "eyes and ears." They see and remember everything parents and others do and say. They are like little sponges. Moreover, fortunately or unfortunately, they want to repeat or model everything parents do. So, we must be careful about what we are showing our children to do. Because many abilities and characteristics developed in childhood last a lifetime, we must be careful about how we model around our children.

One of the easiest ways to prevent a child from displaying maladaptive behavior is to plan ahead of any future problems. Modeling is the easiest and most important way a child learns how to deal with problems. If he sees his primary care givers yelling at each other or hitting one another the child learns that this is the right way to express any angry or negative feelings he may be experiencing and behaving inappropriately.

Since learning consists of imitating the behavior of others, a boy may acquire his father's style of talking, his mothers' tendency to roll her eyes, and his favorite basketball player's moves on the court. In doing so, he also acquires expectations about the consequences of these behaviors. This type of learning has been studied extensively by American psychologist Albert Bandura. His social learning theory emphasizes how learning through observation and imitation affect behavior and thought

As the result of our traditional role models we often have different expectations for boys than we do for girls. In the past, we used to encourage aggression and stoicism in boys and we encouraged dependence and passivity in girls. These roles are changing but we still have few role models of "equality" between the sexes. Our expectations of these roles and even our confusion about them have a profound influence on our children's perceptions.

In the Johnson family there is an eight-year-old boy and a six-year-old girl. When the boy gets hurt and starts to cry, the parents respond by saying, "Stop crying and be a big boy!" Whereas when the girl gets hurt and cries, she is comforted and her tears are accepted.

In this situation, the son is being taught to hide his feelings and to influence people with his strength. The girl is being taught to influence people by using helplessness and dependence. What most children lack are roll models that balance strength, vulnerability and open honest expression of feelings. Whether it is our son or our daughter who gets hurt and cries, we could acknowledge their hurt, allow them to cry and encourage them both to find ways that they could make themselves feel better

Young children learn a great deal about how to act by watching you. Before you lash out or blow your top in front of your children, think about this: Is that how you want them to behave when they are angry? Be constantly aware that your children are observing you. It is important that you model the traits you wish to cultivate in them such as respect, friendliness, honesty and kindness. You must always exhibit unselfish behavior. Do things for other people without expecting a reward, such as taking dinner to a sick neighbor. Express thanks and offer compliments both to your children and to others. Above all, treat your children the way you expect other people to treat you. This principle is reflected in the poem Children Lean What They Live.

CHILDREN LEARN WHAT THEY LIVE

If a child lives with criticism
    He learns to condemn.
If a child lives with hostility,
    He learns to fight.
If a child lives with ridicule,
    He learns to be shy.
If a child lives with jealousy,
    He learns to feel guilty.
If a child lives with tolerance,
    He learns to be patient.
If a child lives with encouragement,
    He learns confidence.

If a child lives with praise,
He learns to appreciate.
If a child lives with fairness,
He learns justice.
If a child lives with security,
He learns to have faith.
If a child lives with approval,
He learns to like himself.
If a child lives with acceptance,
He learns to find love in the world.
Author Unknown

REINFORCEMENT

Reinforcement is the act of presenting the child with a consequence that will **increase** the probability that a certain response (behavior) will reoccur. There are two types of reinforcement: 1) positive reinforcement and 2) negative reinforcement. Remember that both will **INCREASE** behavior. Probably 99% of people confuse negative reinforcement with discipline which is meant to **DECREASE** behavior and which we'll talk about later.

Positive Reinforcement is anything needed or desired by the child which, when presented after a freely emitted response, will INCREASE the probability that the response will reoccur. They are similar to rewards or something we will work for. However, the definition of a positive reinforcement is more precise than that of reward. Specifically, we can say that positive reinforcement has occurred when three conditions have been met:

1. A consequence is presented dependent of a behavior. That is the behavior MUST occur first and without prompting.
2. The behavior becomes more likely to occur again.
3. The behavior becomes more likely to occur because and only because the consequence is presented dependent on the behavior.

How do we know if a behavior has been positively reinforced? IT INCREASES! One caution parents do need to take when using positive reinforcement is that rewards such as money, candy, special privileges, etc must be used carefully. This is so that the child does not become a "carrot seeker" who is always looking for a reward every time they do something right or well. We don't want children to do good things simply for a reward. When it comes to behaving properly or doing things in the home it is best when the motivation comes from within. Once we start paying children for acceptable behavior or for tasks they should be doing simply because they are part of the family we may find ourselves riding a tiger. And as someone pointed out, "He who rides a twelve year old tiger finds it hard to get off." To prevent this from happening, the best reward is ENCOURAGEMENT.

ENCOURAGEMENT VS. PRAISE AND REWARDS

There is a subtle distinction in the parental attitudes and guidelines between praise and reward vs. encouragement. To illustrate this principal let's take a look at examples of the two situations.

When I first began studying this concept, it was very difficult for me to grasp. I thought it was always good to give your children "praise." Now I'm learning to understand it better. I hope I can explain it to you. Rudolf Driekers, the author of "Children: the Challenge" said, "Children need encouragement like a plant needs water."

First let me begin with the concept of encouragement vs. praise and rewards. We will nearly always reward a child for a job well done or to a child who is behaving well. I say, "There is nothing wrong with this." The trouble is that it is only one side of the coin. What do we do with the child who is misbehaving and feeling poorly about himself? This child needs encouragement the most.

It would be easy for him to get discouraged and we know that a discourage child is very apt to misbehave. The child who receives a lot of praise and rewards quickly learns what they need to do to get the approval of others. They depend on the approval of those around them to make them feel good about themselves. Whenever anything or anyone gets their way most of the time they can express very aberrant behaviors. It also causes them to avoid making mistakes instead of learning from their mistakes. This inhibits them from reaching their full potential. On the other hand children who receive a lot of encouragement learn it is OK to make mistakes. They do not lose any love from others. They are not afraid of trying for fear of losing. These children develop good self-esteem and social skills. Encouragement is given when the child tries hard to do better at a task then the first time. He is not reliant on the praise of others to feel encouraged. An example of encouragement would go something like this: "Hey anyone can have a bad day. You tried your best and we are proud of you!"

EXAMPLES USING REWARDS VS. ENCOURAGEMENT

USING REWARDS
Company is coming so to get ten year old Suzy to cooperate, mom just offered her $10.00 to clean up her room. Of course Suzy willingly completes the task. Mom is happy because her room is clean and Suzy is happy because she is $10.00 richer. The next week after cleaning her room Suzy goes to mom and asks for her $10.00.

USING ENCOURAGEMENT
Let's take another look at how mom's reaction differs when she uses encouragement rather that reward. In this case mom would simply ask Suzy to clean her room because it needed to be done. She would not dangle a carrot in front of her. When Suzy finished the job and did it well mom would say something like this: "Suzy what a fine job you did of cleaning your room. It looks very nice. I'll bet you are proud of yourself for doing such a good job. I appreciate your work so much. Thanks honey." This encourages Suzy to do other jobs well in the future simply for the satisfaction, not for money or some other reward.

Notice that in this case, mom puts the emphasis on the job Suzy did, not on Suzy herself. She does not link Suzy's goodness or worth as a person to what she has done. Mom does not say, "Suzy you are such a good girl for cleaning your room." This would be dangerous because if, say the next time, Suzy did not do such a good job (as can easily happen with a ten-year-old) mom would have to tell her. Suzy would then think that because she did a bad job of cleaning her room she is a bad person. She would think that if doing a "good" job makes her a good person then doing a "bad' job makes her a bad person.

We must not make children feel they are loved only when they perform correctly. Our love must be unconditional and children should feel that they could come to us even when they make mistakes. It is important to avoid giving children a message that says, "I love you when . . ." or "I love you if . . ." Remember that reward centers on the child herself and encouragement centers on the child's behavior.

Kahlel Gebran wrote:

Your children are not <u>your</u> children
They are the sons and daughters of Life's longing for itself.
They come through you but not from you
In addition, although they are with you yet they belong not to you

KEY POINTS TO POSITIVE REINFORCEMENT

1. Positive reinforcement can be tangible: toys, special food, TV, etc. Tangibles should be used in moderation, for special projects or with young children.
2. Positive reinforcement can be intangible: praise, hugs & kisses or notes of thanks, etc.
3. It strengthens (increases) the behavior it follows. For an example, a child who gets a big kiss and a hug when he changes clothes after school, without being told, is more likely to change clothes the following day. The key words here are, "without being told!" If you have to tell them, then reinforce them, you will need to tell them each time you want them to do the behavior.
4. Positive re-enforcers tell children what they are doing right.
5. It is a way of teaching rather than punishing.
6. The reinforcer needs to be something the child wants not what we THINK the child wants.
7. The reward or consequence needs to be specific. For example: "You and your brother have watched TV together for half an hour without fighting. You can have another half hour to watch what you want."
8. Give the positive reinforcement immediately after the good behavior. If it is something that is not available right then, use some kind of a "token" for later.
9. Positive reinforcement reminds parents of the good things their kids do. It is also an opportunity for those quiet children who don't get much attention to get some needed recognition.
10. The child must be in a condition for learning.
11. The child must be able to perform the task you want him to learn (age appropriate.)
12. Avoid punishment except as a last resort or to prevent the child from being killed or seriously hurt.
13. Instead of punishment, when you want to get a child to stop doing something undesirable, use extinction techniques. We will talk about extinction techniques later.
14. The teacher must give reinforcement to the learner.
15. Reinforce what ever you want the child to do and pay no attention to what the child does that you don't want him to do. This is especially true of young children exhibiting a new behavior that is not really too bad to require giving attention to.
16. Reinforce every move in the direction of the goal. Do not wait for your child to get all the way to the goal before you reinforce him.

17. In the early stages of training, it is important to reinforce every desirable response. Once learning is well under way, the reinforcement may be spaced out.
18. Arrange for the prospective learner to be successful in the initial stage of the activity that is to be learned. Do not set them up to fail.

POSITIVE REINFORCEMENT EXERCISE

Decide if the following situations are examples of positive reinforcement. Focus on the underlined target behavior and determine if it was positively reinforced.

Q. Miss Jones, a preschool teacher, was teaching the class underline{correct color names.} In order to encourage the children to use these names she began giving objects and materials to the children only when they had asked for the materials using the correct color name. For example, little Amy's requests for a "ball" were not honored but her requests for a "blue ball" were. As a result of this procedure, Amy and the other children used the correct color names much more often than they had before. Is this an example of Positive Reinforcement?

A. TRUE. This is an example of positive reinforcement because the response of using the correct color name produced a dependent consequence, receiving the desired objects or materials, and this if-then relationship between response and consequence resulted in an INCREASE in the level of correct color naming.

Q. James was handing in less than 50% of homework assignments in his sixth grade math class. His parents told James that for any day on which he did not hand in his homework he would be sent to bed right after dinner. As a result of this procedure, James handed in his assignments 95% of the time. Is this an example of Positive Reinforcement?

A. FALSE. This is NOT an example of positive reinforcement. In positive reinforcement a stimulus is presented dependent upon a target (desired) behavior and this dependency causes that behavior to increase in frequency. In this illustration no stimulus is presented dependent upon the target behavior, handing in the assignments. Instead, the stimulus is presented dependent upon NOT handing in assignments. Therefore, the stimulus, sending James to bed right after dinner, is not a positive reinforcer.

Q. In Megan's first grade class the children were given building blocks and invited to play with them. The teacher began expressing delight and enthusiasm when the children had constructed a shape or form they had not constructed before. As a result of this procedure, the number of novel forms increased. Is this an example of Positive Reinforcement?

A. TRUE. This is an example of positive reinforcement because the response, constructing novel forms, produced a dependent consequence, teacher's praise and approval, and this procedure resulted in an increase in the number of novel forms.

Q. In a junior-high English classroom the noise was often so high that the students' work was impaired. In order to solve this problem the teacher constructed an apparatus to measure the overall noise level in the room. If the students made little or a moderate amount of noise music would come on. As a result of this procedure, the students made little or a moderate amount of noise much more often than they had before. Is this an example of Positive Reinforcement?

A. TRUE. This is an example of positive reinforcement because the response that resulted in low noise levels produced a dependent consequence, the radio music and this procedure increased the amount of duration of low noise levels. This is an illustration of using positive reinforcement to STRENGTHEN a desired "mirror image" of an unwanted behavior.

Q. David sometimes <u>teased Lori about her weight</u>. One day Lori got so mad about this that she slapped David in the face and she continued doing this whenever he teased her. As a result of this David teased Lori about her weight more often than he ever had before she began slapping him. Is this an example of Positive Reinforcement?

A. TRUE. This is an example of positive reinforcement because the slap was a consequence dependent upon teasing and because this caused teasing to become more frequent. As illustrated in this example, sometimes stimuli that are painful and seemingly unpleasant can act as a positive reinforcer.

Q. Mark had just bought a new car. One feature it had was a computer with a voice that told Mark to buckle his seat belt when he started the car. As a result of the computer voice, Mark <u>buckles his seat belt</u> much more often than he did before. Is this an example of Positive Reinforcement?

A. FALSE. This is NOT an example of positive reinforcement because the computer voice presentation was not dependent upon buckling the seat belt. This is an example of the use of a rule or instruction to engage in a behavior.

NEGATIVE REINFORCEMENT

Negative Reinforcement is a way to increase behavior by making a response available that will terminate (stop) an adverse event. In other words, you increase the behavior by making an escape possible. A danger inherent in negative reinforcement is called the negative reinforcement trap. For example: Three-year-old Sara is in the kitchen with mom and begins to fuss and cry. To stop Sara's crying mom gives her a cookie. Mom has been negatively reinforced because giving the cookie terminates the adverse event (crying) and increases the probability that mom will give cookie next time the child cries. Mom is negatively reinforced AND Sara is positively reinforced. She just learned that crying can get her something she wants. Learning theories provide extremely useful ways of understanding how developmental changes in behavior and thinking occur and, for some children, why behavior problems arise. These theories can be studied scientifically and practically applied. Critics point out, however, that because of their emphasis on the guidance of the social environment, learning theorists sometimes neglect children's active role in their own understanding and development.

<u>WHY IS IT IMPORTANT TO TEACH CHILDREN ACCEPTABLE BEHAVIOR?</u>

1. To maintain order in the home.
2. To learn to follow rules.
3. To learn to become independent.

WHY DOES IT SEEM THAT THIS JOB IS SO DEMANDING?

1. We often, unwittingly reinforce unwanted behavior.
2. We model unwanted behavior.
3. We spend too much time trying to decrease unwanted behavior rather than working to increase the "mirror image" or wanted behavior.

One of our main jobs as parents is to encourage our children and strengthen their self-esteem or self-concept. Some things that can strengthen a child's self-concept are:

1. An individualized approach to each child promotes a good self-concept in that child.
2. Giving a child freedom to explore his environment and assume self-regulation as soon as he is able at each stage of development builds a positive self-concept.
3. Treating the feelings of your child differently from the way you treat his actions builds a positive self-concept.
4. Relying on the powerful force of unconscious imitation is a great builder of a positive self-concept in a child.
5. Emotional support from his parents helps a child to overcome feelings of inadequacy and to build a strong self-concept.
6. Letting your child learn by natural consequences helps to build a strong self-concept.

Just remember that behavior is simply a tool we use to have one or our needs met. Behavior is a learned response and therefore can be unlearned or redirected by using Positive Effective Parenting techniques. This will help them know their worth in the world. An encouraged child is a well-behaved child.

BED TIME BLUES

I think this may be a good time to discuss a challenge that all parents face and that is bedtime.

First tell each child exactly what their bed time is and discuss before hand the appropriate bed time rituals such as reading a story, singing some songs, going to the bathroom etc. Be careful though, some children will actually get stimulated with these things and find it hard to fall off to sleep, so all stimulants must be eliminated.

About 30 minutes before bed time go ahead and begin the bedtime rituals. Make sure they are quiet non-stimulating rituals. No homework, housework, TV or radio because these can cause a child's mind to become over stimulated. They must keep not only their bodies still but also their minds.

If you have one child that goes to bed easily due to their temperament and another that is difficult due to theirs, be careful not to ignore the "good" child just because you are paying so much attention to the difficult one.

This is the time to make sure teeth have been brushed, they have gone potty and have had something to drink because these are the requests they usually use to get up out of bed.

Now bedtime has arrived. Be careful to watch the clock and no matter what you are doing stop and prepare children for bed. Depending on age have or help kids get dressed for bed, again with as little verbal stimulation possible. Use very few words. This is the time to give hugs and kisses and say "I love you, sweet dreams, see you tomorrow." It is very important, especially for young kids, because many times they are afraid they will not see you tomorrow. Next, leave the room even if they are crying. If they get up the first time just immediately put them back in bed. Talk a little about why they must go to bed now. So they won't be tired tomorrow and that every one will be in bed shortly. Once again hugs and kisses. If they leave the room or get out of bed again, no more talking from you. Just put them back in bed and leave the room. Second time they get up. NO TALKING. Just gently put them back in bed and leave the room, do not even give hugs and kisses or other stimulation. Any future time they get up do the same thing. Keep doing this until they stay in bed. Be prepared because this can be even up to 30 minutes at first. Be ready because it will get worse before it gets better. They could get up 30-40 times before they stay in bed. Just keep doing the same things. DO NOT GIVE UP. And if you stick to the plan it will work. After two or three nights they will get the picture and go on off to sleep.

Being a parent is the most demanding job in the world, yet most of us trained on the job. When things are going well, savor the moment. Give your child hugs and plenty of encouragement. Be generous with pats on the back for yourself and the other adults in your life, and don't be afraid to admit mistakes. Your child will respect your honesty. Now is the time we must begin to nourish and nurture so they will blossom into loving, caring, self sufficient adults. The lesson is to critique don't criticize. We know that we are only human and will make mis-steps along the way, but practice makes perfect so keep up the good work.

POSITIVE EFFECTIVE PARENTING
P.E.P.

CHAPTER FOUR
Temperament

CHAPTER FOUR

Temperament

The main reason that teaching our children acceptable behavior is so demanding is because too often we work against their temperament. To learn to work with our child's temperament we first need to know what temperament is and how to recognize each child's temperament traits.

DEFINITION OF TEMPERAMENT

Temperament is that part of our personality that we were born with (hard-wired) and remains constant over a lifetime. Temperament shows up in the way an individual responds to their environment. That is, what behavior they exhibit when something or someone around them creates a stimulus (does something.) It is not the way caregivers WANT the child to respond, it is the way the child responds most of the time. Scholars have long debated the relative importance of nature (hereditary influences) and nurture (environmental influences) in child development. The environment can be modified and traits can be somewhat modified but the basic temperament will remain the same throughout one's lifetime. Since neither the parent nor the child can change the temperament, parents need to work WITH not AGAINST the child's temperament. Personality is determined by the interaction of temperament traits with the environment. Each person (including your child) comes with a factory installed wiring. We call this hard wiring. How your child is wired can determine how a child sees himself and others.

WHAT IS TEMPERAMENT?

Temperament is a set of in-born traits that organize the child's approach to the world. They are instrumental in the development of the child's distinct personality. Our personality is a combination of our temperament, our physiology and environment. Environment includes everything such as family, school, neighbors, ecology system, socioeconomic, etc. Behavior is the outward manifestation of personality. It's what personality "looks" like. These traits also determine how the child learns about the world around him. If a child is found to be introverted they will never become extroverted. They may be less introverted at times, depending on their environment but they will never be what we think of as extroverted. We have no influence over temperament. We cannot change it. We do have some influence over environment. We can change it. Since behavior is the result of personality and if personality is a combination of temperament and environment, since we can change our environment then we can change behavior. Since we can't change our genetic codes, if we want to change anything in personality, we must change our environment.

Our personality is never considered good or bad. How it is perceived and understood by the significant people in their lives that influences how children feel about themselves. Since temperament changes little over the years our personality will remain relatively stable from birth unless something in our environment changes dramatically. When parents understand how their child responds to certain situations they learn to anticipate issues that might present difficulties for their child. They can prepare the child for the situation or in other cases they may avoid a potentially difficult situation all together.

Parents can tailor their parenting strategies to the particular temperament or characteristics of the child. When the demands and expectations of people and the environment are compatible with the child's temperament there is said to be a "goodness-of-fit." When incompatibility exists you have what is known as "personality conflict." Early on, parents can work with the child's temperament traits rather than in opposition to them.

WHY ARE CHILDREN SO DIFFERENT?

Children are different because each has his or her own temperament. This accounts for why infants and children need to be raised in different ways. Parenting methods and techniques must be compatible with their personalities.

Researchers have long wondered why some children with very supportive and nurturing homes still have done poorly, while some from cold and barren home environments have excelled. Part of the answer is that infants are born with differing levels of resilience in their personalities. Another part of the answer is the "goodness of fit" between the child's individual behavior and the way they are reared. Generally, the better the "fit" the better the results.

Temperament is important in parenting in two ways: 1) knowing the proper parenting techniques and how to discipline and; 2) how it affects the parent's view of the child and themselves as parents. Both of these dimensions are critical in determining how the parent-child relationship evolves over time.

First, since parents cannot change or determine the child's temperamental style, parenting needs to be molded around the child's temperament. Parents who try to make the child fit their concept of the "perfect child" usually end up feeling very frustrated. A better approach is to observe and learn about the infant's behavioral style and then change the way the parent reacts to the situation.

Temperamental characteristics can be very positive in some situations and challenging in others. Only by sensitizing themselves to the infant's personality can parents learn how to respond to her in a helpful way. Most parents learn this through a period of trial and error but when conflict continues to increase rather than resolve itself or when it appears unexpectedly, assistance may be welcome.

Key points:

1. Do not punish the child for her temperamental style. If a child is shy, she should not be reprimanded for being hesitant toward a stranger. If the child adapts gradually, do not punish her for not obeying completely. If her response is better than last time so long as she is moving in the right direction encourage her. If the child is intense she shouldn't be criticized for being loud when she feels upset, just as she isn't punished for being loud when she is happy. If a child is irregular, she shouldn't be punished for not being hungry at every meal or not ready to sleep at every bed time.

2. Notice the times when things are going well. How are you reacting at the times when you and she are feeling good about each other? There are clues there about what the infant or child needs.

3. Recognize and accept the way the child really is. If parenting is stressful and your child doesn't act like the one next door, she may be "spirited" and need specialized parenting techniques. You may need to learn more about how to parent a spirited child than the parent next door.

4. Recognize your feelings toward the child. It can be isolating to feel that you are frustrated rather than fulfilled as a parent, that you are stressed by parenting rather than energized by it and that you sometimes wish that your child was different. Lots of other parents have these feelings. Find a way to discuss these feelings honestly. It will probably benefit your child also, if you do.

NINE BASIC TEMPERAMENT TRAITS

There are nine basic temperament traits, which can be observed in the way an infant, child or adult INITIALLY reacts to a stimulus situation MOST of the time. Remember that the child's reactions to its environment are a certain way because the child has a predisposition to that behavior; his temperament. As you read over these, think about one of your children and circle the appropriate number where you think he falls on the continuum. Please understand that these descriptions do fall on a continuum and, although we seldom find a child at either of the extreme ends, the entire continuum is considered "normal" and acceptable. Nothing is good or bad. It just is a simple fact and will help you determine his temperament. The conclusion that strongly inherited characteristics are somewhat changeable has important practical implications. For instance, even though many features of personality are based on inherited temperament, the family environment is an important influence on a child's personality development. Thus, even a child with a difficult temperament can develop positively in a warm and caring family environment.

1. *Activity level*   <u>ACTIVE 1 2 3 4 5 6 7 8 9 10 QUIET</u>

An active child is comfortable when active. A quiet child is comfortable being still. They need to be encouraged to act or move. This is the child's idle speed or how active the child is generally. Does the infant always wiggle, and squirm? Is the infant difficult to diaper because of this? Is the infant content to sit and quietly watch? Does the child have difficulty sitting still? Is the child always on the go? Or, does the child prefer sedentary quiet activities? Highly active children may channel such extra energy into success in sports and may perform well in high-energy careers and may be able to keep up with many different responsibilities.

2. *Regularity*   REGULAR 1 2 3 4 5 6 7 8 9 10 IRREGULAR

This trait refers to the predictability of biological functions like appetite and sleep. Does the child get hungry or tired at predictable times? Or is the child unpredictable in terms of hunger and tiredness? As grown ups, irregular individuals may do better than others with traveling as well as be likely to adapt to careers with unusual working hours. A regular child is predictable. Their needs can be determined, in part, by the predictable nature of their bodily functions such as regular sleep times, eating times, amount of sleep and elimination. Or, is the child unpredictable in terms of hunger and tiredness?

3. *Adaptability*   QUICKLY 1 2 3 4 5 6 7 8 9 10 SLOW TO ADAPT

Adaptability is related to how easily the child adapts to transitions and changes, like switching to a new activity. Does the child have difficulty with change in routines or comfortable to new situations? A slow-to-adapt child is less likely to rush into dangerous situations and may be less influenced by peer pressure. When faced with changes in a schedule or routine, new food, new people or new places, the adaptable child quickly accepts the change. Slow to adapt children take more time to "get used to" things. As grown-ups irregular individuals may do better than others with traveling as well as be likely to adapt to careers with unusual working hours

4. *Approach/Withdrawal*   APPROACH 1 2 3 4 5 6 7 8 9 10 WITHDRAWAL

This refers to the child's characteristic response to a new situation or strangers. Does the child eagerly approach new situations or people? Or, does the child seem hesitant and resistant when faced with new situations, people or things? Slow-to-warm up children tend to think before they act. They are less likely to act impulsively during adolescence. Does the child have difficulty with changes in routines or with transitions from one activity to another? Does the child take a long time to become comfortable to new situations? When faced with something new, the approach-oriented child "goes for it," is eager to reach for the new. At the opposite end, a withdrawal-oriented child will back away from something new or may even seem fearful at first.

5. *Physical Sensitivity*   LOW 1 2 3 4 5 6 7 8 9 10 HIGH

Physical sensitivity is related to how sensitive this child is to physical stimuli. It is the amount of stimulation (tastes, touch, temperature changes) needed to produce a response in the child. Does the child react positively or negatively to particular sounds? Does the child startle easily to sounds? Is the child a picky eater or will he eat almost anything? Does the child respond positively or negatively to feel of clothing? Highly sensitive individuals are more likely to be artistic and creative. A child who does not seem to notice pain has a high sensory threshold. It takes a lot of stimulus to cause a reaction. A low sensory threshold results in a very sensitive child who is bothered by lots of things. This sensory threshold determines how one experiences noise, temperature, differences in taste, the feel of clothing, etc.

6. *Reaction Intensity*   HIGH 1 2 3 4 5 6 7 8 9 10 MILD

The energy level of a response whether positive or negative. Does the infant react strongly and loudly to everything, even relatively minor events? Does the child show pleasure or upset strongly and dramatically? On the other hand, does the child just get quiet when upset? Intense children are more likely to have their needs met and may have depth and dramatic arts. Intense children tend to be exhausting to live with. A child's reaction does not represent the intensity of his feelings. A child with high intensity reacts loudly and with great emotion to everything. He laughs loud, cries loud and screams loud regardless. The mild reactor is quiet and reacts quietly. However, the child who reacts mildly to stimuli does not feel less or experience less.

7. *Distractibility/Adaptability*   HIGH 1 2 3 4 5 6 7 8 9 10 LOW

This is the degree of concentration and paying attention displayed when a child is not particularly interested in an activity. This trait refers to the ease with which external stimuli interfere with ongoing behavior. Is the infant easily distracted by sounds or sights while drinking a bottle? Is the infant easily soothed when upset by being offered alternate activity? Does the child become sidetracked easily when attempting to follow routine or working on some activity? High distractibility is seen as positive when it is easy to divert a child from an undesirable behavior but seen as negative when it prevents the child from finishing school work. It is related to how easily the child adapts to transitions and changes, like switching to a new activity. Does the child have difficulty with changes in routines or with transitions from one activity to another? Does the child take a long time to become comfortable to new situations? It is the degree of concentration and paying attention displayed when a child is not particularly interested in an activity. Some children can be easily distracted from their current interest. They notice everything. Some children are non-distractible. It is very hard to get them to notice any thing other than what is immediately in front of them.

8. *Positive/Negative Mood*   POSITIVE 1 2 3 4 5 6 7 8 9 10 NEGATIVE

This is the tendency to react to the world primarily in a positive or negative way. Does the child see the glass as half full? Does he focus on the positive aspects of life? Is the child generally in a happy mood? Or, does the child see the glass half empty and tend to focus on the negative aspects of life? Is the child generally serious? Serious children tend to be analytical and evaluate situations carefully. Mothers have always known that some babies are happier at birth than others. A person with a positive mood tends to react to things in a positive spirit. The initial reaction is positive. A child with a negative mood reacts to things initially with a negative reaction.

9. *Persistence*   LONG 1 2 3 4 5 6 7 8 9 10 SHORT

This is the length of time a child continues in activities in the face of obstacles. Does the child continue to work on a puzzle when he has difficulty with it or does he just move on to another activity? Is the child able to wait to have his needs met? Does the child react strongly when interrupted in an activity? When a child persists in an activity you asked him to stop, some say he is stubborn. On the other hand, if a child continues to work on a tough puzzle others say he is patient. The highly persistent child is more likely to succeed in reaching goals. A child with low persistence may develop strong social skills because he realizes other people can help. Some children are capable of sustained effort from the beginning. Other children give up quickly. Children come with varying degrees of attention span, persistence or stubbornness, children come with varying degrees.

Babies, children and adults will thrive with a reasonable match between their temperament and their environment. However any trait can become a hazard. For example, in this fast changing culture, we value high adaptability. But those with a fast adapting temperament can get to the end of the day and realize they have adapted so readily to their surroundings that their own personal needs have not been recognized. On the other hand, those who by nature are slow to adapt can become overwhelmed by demands for change. Or they can become natural planners who learn to respectfully pace the amount of change in their lives

To live and work optimally with children, we need to integrate both nurture (environment) and nature (inborn.) We need to adapt our interaction to the inborn characteristics of each individual.

GENERAL TEMPERAMENT CATEGORIES

While some children have no specific groupings of traits, most fall within some general categories.

1. The Easy Child: (40%)

    * Has a moderate activity level.
    * Is regular.
    * Is adaptable.
    * Is approach-oriented.
    * Has a positive mood.

Given traits like these who could not be a good parent? Fortunately, most children are not that difficult to parent. For these situations, good enough parenting will work. When the child is adaptable, a parent's techniques will work because the child adapts easily. Not all children fall into this category so let's take a look at the other categories.

2. Slow to warm up: (15%)

    * Has a moderate activity level.
    * Is slow to adapt.
    * Shows initial withdrawal.
    * Has moderate intensity.

There are special parenting skills that will make life better for these kids and we will discuss them a little later.

3. Difficult child: (10%)

- Has a high activity level.
- Is unpredictable
- Has initial withdrawal.
- Has poor adaptability.
- Is intense.
- Is negative.

These kids really are difficult to parent. It is important to note that any one of these difficult traits can cause enormous problems by itself. All the traits combined describe 10% of children, but many kids have one or a few of these traits that make daily life difficult. Special parenting skills can make a tremendous difference in the child's behavior and sense of psychological survival. For any parent who is living with such a child it is suggested that you get a complete evaluation for the child by an experienced psychiatrist. Many neurological disorders can cause these very symptoms and the symptoms exist from birth. Treatment is available.

You can use the table below to get an idea on how easy or difficult your child is to raise.

Temperamental Traits	Easy	Difficult
Activity Level (how active the child is generally).	Low	High
Distractibility (degree of concentration and paying attention when child is not particularly interested).	Low	High
Intensity (how loud the child is).	Low	High
Regularity (the predictability of biological functions like appetite and sleep).	Regular	Irregular
Sensory Threshold (how sensitive the child is to physical stimuli: touch, taste, smell, sound, light).	High	Low
Approach/Withdrawal (characteristic responses of a child to a new situation or to strangers).	Approach	Withdrawal
Adaptability (how easily the child adapts to transitions and changes like switching to a new activity).	Good	Poor
Persistence (stubbornness, inability to give up).	Low	High
Mood (tendency to react to the world primarily in a positive or negative way).	Positive	Negative

If your child weighs more heavily on one side of the spectrum than the other, he may be classic example of the easy or difficult child. However, if your child is in-between and his behavior presents you with problems, you may be in need of some new management techniques.

COPING WITH YOUR CHILD'S PERSONALITY

To become a "manager of your child's temperament", make sure that you step back from his objectionable behavior for a minute and remind yourself that his shrill shrike of excitement or his irregular sleeping habits are not deliberate reactions but ones he can not yet control. The key is to switch on the objective part of your mind rather than to become emotionally embroiled in his temperament difficulties. Through this emotionally "neutral" stance," you'll be better able to help him modify his reactions because you'll be thinking rationally.

Learn to distinguish between behavior that is temperamentally induced and that which is learned. If a child knocks over your best vase by mistake because he is a high-energy child and was running gleefully through the living room your response should be different than if he broke your vase deliberately. In the first case you may have to give some thought on how to prevent your child from running through the living room and remembering other ways he can work off his energy while in the house. In the second scenario, you will probably want to discipline the child for his deliberate destruction of your personal property to impress upon him that this behavior is socially unacceptable. With temperament the goal is always to manage rather than to systematically punish.

PARENTING STRATEGIES FOR VERY INTENSE CHILDREN

- Provide activities that are soothing such as warm bath, massage, water play, stories.
- Recognize cues that signal that intensity is rising.
- Help child learn to recognize cues that signal when intensity is rising.
- Use humor to diffuse intensity.
- Teach child to use time-out as a time to calm self-down.
- Avoid escalating intensity of child by reacting intensely to his/her behavior. Give calm, and clear feedback.

PARENTING STRATEGIES FOR SLOW-TO-ADAPT CHILDREN

- Establish clear routines.
- Prepare child by discussing plans for the day when routines change.
- Prepare child for transitions.
- Give warnings a few minutes before transition from one activity to next.
- Allow time for closure of one activity before going on to next.
- Stay aware of number of transitions required, and keep transitions to minimum if possible.

WORKING WITH YOUR CHILD'S TEMPERAMENT

A child's temperament, in large part, determines the special parenting skills needed to work effectively with the child rather then against him. All children must be accepted "as is." Problems develop when the environment (or adult) puts demands or expectations on the child that do not fit or work with the temperament. So let's take a look at the three "groups" and discuss some parenting skills necessary to parent these children effectively.

1. Easy Child—(40%)

This child can be described as positive, approach oriented, predictable, average intensity, and extremely adaptable. The "easy child" can fit most any environment, most any demands. Parents and teachers feel competent when working with an easy child, even grateful since care of this child requires little time, effort or attention. Danger: child's needs may be overlooked because they are so "good".

2. Slow to Warm Up—(15%)

This child can be described as passive, shy, afraid of new people and situations, cautious, mild-mannered, negative and slow to adapt. If this child is not given time to adapt, the time the child needs, a problem child will be the result. For every step this child is forced to take forward he or she will take two steps backward. If, however, no demands are ever placed on this child he will not make any progress.

The slow to warm up child needs an environment where stimuli are presented gradually and repeatedly, in a positive manner, over and over and over and over. Danger: Too much pressure will increase the negativism. This child must be encouraged, never forced. This is a difficult child to "hurry up" and the child's responses to the demands of socialization will wear on adult patience. Flexibility is the prime requirement for the parent of a slow to adapt child. Otherwise, frustration with this child can create a great deal of anger.

3. Difficult—(10%)

Withdrawing, and non-adaptable to change, extremely negative and very intense, nothing seems to work with the difficult child. Gradual and repeated demands presented with patience, consistency and objectivity are required.

Flexibility is the key attitude in coping with such as child. No one however, should be with this child for extended periods of time. Dangers: Without assistance, this child will receive nothing but negative feedback from his environment. Adults often communicate a host of negative feelings to this child such as hostility, impatience or bewilderment. Parents feel; 1) threatened, anxious and guilty. They believe that they are unconsciously rejecting the child; 2) resentful or; 3) intimidated (inadequate, lost, hopeless and confused). Parents must spend time away from this child to maintain sanity and perspective. Nurturing the difficult child is infinitely difficult.

When a child fits with the demands of his or her environment, that child grows. When the child does not fit, problems in interaction with that environment occur. Positive traits can be enhanced and negative traits can be subdued. The child's style of reaction, however, cannot be changed.

Adults, parents and teachers can intervene between the child's personality and the demands of the environment. If a child is coping with the demands of the environment it is a healthy situation and the child should be left to cope. If the child cannot cope with a situation and problems are developing and negative traits and behaviors are intensifying, adults must intervene and change the demands of the environment. When the child's problem behavior or symptoms cause the adult to react to the child with undesirable management practices such as impatience, inconsistency and rigidity, unreasonable demands can be identified and corrected. Harmful attitudes such as guilt, anxiety and hostility toward a "difficult child" can also be changed. The child will not change but the adult's reaction to the child's actions will be altered and the number of problems will decline.

A child who is identified as lazy, inattentive and lacking interest may be a child whose restlessness and shifts in attention are to be expected. If the child is highly active and distractible demands on the child to sit still or concentrate for long periods of time will be unreasonable. The child will need high activity outlets and may need to learn cues for returning to the task at hand.

Children can be taught ways to subdue negative traits. Mild-mannered children can be taught to speak up repeatedly until their needs are noticed. Non-persistent children should be encouraged to take breaks and breathers with a difficult task as often as necessary until the task is completed, rather than just giving up.

Before labeling your child as having "bad" behavior take a good look at their temperament and ask yourself, are you working WITH it or AGAINST it.

What type of temperament style do you identify with your child?

_____
_____
_____
_____

ONE ZOO, TWO FAMILIES, TWO VERY DIFFERENT KIDS

This is a story showing how important it is to work WITH a child's temperament.

One day two families make a special outing to the zoo. The weather is beautiful and this will be the first zoo experience for their children. The Smiths and the Browns have three year olds and high expectations for a wonderful day.

As they approach the zoo, the Browns have a difficult time keeping their child in check. Jamie Brown pulls away from her parents and runs through the front gate. They bump their way through the line and catch Jamie just as she is leaning through the guardrail over the alligator pond.

Back at the gate, the Smiths are still trying to convince Billy to get down and walk like a big boy. Billy is overwhelmed by all the sights, sounds and smells and is suddenly very clingy. As his parents try to show him the alligators, Billy cries and buries his face in his father's shoulder.

Jamie is having a wonderful time. Billy hates the zoo. Both sets of parents are exhausted from trying to cope with their children. While it may be difficult to have children like this, both kids are very normal. They simply have extremely different reactions to new situations. Kids respond to "new" differently

A great deal can be discovered about the personality of a two or three year old by watching them in new situations. One way of looking at personality differences is to observe the child's response to the unfamiliar

This response can fall anywhere along a continuum with extreme approach behaviors at one end and extreme avoidance behaviors at the other end. While most children are somewhere in between, the extremes do exist.

EXTREME APPROACH/WITHDRAWAL BEHAVIORS ARE DIFFICULT FOR PARENTS

Jamie is an extreme approach-oriented child. This personality type is going to be an adventurous, exploring adult. As a child, they are quite difficult to parent because they know no fear and will get into anything. They can unlock all the child-safety restraints. They like to go, to see, to do.

Parents often "lose" these kids without knowing the child is gone. Jamie probably got up from a nap at least once and left the house without her mother knowing it. A neighbor a few blocks away brought her back, much to her mom's embarrassment and relief. Keeping these kids safe is difficult and parents often feel incompetent and exhausted by the effort it takes.

THE CHALLENGE OF AN EXPLORING CHILD

Jamie will never meet a stranger. She has been told not to talk to strangers but she thinks a stranger is someone you haven't talked to yet. It is hard to protect her.

When she learned to ride her tricycle, Jamie left the street even though she had been told to stay on the driveway. Her parents were watching as they worked outside but in a split second she was gone. She didn't do it on purpose. She saw something interesting down the street and she needed to see what it was.

Jamie will not hold her parent's hand. A safety harness that connects child to parent is almost necessary in malls, parks and large crowds. The child can be required to wear the connecting strap until they learn to stay by the parent. Jamie's natural tendency is to explore, but she can learn appropriate behaviors. If she doesn't like the wrist strap, the solution is to let them hold her hand or to stay by her parents. She'll learn.

PROTECTING THE CHILD WHO IS DIFFICULT

Jamie's parents will need to provide close supervision, put good locks on doors and windows and set firm rules about what is and what is not allowed. They will never be able to assume she is in the backyard playing. They will need to check frequently.

When Jamie rode off on her tricycle, her parents put the tricycle up for two days. When she asked for it, they reminded her of the reason that her tricycle had been away; it was because she did not stay on the driveway. Then tell her that she would get another chance later. Always re-introduce the activity when it is appropriate.

We need adventurous people in the world; the explorers open new frontiers in every field. However, when you are the parent of a little one, their safety is a constant concern. Jamie's parents will not change her personality. They WILL have to watch her carefully and provide experiences that allow her to explore in safety.

THE WORLD IS DIFFICULT FOR SOME KIDS

While Jamie's parents will have a hard time keeping her safe in spite of her sense of adventure and Jamie will experience many consequences as a result of her behavior, Billy is the child who will come to see the world as a difficult place.

If Billy's parents had a personality to match his, they would understand that he needed time to get used to new things. They would understand his need to remain close to them until he is comfortable in new surroundings. They would allow him the time and the protection he needs without forcing him to participate too soon.

Billy has a personality trait that makes him cautious and reserved. He came this way!

His usual first reaction is to withdraw from or avoid new situations and he has trouble adapting to changes. Billy's parents, however, find his behavior hard to tolerate and are embarrassed by his responses.

Researchers in temperament studies call this reaction "slow to warm up." This has nothing to do with being male or female. If the slow-to-warm-up child is a girl, our culture is more tolerant. When the slow-to-warm-up child is a boy, like Billy, he is often subjected to ridicule for being a sissy, coward or baby.

This is unfortunate because there is nothing wrong with being slow-to-warm-up. If given a chance to get used to things gradually, to adapt at a slower rate than the average person, these children WILL accept new things and adapt to changes. If they are forced beyond their comfort zone, they will be stressed emotionally and become even more resistive.

Billy's father is afraid that Billy will never "act like a man." Frustrated in his efforts to force Billy to accept the zoo experience, Dad berates Billy for his natural response. Billy will have to cope with his fears and with his father's rejection. Billy's future does not look promising.

SLOW TO WARM UP KIDS NEED UNDERSTANDING AND TIME

Adam is another three-year-old who is visiting the zoo for the first time. His parents have watched him for three years and they know he needs time to get used to new things. When Adam needs to be picked up in order to feel safe his parents pick him up and say, "This is all new and unusual. Let's sit on the bench over here and spend some time looking around before we see the animals."

On the bench, they talk to Adam about everything he is seeing and smelling and hearing and wait for him to make the next move. They do not care how many animals they see in one day. They know this is Adam's day.

Eventually Adam begins to feel comfortable and wants to see the elephants. They hold Adam's hands and walk to the elephant's area. Instead of walking up to the rail, they stop at a bench when the elephants come into view. After a few minutes, Adam wants to see closer. His dad picks him up and they walk slowly to the rail. Adam loves the elephants.

Although they did not see much of the zoo that day, the next trip will be better. On the way home, Adam talked about how much fun he had and how he wanted to go back tomorrow. Billy's experience was not so pleasant.

Slow-to-warm-up children need understanding and time. They do not like surprises and need advance warning before things change. As they get older, they will learn coping skills and adapt to the pressure demands of society, but when they are small, they need our help, understanding and patience.

ACCEPTING CHILDREN "AS IS"

While most children are somewhere in between, the extremes do exist. These extreme approach/withdrawal behaviors are difficult for parents. Remember however, for children it is their natural response. They are not doing it on purpose. You just must learn to work with them rather than against them

Circle each answer below that pertains to your child.

THE EASY CHILD

1. Moderate activity level.
2. Regular.
3. Adaptable.
4. Approach-oriented.
5. Positive mood.

SLOW TO WARM UP

1. Moderate activity level.
2. Slow to adapt.
3. Initial withdrawal.
4. Moderate intensity.

DIFFICULT CHILD

1. High activity level.
2. Unpredictable.
3. Initial withdrawal.
4. Poor adaptability.

5. Intense.
6. Negative.

Based on the above information I feel my child is:

1. An easy child.
2. A slow to worm up child.
3. A difficult child.

How are you going to work with your child so that you are working WITH your child's temperament not AGAINST it?

_____

_____

_____

_____

Finally remember that one of the most important jobs a parent can do is help his child develop self-esteem. That doesn't mean over-inflating his ego but rather helping him develop a positive sense of himself with a fair sense of his strengths and weaknesses. Understanding a child's temperament is the first step toward enhancing his self-esteem because you will be able to deliver encouragement sensitively in accordance with his innate tendencies and help him build upon those traits in a positive way.

POSITIVE EFFECTIVE PARENTING
P.E.P.

CHAPTER FIVE
Discipline & Consequences

CHAPTER FIVE

Discipline vs. Punishment

DISCIPLINE VS. PUNISHMENT

As we discussed in chapter three, all behaviors are learned and they have a purpose. Behavior is simply a tool we use to communicate our needs to others and to have these needs met. We also talked about the fact that it is easier and more effective to INCREASE a wanted behavior than have to DECREASE an unwanted behavior. Unfortunately, there are times when we need to decrease or eliminate inappropriate behavior. To do this Positive Effective Parents use Positive Effective Discipline. Notice I said DISCIPLINE not punishment! There is a huge difference. Punishment focuses on the child and discipline focuses on the behavior. Discipline involves using natural and logical consequences where as punishment involves using retaliatory consequences. The most important difference however, is that if our goal is to guide and teach, discipline WORKS and punishment does not. The only way punishment works is if our goal is to get even, get rid of our own frustrations or simply to halt the behavior for the time being. However, the negative side effects of punishment are numerous and should be considered carefully. Studies have shown that physical punishment, such as hitting and slapping and verbal abuse, is not effective and has dangerous side effects. Physical punishment erodes the bond of trust between child and parent. Now the parent isn't a source of care giving, protection and comfort but rather a source of danger and pain. The child feels betrayed, becomes resentful and fails to mature optimally. Physical punishment can discourage, embarrass and humiliate children and they can develop low self-esteem. Most experts argue that it also promotes physical aggression in children by showing them that violence is acceptable and that "might makes right."

All too often when parents "punish", it comes from a desire to control children rather than guide, teach and nurture, this is often when they will "punish." Parents who use punishment as their first choice of discipline technique generally prefer the child who is submissive, palatable and easy to lead—sort of like a puppy dog. Of course we want children to be well behaved but not necessarily easily controlled by others.

To be prepared for the challenges of adulthood they need to be able to stand-alone, be responsible and mature and to think for themselves. If your child obeys simply because "you say so" or because he is afraid of you, what will happen when you are not around to tell him what to do? If punishment worked we would only have to punish once for an infraction of the rules. The child would learn after the first time. Punishment seems to work for the moment but it creates resentment. Thoughts are running through the child's mind like, "OK mom you won this time but I'll get you later." Punishment teaches children that because we are bigger and more powerful than they are that we can force our will on them. With punishment there has to be a winner (the parent) and that makes the child the loser. No one wants to be a loser. On the other hand, Positive Effective Discipline sets up a WIN WIN situation and the parent then becomes much more effective. Now we'll take a closer look at the differences between disciplining and punishment.

PUNISHMENT

Parents punish children for three basic reasons.

1. We are modeling our parents. Many of the parents I work with say things like, "My parents punished me and I turned out OK." If the old ways worked, we would not be experiencing the problems we find in children's behavior today. As we discussed earlier, the traditional parenting techniques of the past are no longer working.
2. We are negatively reinforced. Since punishment seems to work at the moment we become negatively reinforced and the probability that we will use it again INCREASES
3. Parents don't know what else to do. Most parents were never taught things such as child development, human behavior and communication skills when growing up. That is why books like this are so valuable. Disciplining is difficult and does require some skills. This book can help you learn these skills and learn ways to discipline your children in all kinds of situations.

DISCIPLINE

I want to make it clear that not using physical punishment does not mean our children can just do as they please! It is still our jobs as parents to teach and guide them using positive effective discipline. The purpose of discipline is to teach children acceptable behavior so they can become self-disciplined.

First of all let's define discipline. It is a set of behavioral rules and stated or implied consequences for minor children, which may be enforced (or not) by one or more parenting adults.

Why is child discipline needed? This may seem like a stupid question yet many parents can't clearly answer it. There are many reasons for child discipline. Let's look at some.

- To teach each minor child that their actions have consequences which they're responsible for, and can control.
- To help maintain order and harmony within the home, family and to promote a feeling of security in the kids.
- To enhance the self and mutual respect of the child and parent(s).
- To protect the inexperienced child, property and other people from harm.
- To model how parents lovingly guide, protect and care for minor children.

- To show the child that people have limits to what they'll tolerate and what happens when the limits are exceeded.

Notice that these objectives all have a positive flavor rather then things like, "to punish, to force or make pay for."

Positive Effective Discipline uses techniques that foster the 5 principles of Positive Effective Parenting, 1) Nurture; 2) Empower; 3) Validate; 4) Encourage; and 5) Respect. Using these five principles, parents are able to teach, guide and care for children until they are able to be self-regulating adults. Discipline is free from power struggles. It does not breed resentment. Moreover, when used correctly, is EFFECTIVE! So what <u>do</u> we do to discipline our children?

NATURAL & LOGICAL CONSEQUENCES: A METHOD OF DISCIPLINE THAT WORKS

In the past, most parents used rewards to get children to obey them and punished children when they disobeyed. We have already discussed the fact that this approach no longer works and why. Now the question is, "What do parents do when children are behaving inappropriately?" The most effective way to teach children acceptable behavior is to use natural and logical consequences. This method has several advantages over the traditional reward and punishment method. First, it allows children limited choice when making decisions about what courses of action are appropriate. Second, it permits children to learn from the natural or social order of events, rather than forcing them to comply with the wishes of other persons. Third, using natural and logical consequences gives children the mutual respect and dignity they deserve.

Whenever possible let natural consequences apply. Natural consequences are those which are solely the result of one's own behavior. Natural consequences involve a natural flow of events. They permit children to learn from the natural order of the physical world. For example the child who refuses to eat lunch gets hungry before dinner is served. Or the child who refuses to get up on time will be late for school. Always keep in mind that it is NEVER appropriate to use natural consequences if they would endanger the child or others in any way!

In situations devoid of natural consequences or if the child would be in danger, logical consequences can be used. For the consequence to be effective, the child must see it as logically relating to their unacceptable behavior. In other words, it must "fit the crime." Logical consequences involve guidance and arrangement by adults, discussion, understanding and agreement by your child. When a good relationship is in existence, you can use logical consequences as long as they are relevant to the behavior.

EXAMPLE OF USING NATURAL AND LOGICAL CONSEQUENCES

Sara is playing roughly with her doll and breaks it. Mom comes into the room and yells, "How many times have I told you to be gentle with your things? Go to your room!" Sara runs off crying while mom picks up the toy and throws it into the garbage. A half hour later mom comes into the room and says, "I hope you've learned your lesson! Tomorrow we'll go the mall and get you another doll if you're good the rest of the day." Mom would like to think Sara has learned her lesson and she did learn something but not exactly what mom had in mind. Sara learned to associate breaking things with anger toward mom for punishing her and joy that she gets a new doll. Mom has been negatively reinforced and Sara was positively reinforced. This means that both of them will increase the target behavior in the future. The only thing Sara learned was that if she breaks another toy, she will be sent to her room then be taken to the mall to buy a new toy.

In this case natural and logical consequences should be used to decrease the unwanted behavior. A natural consequence would merely be that Sara now has a broken toy. Natural consequences refer to things that happen as a result of the natural flow of events.

In this case mom didn't even need to do anything. She can just say something like, "I am so sorry you broke your doll" and leave it like that. You stay in control and there is no need for a power play (just no toy, no yelling and no discipline.) Let natural consequences take over.

Logical consequences are slightly different. They are logically related to the behavior. Let's say that Sara had actually been playing with her sister's doll. A proper logical consequence would make Sara buy her sister a new doll with her allowance. Once again the consequence is directly related to the act, and doesn't make the child a "bad" person.

Natural consequences are the best because no discipline is necessary and the behavior will decrease. If a logical or natural consequence cannot be thought of or is not obvious, then a consequence is not appropriate at this time. It is better to look for solutions.

Natural and logical consequences have several advantages over punishment. They both apply to the behavior not the child herself. They make sense and they decrease behavior without getting into a power struggle. Sara also gets to own her behavior and she feels as though she has some power over the situation. On the other hand punishment is rarely related to the behavior. Since natural and logical consequences are related to the child's behavior a good lessen will be learned. If Susie leaves her bike in the driveway after being told not to, you could take her TV privileges away. By doing this however, Sara will not learn to always put her bicycle away in the future. On the other hand a logical consequence would be to take her bike away for two days. When Johnny doesn't eat dinner he will go hungry. If Suzy does not put her dirty cloths into the hamper, she will have to wear dirty smelly cloths. After leaving her lunch at home Mary will go hungry for three days and then she will remember the next time. The parents don't have to use any punishment and they won't be the "bad" guys. Punishment will likely result in resentment and increase the chance that the child will start to feel badly about himself. The behavior will cease for the moment only to return in the future. The child learned no lesson.

To apply natural consequences, Rudolph Dreikurs recommends that parents simply ask the question, "What would happen if I didn't interfere?" There are many inevitable consequences that don't require the intervention of the parent. Of course, if the child is likely to hurt himself or others with no parental interference, logical consequences are warranted.

View misbehavior objectively, rather than as a personal affront and you will be much more effective. If you were trying to teach your child a new skill, such as playing the piano, you would probably be patient. You would expect and accept mistakes. If you will learn to approach any sort of mistaken behavior this way, you will find it easier to regard inappropriate behavior as a learning experience rather than a violation of parental authority.

SETTING CONSEQUENCES

To be effective, consequences must be:

1. Related: to the behavior.
2. Respectful: to the child.
3. Reasonable: age appropriate.
4. Reachable: can be attained.
5. Measurable: can be measured in time and space.
6. Meaningful: the consequence is meaningfully connected to the behavior.
7. Maintainable: can be maintained over a long period of time.

We must get children involved in setting consequences. They will be more willing to follow a rule if involved in the consequences that would follow the misbehavior. They are more likely to keep agreements in which they have ownership. Of course children must be guided in this process. They will probably be likely, at first, to want to set limits which are not acceptable or which do not contain the 4 R's and 3 M's

A good example of children participating in setting consequences may go something like this:

Mother: "What problems do you think we may have if you don't put your bicycle in the garage?"

Child: "It could get stolen or someone cold trip and fall on it. If in the driveway the car could run over it?"

Mother: "What solutions do you have for solving this problem?"

Child: "I must put it in the garage."

Mother: What do you think would be a reasonable, respectful, related and reachable consequence if you do not follow the rule of putting your bike in the garage?"

Child: You can take my bike away for a day."

Mother: "What do you think an appropriate consequence would be if this continues?"

Child: "Take my bike away for a longer period of time."

Mother: "That is a very good, responsible consequence. I'm proud of you."

PRINCIPLES OF NATURAL AND LOGICAL CONSEQUENCES

1. <u>Relate the consequence to the behavior</u>. Example: If Sally leaves her bike on the front lawn, a logical consequence would be that she could not ride her bike for two days.
2. <u>Make no moral judgment</u>. Example: a retaliatory consequence would sound like, "You're really a bad kid. I told you not to . . ." When using a logical consequence the parent would stay cool, explain what the unwanted behavior was, and give a logical consequence.

3. <u>Consider misbehavior a mistake not a SIN</u>. This separates the doer from the deed.

4. <u>Stay in the present</u>. Don't use the incident as a springboard for gloomy forecasts or as an opportunity to dredge up ancient history. Say, "I'm disappointed in this report card" not "Your report cards are always bad" or "At this rate, you'll never amount to anything."

5. <u>Use a neutral tone of voice</u>. You CAN show or say you're disappointed, angry, etc. without yelling. Be both firm and kind. When you PUSH you only get resistance and end up in a power struggle.

6. <u>Give choices</u>. Giving choices enhances communication. Don't give "yes" or "no" only choices. Logical consequences follow the three "F's": 1) FIRM; 2) FAIR; and 3) FREEDOM to make a choice.

7. <u>Encourage independence</u>. Children will be better prepared for adulthood if you let them become independent and self-reliant.

8. <u>Talk less and act more</u>. Parents hinder their effectiveness by talking too much. A child can easily become "parent deaf." When using logical consequences, keep talk to a minimum as you follow through with action.

9. <u>Refuse to fight or give in.</u> Set limits and allow the child to decide how to respond to them. When offering limited choices only offer those which you are willing to accept. Remember that you do <u>not</u> have to WIN because you are not in a contest.

What are some natural consequences your child experienced in the last week or two?

_____
_____
_____
_____

What are some logical consequences you have used lately to teach your child acceptable behavior?

_____
_____
_____
_____

RETALIATORY VS LOGICAL CONSEQUENCES

There are several major differences between logical consequences (discipline) and retaliatory consequences (punishment.) Below you will find several examples.

RETALIATORY CONSEQUENCES express the power of authority. Example:

Father: (yelling) "Jimmy, you are really stupid for taking that $5.00 out of my wallet without asking! You go up to your room right now and don't come down for dinner or watch any TV tonight!"

LOGICAL CONSEQUENCES express the reality of society. Logical consequences acknowledge mutual rights and mutual respect. Example:

Father: (speaking calmly) "Jimmy, you took $5.00 out of my wallet without asking. Now you will have to pay me back from your allowance and give an additional $5.00 to the church."

RETALIATORY CONSEQUENCES are arbitrary or barely related to the behavior. Example:

Mother: "Amy, I have told you a hundred times to put your bike away. You never listen. Go up to your room right now and don't come down for dinner or get on your computer tonight."

LOGICAL CONSEQUENCES are directly related to the behavior or logic of the situation. Example:

Mother: "Amy, you did not put your bike away after you came home from school. Now you can't ride your bike after school for two days."

RETALIATORY CONSEQUENCES are personalized and imply moral judgment. Example:

Father: "Billy, your teacher called today and said you didn't turn in your homework AGAIN. You are so stupid. How do you think you are going to pass 7th grade if you never do your homework? From now on you can't play outside until I get home and inspect your work."

LOGICAL CONSEQUENCEs make no moral judgments. They are impersonal. Example:

Father: "Billy, your teacher called and said you didn't turn in your homework today. Since you seem to be having trouble finishing your homework, from now on you will have to do it and let me look it over before you go out to play."

RETALIATORY CONSEQUENCES are concerned with past behavior. Example:

Ryan had made an agreement to be home at ten o'clock last Friday night, but did not arrive until eleven o'clock. It is now Saturday night and Ryan has asked to go to a party.

Mother: "Ryan, don't even ask to go out this weekend. You never can come home on time. You never do what we ask of you. You can just stay home for the next week. And by the way, you can forget that new boom box we talked about!"

LOGICAL CONSEQUENCES are concerned with present and future behavior. Example:

Mother: "I'm sorry Ryan but you're not ready to take responsibility for coming home on time so you can't go out tonight. We'll try again next weekend."

RETALIATORY CONSEQUENCES threaten the "offender" with disrespect or loss of love; they are a put-down. Example:

Father: (moralistically and disrespectfully) "Kevin you did not feed Spot so you may not play with him today. Maybe this will teach you the value of being responsible for your pet."

LOGICAL CONSEQUENCES use a calm voice and imply good will and mutual respect. Example:

Father: (matter-of-factly and in a calm voice) "No, Kevin you can't play with Spot you haven't taken time to give him his food and water today. We'll try again tomorrow".

RETALIATORY CONSEQUENCES demand obedience. Example:

Jenny and Jamey are disturbing the dinner meal by kicking each other under the table.

Mother: "You two knock it off right now or you'll go to bed without supper!"

LOGICAL CONSEQUENCES permit limited choice. Example:

Mother: "Jenny and Jamey you two may settle down or leave the table until you're ready to join us and act appropriately."

In addition to these more obvious differences there are subtle yet important differences between retaliatory and logical consequences. Without meaning to, parents can nonverbally turn what may appear to be a logical consequence into one that is retaliatory. Anger, warnings, threats and reminders may turn a logical consequence into a punishment. Example:

Mother (after Dylan missed his school bus) "Looks like you'll have to walk today. I knew you'd miss the bus, that's what happens when you don't get up on time!"

This is an example of a mother who is shouting with her mouth shut. These kind of hidden messages imply that the child has committed a crime and needs to be punished. It is directed at the child rather than the behavior.

DISCIPLINE USING LOGICAL CONSEQUENCES

The whole purpose of designing logical consequences is to teach children to make responsible choices, not to force them into submission. If a person is offered a choice they can be held accountable for their decisions. Most of us will learn more from our mistakes than our successes. The same is true for children. If we make all of their decisions for them how will they learn to be self-regulatory?

Timing is extremely important to make logical consequences work effectively. Unless the behavior must be stopped immediately due to safety factors, never discipline a child when you are angry or frustrated. The child will see you as being out of control and will control the situation as they wish. Any time you are OUT of control the child is IN control. Remaining matter-of-fact and firm yet non-punitive is important. It will help to have a "pocket discipline" ready to use in those instances when you are caught off guard. For instance, before taking your five-year-old to a restaurant have in mind what you will do if he begins acting inappropriately.

View misbehavior objectively, rather than as a personal affront and you will be much more effective. If you will learn to approach any sort of mistaken behavior this way, you will find it easier to regard inappropriate behavior as a learning experience rather than a violation of parental authority.

Plan ahead, with the whole family, about the rules, guidelines and boundaries. Everyone must understand. Explain the OCR of discipline.

O = OPPORTUNITY: to make a choice and which carries with it;

R = RESPONSIBILITY: which leads to;

C= CONSEQUENCE

Let the children be involved in setting consequence as much as possible in advance of the opportunity. For instance, the child will have the opportunity to ride his bike after school for 30 minutes. He has the responsibility to put the bike in the garage after riding it. If he does not do so you can take the bike away for one day, (time must be age appropriate.) Remember one day to us seems like 100 days to them. This is the consequence. If the child does wrong for the first time, discuss with him that everyone can make a mistake. Then go over the ORC again. After that calmly remind him of the consequence that will take place the next time and stick to it.

When it is time to enforce the consequences remember the 3 C's.

1. CARING: Teach the child with respect and dignity
2. CLARITY: Make sure he understands exactly what the consequence will be.
3. CONSISTENCY: This is the most important one and must be used <u>EVERY</u> time.

BASIC PRINCIPLES GOVERNING THE USE OF LOGICAL CONSEQUENCES

1. <u>The consequences should be reasonably consistent</u>. The same consequence should follow the same behavior. If your child is sent to his room one day because he yelled at his sister then was laughed at indulgently the next day for doing the exact same thing it will be very difficult for him to learn to stop yelling at his sister and others.
2. <u>The consequences should be immediate</u>. The more closely related in time, a consequence is the more it will help a child to learn new behavior. When you say something like, "You can't watch TV tomorrow," your child often does not see the connection.
3. <u>Don't deprive him of something important</u>. If you deprive a child of something important to him, the amount of time the deprivation lasts should be reasonable. To deprive a five-year-old of watching TV for a month is unreasonable and the discipline becomes meaningless to him. He has no incentive to improve his behavior any time in the near future.
4. <u>Never deprive a child of something really crucial to him as a punishment</u>. To deprive a child of a birthday party for instance is cruel and unusual punishment. He will react only with deep hostility and a desire for revenge.
5. <u>The unpleasant consequences should be as relevant as possible to the misbehavior</u>. If a child has scribbled on the wall with crayons, it is relevant for him to be deprived of the use of his crayons for several days. It is not relevant to not let him watch TV.
6. <u>Give your child a positive model for what he SHOULD do</u>. We need to phrase our instructions to a child so that we tell him what TO do, and refrain from telling him what NOT to do. Instead of saying, "Don't hit Larry with the block" you can say, "Blocks are for building, not for hitting."
7. <u>Handle danger situations wisely</u>. It is important to help your child learn to cope with danger situations such as crossing a street, fires, sharp knives and poisons. And, to teach him a healthy respect for the danger, without developing excessive fears in him. Allow him

to experience minor unpleasant consequences of his actions in situations which are not dangerous and he will be more likely to be cautious and listen to you in really dangerous situations.

8. Use natural consequences. Natural consequences are those that permit children to learn from the natural order of the physical world. For example, that not eating is followed by hunger.

9. Use logical consequences. Logical consequences are those that permit children to learn from the reality of the social world. For example, children who do not get up on time may be late to school and have to make up work. For consequences to be effective, the children involved must see them as logical.

10. Motivate children. The purpose of using natural and logical consequences is to motivate children to make responsible decisions, not to force their submission. Consequences are effective only if you avoid having hidden motives or winning and controlling.

11. Provide acceptable choices and accept the child's decision. Use a friendly firm tone of voice that communicates your good will.

12. Follow through. As you follow through with a consequence, assure children that they may try again later. This is very important

13. If the misbehavior is repeated, extend the time that must elapse before the child tries again.

Be patient. It will take time for natural and logical consequences to be effective. Some behavior even gets worse before it gets better. Just NEVER give up.

What are some natural consequences your child experienced in the last week or two?

_____
_____
_____
_____

What are some logical consequences you used lately to teach your child acceptable behavior?

_____
_____
_____
_____

To summarize, just remember to use natural and logical consequences whenever possible. If you cannot find a natural or logical consequence perhaps no discipline or consequence is necessary at the time. Look for solutions instead.

POSITIVE EFFECTIVE PARENTING
P.E.P.

CHAPTER SIX
Discipline

CHAPTER SIX

Discipline

APPROPRIATE WAYS TO DISCIPLINE

In addition to natural and logical consequences there are other appropriate ways to discipline positively and effectively. The way you choose will depend on many things such as the age of the child, the severity of the situation, time and place restrictions and WHAT WORKS. Let's take a look at some specific techniques you may use.

EXTINCTION: decreases behavior by removing the positive reinforcer which is sustaining or increasing the target behavior; pull away the "goodie." Instead of punishment, when you want to get a child to stop doing something undesirable, use "extinction techniques." Extinction is the best yet hardest way to decrease behavior. The reason it is so difficult is that most of the time the behavior will INCREASE before it decreases. However, if you can "hang in there" it is very effective. Extinction simply means not acknowledging the child or their behavior at all. Of course NEVER use extinction if the child or others will be in danger. For instance, if your ten-year-old is balanced on a high wall to get your attention you can't just ignore him. This technique is especially effective for behaviors that are new such as a five year old using a "dirty" word for the first time. Remember that actors don't continue acting when the audience has gone home! Extinction reduces or eliminates the behavior because you have stopped reinforcing it. For instance, take a four-year-old who discovered the electrical effect that the use of four-letter words can have on his parents. He comes home with these words for the first time. Does he get reinforcements from them? You bet he does! Even though it's negative punishment, the attention acts as a reinforcer and the behavior will increase.

How can Mom get him to stop? Merely stop reinforcing him. Ignore him at this point and play it cool. Sooner or later, when her little boy sees that he doesn't irritate mother any more, he will stop using them. If not, you can always try a different method. You have nothing to lose.

TIME-OUT: decreases behavior by response-contingent withdrawal and re-presentation of the positive reinforcer. Time out is a very good form of discipline. Unfortunately, it has been overused and used incorrectly. Let's take a look at the important points about time-out:

1. Very effective, especially for behaviors that can't be ignored, such as harmful or disruptive behaviors (kicking, hitting, biting, etc.)
2. Should be encouraging and empowering instead of punitive and discouraging.
3. As soon as children are able to understand, explain to them (not at the time of the upset) that sometimes we all get upset or act disrespectfully and may need time to cool off or settle down until we feel better. We behave better when we feel better.
4. Get the child to help design a time out area that will help them feel better. And let them know they can come out when they are ready to behave better.
5. Ask the child how long he thinks he needs in time-out to feel and behave better. Or let him set a timer.
6. Use sparingly! Never use when accompanied by anger in voice inflection, words or looks. Use a calm yet firm voice.
7. Time Out means isolating your child in a boring place for a few minutes. It has the advantage of providing a cooling off period for both you and your child.
8. The best PLACE for "time-out" is anywhere out of the mainstream (withdrawal from reinforcement) such as, playpens (without toys) or chair. Never use their bedroom. That should be a nice, peaceful, safe place for them.
9. First, "time-out" should be about one minute per year of age, with an upper limit of 5 minutes.
10. Call time out each and every time the child performs unwanted behavior. Expect the behavior to increase initially. Something in the environment has been reinforcing that behavior. When reinforcement is removed, the behavior escalates in an attempt to get reinforced.
11. When you call time out, state the behavior. Be brief. Example: Lisa, biting, time out.
12. If the child refuses to go to time out or performs another behavior on the way that is hurtful, add one minute. Tell the child (be brief). Do not show anger in either tone of voice, words or expression. Example: "Lisa, biting, time out." If Lisa ignores say: "Lisa, ignoring, that's one more minute."
13. Be sure your child stays in "time-out" for the full amount of time. Some strong willed toddlers initially need to be held gently in the chair with a hand on their shoulder. Do not be discouraged, this teaches your youngster that you mean what you say.
14. Remember: time out is quiet. If the child talks, plays, etc., start time out again. Example: "Lisa, talking, time out starts over now."
15. When "time out" is up, go to your child and tell him, "Time-out's over. You can get up now." Always re-present the child to the task!
16. Watch for any good behavior from the child and praise him for it.
17. Recognize any semblance of the wanted behavior. This reinforces the behavior you do want and helps it replace the unwanted behavior. Example: "Lisa, you wanted that toy and you remembered to use your words!" This should be accompanied with a smile and if appropriate a hug. Try to recognize wanted behavior in as many situations as possible and reinforce it.
18. Teach other, appropriate, ways to get the needed effect.
19. If necessary practice "time-out" a head of time.
20. Identify a specific behavior to be changed. Example: Biting
21. Identify a specific behavior to replace the unwanted behavior. Example: saying that you are angry, asking for what you want.

22. Talk to the child. Explain what behavior is not acceptable and why. Then explain to the child what behavior to use instead. Also, explain that every time the child does the unwanted behavior time-out will be called.

23. Explain to the child what he will be expected to do when time-out is called. Example: "Lisa, biting hurts! You can't do that here. It's okay to be angry. I feel angry sometimes too. When you are angry, you can say: "I'm angry, I feel like biting you." You can ask for what you want. Biting is too hard for you and for other people. Whenever you bite, I am going to say: "Lisa, biting, time-out." You will need to sit down (where) right away. If you argue or if you don't go to time-out, I will have to add another minuet to your time.

   - Practice with the child.
   - NOTE: this is done only in **advance** of the actual occurrence.

OVERCORRECTION: to decrease behavior using one, two or three levels of "fixing" what is wrong. You can use only one or a combination.

1. Restitution: you must correct or restore what ever it is you "goofed" i.e., the kid spilled milk, must clean up the milk; or the kid stole money from your purse, must pay back the money from his allowance.

2. Over Correction: restitution +. Example: kid steals $5.00 from your purse; he has to pay back the $5.00 plus give $5.00 to charity. If he only has to pay back the $5.00, if he is caught, he really hasn't lost anything.

3. Positive Practice: do restitution and/or over correction AND add the step of positive practicing the proper behavior. Example: kid spills milk, he has to clean it up (restitution); he has to clean up the rest of the kitchen; then you practice how to pour the milk properly. NOTE: do the practice a little later after the incident happens. Do not use it as a punishment.

POSITIVE PRINCIPLES OF DISCIPLINE

In addition to consequences, this list of techniques is designed to help children learn to discipline themselves and their actions.

1. When/Then—Abuse it/ Lose it principle. "When you have finished your homework, then you may watch TV." No homework = No TV

2. Incompatible Alternative Principle. Give the child something to do that is incompatible with the inappropriate behavior. "Help me pick out six oranges instead of running around the grocery store."

3. Extinction Principle. Ignore minor misbehavior that is not dangerous, destructive or embarrassing. Look the other way. Play deaf. Like we learned before, the actor stops acting when the audience goes home

4. Satiation Principle. Allow the behavior to continue (if it is not dangerous, destructive or embarrassing) until the child is tired of doing it. Without your reinforcement, the child will get board sooner than you think.

5. Positive Reinforcement Principle. Make a big deal over responsible, considerate, appropriate behavior with attention, thanks, praise, recognition, hugs, incentives, special privileges NOT food.

6. <u>Successive Approximations Principle</u>. Do not expect perfection. Acknowledge small steps in the right direction.

7. <u>Encouragement principle</u>. Give encouragement as often as possible. Help the child to see the progress that he has made. "You got 5 spelling words correct. That is better then last week!"

8. <u>Logical Consequences Principle</u>. Teach the child that behavior has consequences. For the child to remember the "lesson" the consequence must be logical. "If you forget your sweater, you get cold."

9. <u>Anticipation Principle</u>. Think about whether or not the child is capable of handling the situation. If not, do not take him to places like expensive restaurants, ballet, etc.

10. <u>Preparation Principle</u>. Let the child know ahead of time what he can expect "you will be able to spend $20 on shoes and may have one drink at the mall."

11. <u>Follow Through/Consistency Principle</u>. Do not let the child manipulate you out of using your better judgment. Be tough but kind.

12. <u>Choice Principle</u>. Give the child two choices, both of which are acceptable to you. "Would you rather tip toe or hop upstairs to bed?" "Would you like to wear the red dress or the blue one?"

13. <u>Humor Principle</u>. Make a game out of it. Have fun. Laugh a lot. "How would a rabbit brush his teeth?"

14. <u>Wait Until Later Principle</u>. "We'll discuss this at 5:00 p.m. We both need time to cool off and think."

15. <u>Wants and Feelings Principle</u>. Allow the child to want what he wants and feel what he feels. Do not try to talk him out of it or feel guilty for his wants and feelings.

16. <u>Validation Principle</u>. Acknowledge and validate his wants and feelings. "I know you feel angry with your teacher and want to stay home from school, I don't blame you." "And, you still must go to school. The bus will be here in forty-five minutes." Try to use the word "and" instead of "but".

17. <u>Owning the problem Principle</u>. Decide who owns the problem by asking yourself "Who is it bugging." If it's buggy you then you own the problem and need to take responsibility for solving it. Do not give your power away.

18. <u>"I" Message Principle</u>. Own your own feelings. "When wet towels are left on the bed, the bed gets wet and I feel angry. I would like you to hang them on the hook behind the door from now on."

19. <u>Self-Correction Principle</u>. Give the child a chance to self-correct. Stop talking, preaching and lecturing. Give him time and space. Tell him that you will check back with him later.

20. <u>Keep It Simple Principle</u>. "No hitting allowed." Then STOP TALKING! Give the child time to obey. Do not continue to go on and on about it.

21. <u>Time Out Principle</u>. Tell the child to "Take a break" or a "Time out." Then, give him a place to go until he is ready to come back and behave appropriately or a specific amount of time. Never put your child in his bedroom for time out. His bedroom needs to remain a comforting place.

22. <u>Bathroom Principle</u>. Go to the bathroom and wait for behavior to improve. Take your telephone, books, radio, etc. Do not come out until behavior has changed. Unless the child or others are in any kind of danger or the child is too young.

23. <u>Put It In Writing Principle</u>. If a child can read, write a note to him stating your concerns. Ask for an RSVP talking about what he has done inappropriately. Leave "I love you" notes to him in strange places.

24. <u>Modeling Principle</u>. Model the behaviors that you want to see. Show the child by example, how to behave.

25. <u>Demonstrate Respect Principle</u>. Treat the child the same way that you treat other important people in your life—the way you want him to treat you and others.

26. <u>Privacy Principle</u>. NEVER embarrass a child in front of others. ALWAYS move to a private place to talk when there is a problem especially in a restaurant. Create such a place in your home as well. Sometimes sitting in the car to talk things over is a good idea.

27. <u>Apology Principle</u>. Apologize easily when you are the one at fault or if you make a mistake. However, do not force your child to apologize in return until he is ready.

28. <u>Empowerment Principle</u>. Develop the child's competency, skills, mastery and independence. Encourage him to solve his own problems.

29. <u>Availability Principle</u>. Make sure that your child always knows where she can turn for help. If you are not available, make sure that someone is. Set aside 15 minutes every day to spend together. Let her plan how the time is spent.

30. <u>Positive Closure Principle</u>. At the end of the day, remind your children that they are special and loved. Help them to look for something good about the day that has finished as well as the day that lies ahead.

31. <u>Holding Time Principle</u>. Using this technique, parents hold their child firmly, until he can discharge his emotions. Parents accept the feelings the child expresses, whatever they may be, and continue until everyone is feeling better.

What are some things you think you would be comfortable using to discipline your children?

_____
_____
_____
_____

THOU SHALT NOTS

No matter what kind of discipline we use, we must never do some things to a child if we want him to form a strong self-concept and grow into a self reliant adult.

1. Thou Shalt Not belittle your child.
2. Thou Shalt Not use threats.
3. Thou Shalt Not bribe a child.
4. Thou Shalt Not extract promises of better conduct from a child.
5. Thou Shalt Not insist on blind and instant obedience with a child.
6. Thou Shalt Not talk excessively to a child.
7. Thou Shalt Not pamper and overindulge a child.
8. Thou Shalt Not use inconsistent rules and limits with a child.
9. Thou Shalt Not use rules which are inappropriate to the age of the child.
10. Thou Shalt Not use moralizing and guilt-inducing methods of discipline.
11. Thou Shalt Not give any command to a child that you do not intend to enforce.

REASONS FOR NOT SPANKING CHILDREN

So as you can see there are many ways to discipline our children without using physical punishment. Kathryn Kvols, president of the International Network of Children and Families, is concerned about spanking children. She points out that the latest research from Dr. Murray Strauss affirms that spanking teaches children to use acts of aggression and violence to solve their problems. It only teaches and perpetuates more violence. It can also make the child, especially girls, think it is ok or even natural for others to be violent to her or him even into adult years. His research further shows that children who have been spanked are more prone to low self-esteem, depression and accept lower paying jobs than adults who have not been spanked. In any case, the unwanted behavior may cease, not because they have learned a new and better behavior, but just because they are afraid of you. When you are not there, the behavior can return.

There are many reasons for not spanking children . . .

Spanking can and often does:

1. Lower the child's self esteem.
2. Breed hostility and anger.
3. Fail to stop the undesirable behavior for any length of time.
4. Lead to child abuse.
5. Lead to neurotic disorders.
6. Lead to desire for revenge/retaliation.
7. Teach that Might makes Right.
8. Block the learning process.
9. Lead to fear and avoidance.
10. Fail to teach appropriate behavior.
11. Make the child hit back.
12. Weaken the relationship between the hitter and the one who is hit.
13. Block communication.
14. Give the child a model for aggression and violence.
15. Not stop when the lesson is learned but when the spanker is tired or unavailable.
16. Get misdirected at an innocent party.
17. Not promote inner control.
18. Lead to parent abuse in the future when the roles have reversed and the parent is dependent on the child.
19. Make the child dependent on external controls for his behavior.
20. Backfire on the parent—causing them to suffer emotionally or physically on account of their behavior.
21. Confuse the child because affection, favors or gifts frequently follow it. This teaches a scary message that love involves hitting and hurting, a concept that wife beaters and all consenting victims of battering believe.

List some things you will be willing to do instead of spanking.

_____

_____

OTHER ARGUMENTS AGAINST SPANKING

1. Children who are not hit by their parents are more likely to find non-physical ways to settle their differences with siblings and friends.
2. People who were not hit as children tend to feel proud of that fact and special because of it.
3. When parents learn other successful techniques for discipline they usually like themselves better.
4. When parents learn other successful techniques for discipline, their relationship improves.
5. If a child is usually hit for misbehaving, he may opt to take a spanking and risk being caught if his only reason is to escape punishment. Children can be little gamblers. We want to give our children reasons for behaving not reasons for misbehaving.

When children are spanked, the unwanted behavior may cease, not because they have learned a new and better behavior but just because they are afraid of you. When you are not there the behavior can return. Our goal for discipline should always be future oriented. Teach appropriate behavior rather that merely punishing inappropriate behavior. Always help your child profit from their mistakes and not repeat behaviors that are dangerous or self-defeating. Research shows most parents do not like to spank their children but do not know what else to do

PUNISHMENT CAUTIONS

Whatever types of discipline you use always keep in mind the potential negative side effects of punishment.

1. Suppresses: unless the punishment is VERY, VERY extreme all you do is suppress the behavior for a while; doesn't get rid of it. It only works for a short term.
2. Pain: elicits aggression including psychological pain such as humiliation. The person who is punished may displace the aggression or become passive aggressive.
3. Model: boy hits his brother, mom hits boy and says, "Don't hit brother, it's not right." she is saying one thing but modeling another and the boy is more likely to model her behavior of hitting. You may get a quick decrease in the behavior but look at what you're modeling.
4. Concomitant respondents: the emotional, internal feelings that are paired with the behavior. You may think you are punishing a certain behavior but you are also punishing other concomitant (happening or existing along with or at the same time with something else) things that are going on with the child. Example: child climbs into your lap feeling warm, loved and safe, then begins to suck her thumb; you scold her for sucking thumb (punishment type I); child pairs the punishment with her warm, loved and safe feelings. NOTE: concomitant respondents include enthusiasm, self-confidence, etc.

5. Concomitant Operants: the overt behaviors or approach responses. Example: sitting in your lap, putting her arm around you, etc. The child may think she is being punished for that rather than just sucking thumb.

6. Target Behavior Returns: as soon as the punisher leaves, the target behavior returns. Example: teacher leaves the room. If all you use is punishment, the behavior will only be good if YOU are there.

7. Most Misused Behavior Control Method in The Universe: because it cycles . . . we are negatively reinforced . . . when we punish the behavior decreases for the time being so we get negatively reinforced and keep using it. The behavior INCREASES.

8. Gets Paired With Arousal: pain gets paired with arousal and emotion. Especially for boys because of their physical makeup. Example: caining of young boys in London created a bunch of men who were masochistic.

KEY POINTS OF DISCIPLINE

1. Must be something needed or desired by the child. No TV may be devastating for Johnny, but Suzy doesn't watch TV, for her a better response cost might be no Nintendo.

2. Consequence must fit the age of the child.

3. Parents must be able to follow through and control. If no adult is present when Jimmy gets home from school it is unlikely he will follow your orders not to watch TV.

4. Consequences must be logical: **NOT**: "Since you didn't come home on time you can not ride your bike tonight, you don't get to watch TV." **BETTER**: "Since you didn't come home on time from riding your bike tonight, you don't get to ride your bike for 3 days."

5. Must be consistent. You don't have to always use the same technique but you must always follow through with some form of discipline when rules are broken or the child displays unacceptable behavior.

6. Parents must also teach children what behavior they want the children to show not just discipline for the negative behavior.

7. Must be used VERY VERY sparingly. Pick your battles carefully.

DISCIPLINE TIPS

- Set a good example. You are role models for your children. For example, if you want to teach your child that physical violence is not the way to resolve conflicts or problems, then don't use physical punishment.

- Set limits, but be careful not to impose too many rules. Before making a rule, ask yourself: Is it necessary? Does the rule protect the child's health and safety? Does it protect the rights or property of others? Too many rules are hard, if not impossible, to enforce, especially with younger children. Keep rules simple and understandable.

- Involve children as much as possible in making family rules. They are less likely to break rules that they have helped establish.

- Help your child understand rules and what happens when they are broken. If you and your 4-year-old agree that he shouldn't cross the street alone and he breaks this rule, be ready to enforce the consequences.

- Be flexible. Some rules may work when a child is young, but as children get older, they need and want more independence. Remember, not all children respond in the same way.

- Help your child develop self-control. Young children do not have the self-control needed to follow all the rules all of the time. A 5-year-old may not have the self-control needed not to take a cookie from the cookie jar before dinner. To help the child resist, a parent can move the cookie jar out of sight or offer a snack that is allowed.
- Tell a child about behavior that is annoying to you or others.
- Act quickly when a child misbehaves. Don't let a problem build up over time.
- Be consistent. Agree with other family members on methods of discipline. This way a child always knows what will happen if he or she does not follow the rules.
- Be careful about saying "I'll think about it." If you do you must get back to them with the decision you have made. Otherwise saying, "I'll think about it," makes them think you mean NO and can cause them not to trust you to do what you say you will and it can cause resentment.
- Emphasize do not criticize.
- Teach don't preach.
- Encourage don't discourage.
- Use as few words as possible to get your point across.
- Discuss one thing at a time.
- Tell offense plainly, what consequence will be and use the consequence every time.
- Children are little gamblers they just are not very good at it. They will take the chance that you will not make them do it.
- Always calm down before confronting.
- Pick your battles wisely.
- Use logical consequences that are age appropriate.

Remember that spanking only stops the unwanted behavior for a short period of time. It does not teach a new behavior they can learn to have their needs met. One of the main things is to praise a child for good behavior and accomplishments. Let the child know you appreciate his or her efforts. Use discipline rather than punishment.

POSITIVE EFFECTIVE PARENTING
P.E.P.

CHAPTER SEVEN
Assertiveness Training

CHAPTER SEVEN

Assertiveness Training

ASSERTIVENESS

One of the greatest barriers that parents face in trying to teach their children to behave appropriately is the lack of effective assertiveness training. Children will basically model the parent's behavior style. Most of us have not been taught these skills, which are simple but take a great deal of courage, support and belief in our own control of our lives. Often the parents who do not use effective assertive behavior will find their children modeling their own style of behavior.

In order to raise happy, well functioning children, you must identify the way each family member addresses and interacts with the others. Assertiveness training is a way to make your parenting experience more pleasant by better understanding your family dynamics.

It was once thought that assertiveness was a personality trait; some people had it and some didn't, just like extroversion or stinginess. However, Lazarus redefined assertiveness as, "expressing personal rights and feelings." How we interact with others can be a source of considerable stress in our lives. Being assertive can reduce that stress by allowing us to stand up for our own personal rights. When we are assertive, we can express our thoughts, feelings and beliefs in direct, honest and appropriate ways that respect the rights of the other person.

ASSERTIVE RIGHTS

I have the right to:

1. Have angry or illogical feelings.
2. Be treated as a capable person and not to be patronized.
3. Have my opinions be respected and considered.
4. Make mistakes.
5. Take the time needed to respond to requests.
6. Make quests of others.
7. Determine how to use my time.

8.   Say "no" to requests.
9.   Choose personal values.
10. Have my needs be as important as those of others.
11. Change my thinking and behavior.
12. Strive for personal growth through whatever ethical channels are natural for my talents and interests.
13. Share authentic relationships.
14. Have idiosyncrasies.

What are some assertive rights you feel that we all have and deserve?

_____

_____

_____

_____

ASSERTIVE RESPONSIBILITIES

Along with assertive rights we have responsibilities. Here are some:

1.   To assess my true feelings without exaggeration or underestimation and to express my feelings appropriately without demeaning someone else in the process.
2.   To act in a responsible manner as much of the time as possible.
3.   To think through my opinions and realize others can disagree with them.
4.   To learn from mistakes rather than punishing myself or others because of mistakes.
5.   To reply as soon as possible without taking an unreasonable amount of time.
6.   To accept others' answers respectfully and to carry out any commitments made.
7.   To respect commitments to others as well as to myself and to allow sufficient time to fulfill commitments.
8.   To think through my responses before answering.
9.   To not impose my own vales on others.
10. To express my needs and, if appropriate, work out a compromise.
11. To avoid "boxing in" myself or others by labeling or making judgments.
12. To acknowledge and appreciate each individual's choices and accomplishments and to enjoy the process.
13. To feel appropriate anger and joy and to assert these feelings with the people involved.
14. To recognize anger and joy and see that feelings do not interfere with others' rights and responsibilities.

What are some of your assertive responsibilities?

_____

_____

_____

_____

COMMUNICATION STYLES

The first step in assertiveness training is to identify the three basic styles of interpersonal behavior.

Assertive: Behavior that enables a person to act in her own best interest, to stand up for herself without undue anxiety, to express wants and feelings directly with reasonable comfort and to express wants and feelings directly, and to express personal rights without denying the rights of others. When we are assertive, the basic message we give is: This is what I think, this is what I feel and this is how I see the situation. The message is given without pressuring, controlling or putting down the other person. The assertive message is You're OK-I'm OK.

Passive: Behavior that does not express an individual's rights, wants and feelings directly. It is characterized by silence, no indication of feelings and frequently results in conceding to the wants of others. A person is behaving passively when they let others push them around, when they do not stand up for themselves and when they do what they are told regardless of how they feel about it. Gestalt therapists might refer to this as confluent (flowing together) behavior. Passive or non-assertive behavior is an ego-defense mechanism that prevents people from being authentic. The advantage of being passive is that you rarely experience direct rejection. The disadvantage is that you are taken advantage of and you store up a heavy burden of resentment and anger that can lead to unfinished business and unexpressed feelings. The passive message is you're OK-I'm not OK.

Passive-Aggressive: Behavior that does not express an individual's rights, wants and feelings directly. The person seems to be passive, but there is a mixed message such as, rolling his eyes while saying he would be glad to help. Later, behavior emerges that expresses feelings of anger or hostility. A typical example of passive-aggressive: Alice is ironing when her husband comes in and, in a hostile voice, tells her that she is not doing it right. She said nothing at the time (stuffing her anger.) The next time she "accidentally" burns a hole it. The passive-aggressive message is I'm not OK—You're not OK.

Aggressive: Behavior that expresses personal rights, wants and feelings while infringing on the rights of others. Typical examples of aggressive behavior are fighting, accusing, threatening and generally stepping on people without regard for their feelings. The advantage of this kind of behavior is that people do not push the aggressive person around. The disadvantage is that people do not want to be around him or her. The aggressive message is I'm OK—You're not OK.

One of the main ingredients in assertiveness is RESPECT. There are always two types of respect in assertion:

1. You have respect for yourself by stating your needs and feelings and sticking up for your rights without putting yourself down in any way.
2. You have respect for the other person's needs, feelings and rights by not putting them down.

As you become more assertive, you begin to lay claim to your rights. You're able to have your needs met more often without the pain and frustration that is associated with aggressive or passive behavior.

Before we can stand up for our rights however, we must know just what they are. Here are ten important ones:

PERSONAL RIGHTS

1. You have the right to judge your own behavior, thoughts and feelings. With this right, you must be responsible for it and what happens because of it.
2. You have the right to offer no reasons or excuses for what you do.
3. You have the right to decide if you are responsible for finding solutions to other people's problems.
4. You have the right to change your mind.
5. You have the right to make mistakes. Along with this right goes the responsibility to deal with what happens because of any mistakes you may make.
6. You have the right to deal with others without worrying about whether they like you or not.
7. You have the right to make decisions without having good reasons for the decisions you make. Along with this right goes the responsibility to deal with what happens because of your decisions.
8. You have the right to say, "I don't know."
9. You have the right to say, "I don't understand."
10. You have the right to say, "I don't care."

PERSONAL BILL OF RIGHTS

Along with these rights you also have a personal bill of rights and they are:

1. I have the right to ask for what I want.
2. I have the right to say no to requests or demands I can't meet.
3. I have the right to express all of my feelings, positive or negative, in an appropriate way.
4. I have the right to change my mind.
5. I have the right to make mistakes and not have to be perfect.
6. I have the right to follow my own values and standards.
7. I have the right to say "no" to anything when I feel I am not ready, it is unsafe or it violates my values.
8. I have the right to determine my own priorities.
9. I have the right not to be responsible for other's behaviors, actions, feelings or problems.
10. I have the right to expect honesty from others.
11. I have the right to be angry at someone I love.
12. I have the right to be uniquely myself.
13. I have the right to feel scared and say, "I'm afraid."
14. I have the right to say, "I don't know."
15. I have the right not to give excuses or reasons for my behavior.

16. I have the right to make decisions based on my feelings.
17. I have the right to my own needs for personal space and time.
18. I have the right to be playful and frivolous.
19. I have the right to be healthier than those around me.
20. I have the right to be in a non-abusive environment.
21. I have the right to make friends and be comfortable around people.
22. I have the right to change and grow.
23. I have the right to have my needs and wants respected by others.
24. I have the right to be treated with dignity and respect.
25. I have the right to be happy.

Photocopy the above list and post it in a conspicuous place. By taking time to read the list every day, you will eventually learn to accept that you are, to each one of the rights, enumerated (listed.)

Nearly everybody can be assertive in some situations and yet be totally ineffectual in others. The goal is to increase the number and variety of situations in which assertive behavior is possible and decrease occasions of passive collapse or hostile blow-up.

Many people do not behave assertively because they lack assertive skills. These skills can be learned through assertiveness training. Some people master assertiveness skills sufficiently with just a few weeks of practice. For others, several months of step-by-step work is necessary to experience significant change

Assertiveness training has been found to be effective in dealing with depression, anger, resentment and interpersonal anxiety. People who lack social skills frequently experience interpersonal difficulties at home, at work, at school and during leisure time. Counselors may use assertion training as a form of social-skills training to teach clients ways of interacting with others more successfully.

THREE BASIC STYLES OF BEHAVIOR

Meet Agnes Aggressive: I'm loud, bossy, and pushy. I dominate and intimate people

I violate other's rights. I get my way at anyone's expense. I "step" on people. I react instantly.

To illustrate the aggressive, passive and assertive styles I'll use the following examples of a conversation between a woman who wants help with the dishes from her significant other.

AGGRESSIVE STYLE

Ann: "Listen, I have another bone to pick with you. I've had it with washing and drying dishes. You both pitch in and help me or I'm going out on strike!"

Dan: "Lay off now. I'm watching TV."

Ann: "Who was your maid last week? You don't care what happens around here, as long as your TV works."

Dan: "Shut up, big mouth!"

Note that the opening line is an attack, and Ann is probably replaying the angers of earlier annoyances. Such scenes have no winner because aggressive behavior only aims at hurting another person, creates resentment and resistance to change.

Meet Patsy Passive: I'm unable to speak up for my rights. I don't even know what my rights are. I get "stepped on" often. I'm meek, mild-mannered and very accommodating.

PASSIVE OR NON-ASSERTIVE STYLE

> Ann: "Pardon me, but would you mind terribly wiping the dishes?"
> Dan: "I'm watching TV."
> Ann: "Oh well, all right."

Note that the "Oh, well, all right" only rewards Dan for putting her off. By reacting passively, Ann not only fails to get what she wants, she also loses a little bit of her self respect, and, probably some of Dan's respect. She becomes a silent martyr, and may take it out on Dan later in a slightly overcooked meal.

Meet Annie Assertive: I'm firm, direct and honest. I respect the rights of others and recognize the importance of having my needs and rights met. I speak clearly and to the point. I'm confident about who I am. I realize I have choices about my life.

ASSERTIVE STYLE

> Ann: "I would like you to dry the dishes while I wash."
> Dan: "I'm watching TV."
> Ann: "I would feel much better if we shared the cleanup responsibility. You can
>   get right back to your TV program when we're finished."
> Dan: "They're just about to catch the bad guys."
> Ann: "Well, I can wait a little while. Will you help me when the program is over?"
> Dan: "Sure thing."

Note that assertive behavior does not seek to injure, but to solve an interpersonal problem. Assertive requests include a specific plan and the willingness to negotiate a mutually acceptable contract to solve the problem.

THINKING THROUGH AN ASSERTIVE RESPONSE

A situation in which you would like to act assertively is:

_____

_____

_____

_____

In this situation, the rights I believe I have are:

_____

_____

_____

_____

In this situation, I feel the other person's rights are:

_____

_____

_____

_____

Your feelings before asserting yourself are:

_____

_____

_____

_____

Self-talk that is blocking me from acting assertively:

_____

_____

_____

_____

To challenge these irrational self-statements, I will tell myself:

_____

_____

_____

_____

What is important to me in this situation (What do I want to say or do)?

_____

_____

_____

_____

To respond assertively in this situation (What do I want to say or do)?

_____

_____

_____

_____

After responding assertively, I will probably feel:

_____

_____

_____

_____

GENERAL GUIDELINES FOR ASSERTIVE BEHAVIOR

General questions you can ask yourself as you evaluate your own efforts toward increasing assertive behaviors are:

What did I say?

1. Where my comments concise?
2. Was my statement definitive and firm?
3. Did I make a request for new behavior?

How did I say it?

1. Did I hesitate before saying what I wanted to say?
2. Did I stutter, stammer or lose my train of thought? Or, was I fairly articulate?
3. Was my voice whining, pleading, sarcastic?
4. Was I able to maintain eye contact?
5. Did I talk too loudly? Too softly?
6. Did my physical stance and gestures communicate assertiveness, passivity or uneasiness?
7. Was my facial expression consistent with the verbal message I conveyed?

How do I feel about how I said it?

1. Was I pleased with my performance?
2. Did I feel uncomfortable, uptight or upset afterwards?
3. Did I fell more assured afterwards?
4. Did I feel positive about myself?

EVALUATING AN ASSERTIVE RESPONSE

The following components should be part of assertive behavior. Use this checklist to make sure that your assertive response fulfills the following requirements:

_____ Eye contract: you looked directly at the person to whom you were speaking.

_____ Body posture: You faced the person, stood or sat up comfortably close. Learn forward.

_____ Gestures: You used gestures to give added emphasis but don't overdo it.

_____ Facial expressions: Your facial expression matches your messages.

_____ Content: You accurately expressed how you felt and what you wanted to communicate.

_____ Timing of response: You responded spontaneously, but only after considering the appropriateness of the assertion and how the other person would receive it.

_____ Ask for behavior change: You asked for the change in behavior, but used good judgment. You were sensitive and understanding about the situation and the other person's rights.

AGGRESSIVE, PASSIVE, ASSERTIVE SCENES

To help get a better picture of aggressive, assertive, and passive behavior, I'm going to go over some "scenes." What we're going to do is label person A's behavior as aggressive, passive or assertive.

Scene 1

> A: "Damn it, is that a new dent I see in the car?"
> B: "Look, I just got home, it was a wretched day and I don't want to talk about it now."
> A: "This is important to me, and we're going to talk about it right now!"
> B: "Have a heart."
> A: "We are going to decide right now who is going to pay to have it fixed, when and where."
> B: "Look, I'll take care of it. Now just leave me alone, for heaven's sake!"

How do you think A is acting in this scene? (Right, A is being aggressive.)

The initial hostile statement produced resentment and withdrawal. It doesn't take into consideration the other person's rights and feelings.

Scene 2

> A: I got a letter from Mom this morning. She wants to come and spend two weeks with us. I'd really like to see her."
> B: "Oh no, not your mother! And right on the heels of your sister. When do we get a little time to ourselves?"
> A: "Well, I do want her to come, but I know you need to spend some time without in-laws under foot. I'd like to invite her to come in a month, and instead of two weeks, I think one week would be enough. What do you say to that?"
> B: "That's a big relief to me. Let's invite her."

How is A acting in this scene? (A is being assertive.) The request is specific, non-hostile and open to negotiation and most importantly, it was successful.

Scene 3

> A: "Would you mind helping me for a minute with this file?"
> B: "I'm busy with this report. Catch me later."
> A: "Well, I really hate to bother you, but it's important."
> B: "Look, I have a four o'clock deadline."
> A: "Okay, I understand. I know it's hard to be interrupted."

How is A acting in this scene? (A is being passive.) Complete collapse follows the timid opening line. The file problem must now be dealt with alone.

Step two in assertiveness training is to identify those situations in which you want to be more effective. To better asses the situations in which you need to be more assertive, I would like you to complete the following Assertiveness Questionnaire. Just put a check mark in column "A" by the items that are applicable to you and then rate those items in column "B" as:

(1) Comfortable.
(2) Mildly uncomfortable.
(3) Moderately uncomfortable.
(4) Very uncomfortable.
(5) Unbearably threatening.

Keep in mind that the varying degrees of discomfort can be expressed whether your inappropriate reactions are hostile or passive.

ASSERTIVENESS QUESTIONNAIRE

A	B	
Check here if the item applies to you	Rate from 1-5 for discomfort	

WHEN do you behave non-assertively?

_____	_____	asking for help
_____	_____	stating a difference of opinion
_____	_____	receiving and expressing negative feelings
_____	_____	receiving and expressing positive feelings
_____	_____	dealing with someone who refuses to cooperate
_____	_____	speaking up about something that annoys you
_____	_____	talking when all eyes are on you
_____	_____	protesting a rip-off
_____	_____	saying "no"
_____	_____	responding to undeserved criticism
_____	_____	making requests of authority figures
_____	_____	negotiating for something you want
_____	_____	having to take charge
_____	_____	asking for cooperation
_____	_____	proposing an idea
_____	_____	taking charge
_____	_____	asking questions
_____	_____	dealing with attempts to make you feel guilty
_____	_____	asking for service
_____	_____	asking for a date or appointment

—————   —————   asking for favors

WHO are the people with whom you are non-assertive?

—————   —————   parents

—————   —————   fellow workers, classmates

—————   —————   strangers

—————   —————   old friends

—————   —————   spouse or mate

—————   —————   employer

—————   —————   relatives

—————   —————   children

—————   —————   acquaintances

—————   —————   sales people, clerks, hired help

—————   —————   more that two or three people in a group

WHAT do you want that you have been unable to achieve with non-assertive styles?

—————   —————   approval for things you have done well

—————   —————   to get help with certain tasks

—————   —————   to be listened to and understood

—————   —————   to make boring situations more satisfying

—————   —————   to not have to be nice all the time

—————   —————   confidence in speaking up when something is important to you

—————   —————   greater comfort with strangers, store clerks, etc

—————   —————   confidence in asking for contact with people you find attractive

—————   —————   getting a new job, asking for interviews, rises,

—————   —————   comfort with people who supervise you

—————   —————   to not feel angry and bitter a lot of the time

—————   —————   overcome a feeling of helplessness and the sense that nothing ever really changes

—————   —————   initiating satisfying sexual experiences

—————   —————   do something totally different and novel

—————   —————   getting time by yourself

—————   —————   doing things that are fun or relaxing for you

Later, you can come back and examine the pattern of your answers. Then analyze them for an overall picture of what situations and people threaten you. When you do this, check to see how non-assertive behavior contributes to the specific items you checked on the "What" list. In constructing your own assertiveness program, it will be initially useful to focus on items you rated as falling in the 2-3 range. These are the situations that you will find easiest to change. Items that are very uncomfortable or threatening can be tackled later.

ASSERTIVENESS CHECK LIST

Use the following check list to see when you are assertive, passive or aggressive. Put a Y or N. for yes or no.

_____When a person is blatantly unfair do you usually say something about it to him/her?

_____ Are you always very careful to avoid trouble with other people?

_____ Do you often avoid social contacts for fear of doing or saying the wrong thing?

_____ If a friend betrays your confidence do you tell him/her how you really feel.

_____ When a clerk in a store waits on someone who has come in after you, do you call his attention to the matter?

_____ If you had a roommate, would you insist that he/she do his fair share of the cleaning?

_____ Are there very few people with whom you can be relaxed and have a good time?

_____ Would you be hesitant about asking a good friend to lend you a few dollars?

_____ If someone who has borrowed $5.00 from you seems to have forgotten about it, would you remind this person?

_____ If a person keeps on teasing you do you have a difficulty expressing your annoyance or displeasure?

_____ Would you remain standing at the rear of a crowded auditorium rather than looking for a seat up front?

_____ If someone keeps kicking the back of your chair in a movie would you ask him to stop?

_____ If a friend keeps calling you very late each evening, would you ask them not to call after a certain time?

_____ If someone starts talking to someone else right in the middle of your conversation do you express your irritation?

_____ In a plush restaurant, if you order a medium steak and find it too raw, would you ask the waiter to have it re-cooked?

Go over the questions again to see which type of behavior you use most of the time.

PERSONAL PROBLEM SCENES

Step three in assertiveness training is to describe your own problem scenes. You want to select a mildly to moderately uncomfortable situation that suggests itself from items on the Assertiveness Questionnaire you just completed. Then, write out a description of the scene. Be certain to include: whom the person involved is, when it takes place, what bothers you, how you deal with it, your fear of what will take place if you are assertive and your goal. The important thing is to be specific. Generalizations will make it difficult later on to write a script that will make assertive behavior possible in your given situation. For example, this is a poor scene description:

"I have a lot of trouble persuading some of my friends to listen to me for a change. They never stop talking and I never get a word in edgewise. It would be nice for me if I could participate more in the conversation. I feel that I'm just letting them run over me."

Notice that this description does not specify whom the particular friend is, when this problem is most likely to occur, how the non-assertive person acts, what fears are involved in being assertive and it does not identify a specific goal for increased involvement in the conversation. The scene would be better rewritten like this:

My friend Joan (who), when we meet for a drink after work (when), often goes on nonstop about her marriage problems (what.) I just sit there and try to be interested (how.) If I interrupt her, I'm afraid she'll think I just don't care (the fear.) I would like to be able to change the subject and talk sometimes about my own life (goal.)

It would be helpful now to write your own "Problem Scenes.

_____

_____

_____

_____

_____

_____

_____

LADDER SCRIPTS FOR CHANGE

Now, the **fourth** step in assertiveness training is taking the information from your problem scene and writing a "Script for Change." A script is a working plan for dealing with the problem scene assertively. There are six elements in a script. And they spell LADDER.

1. Look at your rights, what you want, what you need and your feelings about the situation. Let go of blame, the desire to hurt and self-pity. Define your goal and keep it in mind when you negotiate for change.
2. Arrange a time and place to discuss your problem that is convenient for you and for the other person. This step may be excluded when dealing with spontaneous situations in which you choose to be assertive, such as when a person cuts ahead of you in line.
3. Define the problem situation as specifically as possible.
4. Describe your feelings using "I" messages. As we have learned, "I" messages express your feelings without evaluating, blaming others or giving up your power. So, rather than saying something like "You are inconsiderate" or "You hurt me," the "I" message would be; "I feel hurt when my feelings are ignored." "I" messages need to connect the feeling statement with specific behaviors of the other person without placing blame. So, which of these two 'I' statements do you think is best? "I felt hurt because you were inconsiderate" or "I felt hurt when you left without saying good-bye". Number two is best because it does not place blame
5. Express your request in one or two easy-to-understand sentences. Be specific and firm.
6. Reinforce the possibility of getting what you want by stating the positive consequences should the other person cooperate with you. If necessary, state the negative consequences for failure to cooperate.

The first letters of each of the six elements combine to spell "LADDER." You may find this a useful device to recall the steps. "LADDER" scripts are used to rewrite your problem scenes so that you can assert what you want. Initially, "LADDER" scripts should be written out and practiced well in advance of the problem situation for which they are created. Writing the script forces you to clarify your needs and increases your confidence of success.

Here is an example of a ladder script. Let's say that Jean wants to assert her right to half an hour each day of uninterrupted peace and quiet while she does her relaxation exercises. Frank often interrupts with questions and attention-getting maneuvers. Jean's script goes like this:

1. **L**ook at your rights: "It's my responsibility to make sure Frank respects my needs and I am certainly entitled to some time to myself."
2. **A**rrange a time and place: "I'll ask him if he's willing to discuss this problem when he gets home tonight. If he isn't, we'll set a time and place to talk about it in the next day or two."
3. **D**efine the problem: "At least once, and sometimes more often, I'm interrupted during my relaxation exercises even though I've shut the door and asked for the time to myself. My concentration is broken and it becomes harder to achieve the relaxation."
4. **D**escribe the feeling:" I feel angry when my time alone is broken into and frustrated that the exercises are then made more difficult."
5. **E**xpress the request: "I would like not to be interrupted, except in a dire emergency, when my door is closed. As long as it is closed, assume that I am still doing the exercises and want to be alone."
6. **R**einforce: the request by stating positive and negative consequences: "If I'm not interrupted, I'll come in afterward and chat with you. If I am interrupted, it will increase the time I take doing the exercises."

As you can see, these scripts, like the problem scenes are specific and detailed. The statement of the problem is clear and to the point, without blaming, accusing or being passive. The feelings are expressed with "I" messages and are linked to specific events or behaviors not evaluations of the other person involved. "I" messages provide a tremendous amount of safety for the assertive individual because they usually keep the other person from getting defensive and angry. You are not accusing anyone of being a bad person, you are merely stating what you want or feel entitled to.

Successful "LADDER" scripts do the following:

1. When appropriate, they establish a mutually agreeable time and place to assert your needs.
2. Describe behavior objectively without judging or devaluing.
3. Describe clearly using specific references to time, place and frequency.
4. Express feelings calmly and directly.
5. Confine your feeling response to the specific problem behavior not the whole person.
6. Avoid delivering put-downs disguised as "honest feelings."
7. Ask for changes that are reasonably possible and small enough not to incur a lot of resistance.
8. Ask for no more than one or two very specific changes at a time.
9. Make the reinforcements explicit, offering something that is desirable to the other person.
10. Avoid punishments that are too big to be more than idle threats.
11. Keep your mind on your rights and goals when being assertive.

Take some time now to write your own LADDER script. After you've written your script, it's best if you rehearse in front of a mirror and you can even tape record your rehearsal to further refine your assertive style. Then let yourself imagine the worst possible response that could be made to your assertive request and prepare your own countermeasures.

MY "LADDER" SCRIPT

Look at your rights.

_____

_____

_____

_____

Arrange a time to discuss.

_____

_____

_____

Define the problem.

_____

_____

_____

_____

Describe your feelings: "I" messages.

_____

_____

_____

_____

Express your request.

_____

_____

_____

_____

Reinforce the possibility of getting what you want.

_____

_____

_____

_____

DEVELOP ASSERTIVE BODY LANGUAGE

The fifth step in assertive training is to develop assertive body language. Actually practicing with the mirror will be helpful as you follow these five basic rules:

1. Maintain direct eye contact.
2. Maintain an erect body posture.
3. Speak clearly, audibly and firmly.
4. Don't whine or have an apologetic tone to your voice.
5. Make use of gestures and facial expression for emphasis.

BLOCKING GAMBITS

The sixth and final step to becoming an assertive person is learning how to avoid manipulation. Inevitably, you will encounter blocking gambits from those who seek to ignore your assertive requests. Here are some techniques of overcoming the standard blocking gambits:

Broken Record: Calmly repeating your point without getting sidetracked by irrelevant issues. You can say things like "Yes, and . . . Yes, I know, and my point is . . . I agree, and . . . Yes, and I was saying . . . Right and I'm still not interested."

Assertive Agreement: Responding to criticism by admitting an error when you have made a mistake, but separating that mistake from you as a bad person. For example: "Yes, I did forget our lunch date. I'm usually more responsible."

Assertive Inquiry: Prompting criticism in order to gather additional information for your side of the argument. Example: "I understand you don't like the way I acted at the meeting last night. What is it that bothered you? What is it about me that you feel is pushy? What is it about my speaking out that bothers you?"

Content-to-Process Shift: Shifting the focus of the situation from the topic to an analysis of what is going on between the two of you. For example: "We're getting off the point now. We've been derailed into talking about old issues."

Defusing: Ignoring the content of someone's anger and putting off further discussion until they have calmed down. An example of this is: "I can see that you're very upset and angry right now, let's discuss it later this afternoon."

Circuit Breaker: Responding to provocative criticism with one word or very clipped statements such as, "Yes . . . No . . . Perhaps."

Assertive Irony: Responding to hostile criticism positively. You could answer something like: "You're a real loud mouth" with "Thank you."

Assertive Delay: Putting off a response to a challenging statement until you are calm and able to deal with it appropriately. For example, you can say things like: "Very interesting point . . . I'll have to reserve judgment on that . . . I don't want to talk about that right now."

It is helpful to prepare yourself in advance against a number of typical blocking gambits that will be used to attack and derail your assertive requests. Some of the most troublesome blocking gambits are:

Laughing It Off: Your assertion is responded to with a joke.

Gambit Accusing: You are blamed for the problem.

The Beat-Up: Your assertion gets a response with a personal attack, such as: "Who are you to worry about being interrupted. You're the biggest loud mouth around here."

Delaying Gambit: Your assertion is met with, "Not now, I'm too tired. Another time, maybe,"

Why Gambit: Every assertive statement is blocked with a series of "why" questions, such as, "Why do you feel that way. I still do not know why you do not want to go or: "Why did you change your mind?"

Self Pity Gambit: Your assertion is met with tears and the covert message that you are being sadistic. For this one it is best to keep going through your script using Assertive Agreement such as "I know this is causing you pain, AND (not but) I need to get this resolved."

Quibbling: The other person wants to debate with you about the legitimacy of what you feel or the magnitude of the problem.

Threats: You are threatened with statements like: "If you keep harping at me like this, you're going to need another boyfriend/girlfriend."

Denial: You are told, "I didn't do that" or "You've really misinterpreted me." Here you need to assert what you have observed and experienced, and use Clouding by saying something like: "It may seem that way to you, and I've observed . . ."

ASSERTIVE BEHAVIOR

The goal in assertiveness is talking to and relating to the other person as an equal. To do this you must:

1. Give and get respect.
2. Be fair with others and ask them to be fair with you
3. Meet people halfway when there is a disagreement. However, having said that let me say when important values are involved meeting people half-way is not necessary. You need to decide where the line is for you.

There are many reasons for and benefits of acting assertively. Just some are:

1. Assertion builds your own self-respect.
2. It builds your self-confidence, which allows you to feel good about yourself and you won't feel that others HAVE to like you or what you do for you to feel OK.
3. When you act assertively, other people usually look up to you. They respect those who are assertive, who show respect for themselves and others and who take a risk by really saying how they feel and by handling problems and the opinions of others openly and fairly for all concerned.
4. Assertion often results in individuals getting what they want, getting their needs satisfied and getting their choices and feelings respected without hurting or offending someone else.
5. Assertion feels good.
6. It results in closer more satisfying relationships with others.
7. Assertion increases the control you have over yourself by setting personal limits.

Now in addition to verbal assertive messages, there are non-verbal assertive messages that add support to what is being said. These are:

1. Eye contact: You want to look straight at the other person to show that you mean what you say.
2. Body stance/posture: You need to face the person while leaving the right amount of space between the two of you, hold your head up, etc.
3. Personal space: This is an important one. This is the area we all have around us that, when somebody enters it, causes us to feel uncomfortable or uneasy. This is usually about 3 feet.
4. Facial expression: This should match what you are saying.
5. Voice tone and volume: Assertion involves speaking so that the other person can hear what is said without being turned off by your yelling or having to strain their ears to hear you.
6. Gestures: The right use of your hands can add more importance to what you say.

Up to now, I have talked about assertive behavior, which is what we want to be able to demonstrate as often as possible for the reasons I've discussed. However, we need to also understand and be aware of aggressive and passive behavior in ourselves as well as others.

PASSIVE OR NON-ASSERTIVE behavior involves putting down your own rights by not saying what you feel, think and believe. Non-assertion is also when you allow others to disrespect you; talk down to you; shine on what you say, do or want. When you are non-assertive or passive, you are saying: "I don't count . . . you can take advantage of me. My feelings don't matter . . . only yours do.' What I think is not important . . . but what you think is. I am nothing . . . you are more important and better." The non-assertive message is: I'M NOT OK . . . YOU ARE!

With non-assertive behavior there is no respect:

1. No respect for yourself, your needs and your abilities.
2. No respect for the other person, because you act like you believe the other person can't handle their problems.

The **goal** with non-assertiveness is to avoid hassles at any cost.

Not knowing the difference between non-assertion and politeness can cause you to behave passively. Parents may teach children that it is not "polite" to use the word "I." Parents many times teach children that, to disagree with someone older than we are such as a boss, a staff member, a teacher or even our parents is not appropriate. We are said to be "conceited" if we accept a compliment or compliment ourselves. We learn as children that it is not "nice" to refuse a request for help. All of these "lessons" can lead us to act passively. Not knowing or not accepting your own personal rights can also cause you to behave passively.

Children, as well as adults, worry about the bad things that might happen to them if they are assertive such as:

- The other person might get angry at you.
- The other person might not like you anymore.
- The other person might hurt you.
- Not understanding the difference between non-assertion and being helpful.
- Not knowing how to be or simply choosing not to be assertive.

The **results** of acting passively/non-assertively are two fold.

Right Away YOU FEEL BETTER. You are not as uptight because you have ended a tense situation and others praise you for being a "good person" or for "being agreeable" or for not causing them any problems.

Later On YOU FEEL LOUSY. You begin to like yourself less as others use you, walk all over you or take advantage of you. You feel more hurt and/or anger inside and you may get uptight or physically sick from holding your feelings in. You may begin to stay by yourself more because you don't want to be around others who use or hurt you. Finally, others may begin to respect you less and become angry or disgusted with yourself. As with assertion, there are nonverbal parts of non-assertion. The actions of non-assertive people say that they feel uptight and will do almost anything to be liked. They feel weak and are willing to put themselves down. While this may not be what the non-assertive person means, ACTIONS SPEAK LOUDER THAN WORDS. To put it another way, HOW you say something is more important than WHAT you say.

The goal of non-assertive behavior is to soften what is said so that the other person won't get angry or upset with you. This is done through:

1. Eye contact: not looking straight at the other person may say that you do not believe in or feel good about what you are saying.
2. Body stance/posture: covering the mouth when speaking, nervous giggling, etc. may also take away from the importance of what you are trying to say.
3. The look on your face: when it does not go along with what you are saying. An example is laughing when the message is serious.
4. Voice tone and pattern: when your voice is overly soft so people have to strain to hear you or when you use lots of pauses, "uhs," or clearing of the throat.

AGGRESSIVE BEHAVIOR

Now, AGGRESSION involves directly standing up for your own personal rights and expressing your own thoughts, feelings and beliefs in a way that is often dishonest, usually inappropriate and always disrespects the rights of the other person.

With aggression the basic message is, "This is what I think and you are stupid for thinking any differently. "This is what I want and what you want is not important." "This is what I feel and what you feel doesn't count." In other words, I'M OK . . . YOU ARE NOT OK!

The goal when acting aggressively is to win by forcing the other person to lose. They are guaranteed a win by using bullying, putting down or overpowering the other person so that they feel weaker or inferior, they are afraid to say what they feel or stand up for their needs and rights.

The problem is the mismanagement of the anger. Mischief and misbehavior CAN be a problem, but it is also an opportunity to teach responsibility and anger management skills to the child. There are two very effective ways to do this. Give them choices and give them personal examples.

The **reasons** for acting aggressively include:

Fear of losing power or getting hurt. Because they have been hurt before, people fear getting hurt again.

Being non-assertive in the past. When you are non-assertive, hurt and anger can build up over time and you feel that aggression is OK. This is called collecting and turning in stamps.

Your personal ideas about aggression such as:

1. That aggression is the only way to get through to another person.
2. That the world is basically a dangerous place in which others want to hurt you or use you and you must be aggressive in order to survive.
3. You don't know how to be assertive.

There are some situations where aggression is appropriate. We call this ESCALATING, which occurs when: First, you have assertively expressed yourself in, for example, refusing a request from someone else or making your own request. Then the other person does not respond or keeps doing something you would like stopped. Now you can gradually escalate your message to aggression.

The results of acting aggressively are:

Right Away you:

1. Let out feelings.
2. Feel powerful.
3. Get what you want . . . the other person does nothing.

Later On you may:

1. Lose friendships or never get close to people.
2. Become cut-off from friends such as your kids or your loved ones.
3. May get fired from a job.
4. Feel unloved, misunderstood or feel unlovable.
5. May feel guilt, shame or embarrassment and decide to say. nothing in the future because of fearing being "out of control."
6. And others may get back at you in direct or indirect ways so you have to watch your back.

The verbal parts of aggression include using the word "you" a lot to order the other person around or to put the other person down.

The non-verbal parts of aggression include:

1. Eye contact: attempting to stare down the other person.
2. Voice tone: overly strong for the situation and sarcastic.

Many times, our thoughts and irrational beliefs cause us to behave passively or aggressively. We will go over irrational thought later.

ASSESSING YOUR BODY LANGUAGE AND SELF-EXPRESSION SCALE

Assertive body language is congruent with what you are saying verbally, adds strength and emphasis to what you are saying and is generally self-assured.

Aggressive body language conveys an exaggerated sense of self-importance, overbearing, strength and/or an air of superiority.

Non-assertive/passive body language conveys weakness, anxiety and lack of self-confidence. It softens the impact of what is being said verbally to the point that the verbal message loses most of its power. This is particularly true when the person's verbal message and body language are in conflict with each other, for example, laughing when saying, "I'm really angry with you." In general when there is such a discrepancy between a verbal message and a body language message, other people seem to take the body language message more seriously.

Use the following system to check your body language:

OK = Satisfactory level.

S = Some improvement needed.

L = Lots of improvement needed.

Eye Contact

Assertive	Aggressive	Non-assertive
_____ comfortably direct	_____ looking down nose	_____ looking away
	_____ staring off into distance with bored expression	_____ blinking rapidly

Facial Expression

Assertive	Aggressive	Non-assertive
_____ open, frank, relaxed	_____ clenching teeth	_____ constant smiling
	_____ flaring nostrils	_____ laughing
_____winking	_____jutting jaws	_____wetting lip
	_____ pursed, tight-lipped mouth	_____biting or
		_____swallowing

Voice and Speech Expression

Assertive	Aggressive	Non-assertive
_____ appropriately firm	_____ overly rapid	_____ overly soft
_____ appropriately warm	_____ deadly quiet	_____ mumbled
_____ expressive, emphasizing key words	_____ overly loud or strident	_____ whiney
_____ clear	_____ sarcastic or condescending	_____ monotone

Gestures

Assertive	Aggressive	Non-assertive
_____ well balanced	_____ pounding fists	_____ covering mouth or lower face
_____ erect	_____ stiff and rigid	_____ cover face with hand
_____ relaxed	_____ finger waving or pointing	_____ excessive head nodding
	_____ hand gestures	_____ tinkering with clothing
	_____ shaking head	_____ constant shifting of weight
	_____ hands on hips	

Now, as with any new skill, we begin to learn that practice is important so here are 12 Daily Steps To Successful Assertive Behavior. Some people think that assertiveness training turns nice people into irascible complainers or calculating manipulators. This is not so. It's your right to protect yourself when something seems unfair. You are the one who best knows your discomfort and your needs. Just remember the 12 basic steps to successful assertive behavior.

PRACTICING YOUR ASSERTION: 12 DAILY STEPS TO SUCCESSES

1. **USE FEELING TALK:** Express your likes and dislikes by beginning with the word "I". Example: "I think . . ." "I feel . . ." "I believe . . ." "I hope . . ."
2. **TALK ABOUT YOURSELF:** If you do something worthwhile and interesting, you can let others know about it. Just do not brag or hog the conversation.
3. **MAKE GREETING TALK:** If you smile and greet people cheerfully, they will usually see you as friendly and outgoing. It is a lot better then mumbling, nodding sullenly or looking embarrassed.
4. **ACCEPT COMPLIMENTS:** Accept compliments graciously. Example: "Thank you, I like this shirt too". Rather than, "Oh, this old thing?" You want to reward a person who compliments you, not punish them.
5. **USE APPROPRIATE FACIAL TALK:** Look people in the eye when you talk to them. Try to make your voice and face match the feelings you want to express.
6. **DISAGREE MILDLY:** When you disagree with someone do not pretend to agree just to keep the peace. You can show disagreement mildly by looking away, by frowning, raising your eyebrows, shaking your head or changing the topic of your conversation.
7. **ASK FOR CLARIFICATION:** If someone gives you direction, instructions or explanations mixed up, you can ask the person to say them more clearly. Instead of going away feeling confused and dumb (and maybe doing something dumb) you can simply say, "Your directions were not clear to me. Would you please go over them again?"
8. **ASK WHY:** When asked to do something that seems unreasonable or unpleasant, you can ask: "Why do you want me to do that?"
9. **EXPRESS ACTIVE DISAGREEMENT:** When you disagree with someone, and you feel you know what you are talking about, you can express your disagreement by saying: "My opinion is . . . , I think . . . . or I have a different view . . . ."
10. **SPEAK UP FOR YOUR RIGHTS:** Don't let others take advantage of you. You can demand your rights and ask to be treated with fairness and justice. You can say: "I was next in line," or "Excuse me but you will have to leave now as I have a job interview to get ready for."
11. **BE PERSISTENT:** Do not let one or two no's cause you to give up. If you have a legitimate complaint, you can continue to say so until you get satisfaction.
12. **AVOID JUSTIFYING EVERY OPINION:** If someone continually argues and says Why? Why? Why? You can simply state: "That's just the way I feel" or "I don't have to justify everything I say."

COMPARISON OF PASSIVE, ASSERTIVE AND AGGRESSIVE BEHAVIOR

CHARACTERISTIC OF BEHAVIOR:

Passive: Does not express wants, ideas & feelings or expresses them in self-depreciation ways. Intent: to please:

Assertive: Expresses wants, ideas and feelings in direct and appropriate ways. Intent: to communicate.

Aggressive: Expresses wants ideas & feelings at the expense of others, Intent: to dominate or humiliate

YOUR FEELINGS WHEN YOU ACT THIS WAY:

Passive: Anxious, disappointed with yourself. Often angry and resentful later.
Assertive: Confident, feel good about yourself at the time and later.
Aggressive: Self-righteous, superior, sometimes embarrassed later.

OTHER PEOPLE'S FEELINGS ABOUT THEMSELVES WHEN YOU ACT THIS WAY:

Passive;   guilty or superior.
Assertive: respected, valued.
Aggressive: humiliated, hurt.

OTHER PEOPLE'S FEELINGS ABOUT YOU WHEN YOU ACT THIS WAY:

Passive: **irritation, pity, disgust.**
Assertive: **usually respectful.**
Aggressive: **angry, vengeful.**

Many times it is our thoughts and irrational beliefs that cause us to behave passively or aggressively, so I've included a list of some "Thoughts That Cause Problems,"

It's your right to protect yourself when something seems unfair. You are the one who best knows your discomfort and your needs.

THOUGHTS THAT CAUSE PROBLEMS

1. People must love me or I will be miserable.
2. Making mistakes is terrible.
3. People should be condemned for their wrongdoing.
4. It is terrible when things go wrong.
5. My emotions can't be controlled.
6. Self discipline is too hard to achieve.
7. I must depend on others.
8. My childhood must always affect me.
9. I can't stand the way others act.
10. There is a perfect solution.
11. I should be better than others.
12. If others criticize me I did something wrong.
13. I can't change what I think.
14. I should help everyone who needs it.
15. I must never show any weakness.
16. Healthy people don't get upset.
17. There is only one true love.

18. I should never hurt anyone.
19. There is a magic cure.
20. Strong people don't ask for help.
21. People ought to do what I wish.
22. Giving up is the best policy.
23. I need to be sure to decide.
24. People should trust me.
25. I am not responsible for my behavior.

JOURNEY TO ASSERTIVENESS

- Keep track of your assertiveness. Keep a diary for a week. Record each day those situations in which you found yourself responding assertively, those in which you "blew it" and those you avoided altogether so that you would not have to face the need to act assertively. Are you satisfied with your effectiveness in interpersonal need to act assertively? Be honest with yourself.
- Concentrate on one particular situation. Spend a few moments with your eyes closed, imagining how you would handle a specific incident such as: letting a friend "talk your ear off;" asking for a raise, being subjected to harsh and prolonged criticism, etc.
- Find someone who can serve as an effective model and observe how they handle the situations you have imagined.
- Consider alternative responses. What are other possible ways the incidents you have imagined could be handled?
- Imagine yourself handling the situation. Close your eyes and visualize yourself dealing effectively with the situation. Be assertive, but be as much your "natural self" as you can. Repeat this step until you can imagine a comfortable style for yourself that succeeds in handling the situation well.
- Role-play the response pattern you have selected with a friend. Observe your behavior and get feedback from the friend. Keep on role-playing until you get to the point where you feel comfortable dealing with the previously threatening situation.
- Test your new response pattern in the actual situation. If you have repeatedly imagined and practiced your new behavior, you will react almost automatically to the real situation.

WAYS TO SAY, "NO."

1. That's not an option.
2. I am unwilling . . .
3. Say it in a funny way, i.e. "Never in a million trillion years!"
4. Sing, "no, no, no."
5. That's not appropriate.
6. I am not ready for you to do that yet.
7. For a younger child use distraction.
8. Ask: "What do you think you would need to do before I would be willing to say yes to that?"
9. Ask: "What do you think? Is this a good choice for you?" (If you choose to use this make sure you are willing to abide by the answer."

10. For a youngster who has something you do not want her to have, say: "That's not a toy."
11. Ask, "What are your other options?"
12. No, but I would be willing to . . . .
13. I appreciate your asking, however . . . .
14. Give them an alternative. "Walls are not for coloring. Here is a piece of paper."
15. Tell them what to do instead: "Water needs to stay in the tub."
16. This is not negotiable.

Of course realistically we will all behave aggressively and non-assertively sometimes. The goal is simply to use assertive behavior more often in order to have our needs satisfied, to get what we want and to gain respect from others. Assertion will help to build your self-confidence and self-respect without hurting or offending others. It will also allow us to enjoy closer more satisfying relationships with our children and others.

POSITIVE EFFECTIVE PARENTING
P.E.P.

CHAPTER EIGHT
Anger Management

CHAPTER EIGHT

Anger Management

ANGER MANAGEMENT

In order to raise happy functional children you must identify the way each family member addresses how they interact with each other. To have a happy positive experience of raising your children it is important to communicate in a productive manner. Anger management training is a way to make your parenting experience more pleasant by better understanding your anger dynamics.

Productive anger gives us energy to assert ourselves, open up communication and be goal oriented. It protects our self-esteem and sense of fairness while preventing long term frustration. Anger acts as a pressure valve. If conflict can be resolved as it occurs, tension is released in smaller doses and is more likely to be in proportion to the incident. Productive anger can build stronger relationships by increasing trust, honesty and mutual respect.

However, destructive anger can destroy communication, relationships, property and mutual respect. It can accelerate out of control causing physical, verbal and/or psychological abuse. If not dealt with, anger may be expressed indirectly and be misinterpreted.

Effective anger management should lead to improvement in mental health, self-esteem and interpersonal relationships for both adults and children. Anger, when expressed appropriately, can be a good thing. Coping skills can be learned and new strategies implemented. Anger is a feeling in its own right with no underlying cause. It can also be accompanied with other feelings such as fear, hurt, disappointment, despair or depression. Anger is a "feeling" that follows a "thought". A feeling is something we have very little control over. We will go over feelings later. Some of the other feelings that underlie anger are: rage, madness, displeasure, resentment, hostility and fury. These are all forms or degrees of anger.

Anger can be a rational or even a healthy response when it is justified for the situation and expressed appropriately. For a person who is easy to anger they blame others and their anger can be acted out in ways that are physically and emotionally harmful. In reality you are likely to view any anger you experience as rational, even though it may not be. When you feel your anger is justified; strong anger may cloud your reality. When this happens it is hard to get your anger under control.

Each of us has our own way of expressing feelings including anger. Understanding our own style or that of others may make communication easier and heighten our awareness.

Choose one of the styles below or use a combination of styles that best describe you:

1. Expressive Banger: bangs doors, drawers, objects. May also include wall hitters, selective and nonselective thrower
2. Quiet Corner Person: will withdraw when mad and will not tell you why. This person may have learned early as a child that anger is unacceptable and sent to his room or corner for expressing anger.
3. Martyr: sulking, using sarcasm or the guilt trip, passive aggressive tactics.
4. Hipshooter: tells you off then apologizes expecting the incident to be forgiven and forgotten. Not interested in feedback or the other's feelings.
5. Counter Attacker: covers hurt and insecurities by criticizing in return.
6. Blamer: his problems are always because of someone else.
7. Leaker: lets you know why he is angry little by little.
8. Self-Hater: verbally berates self.
9. Body: anger translated into physical symptoms.
10. Creators: stir up conflict due to boredom or irritability.

No matter what kind of anger you experience it is possible to change how you deal with it. Everyone handles anger differently. While traveling down the freeway a car suddenly cut Jim off. Jim gets so angry he had to pull over. In the same situation Sarah just thought maybe the other driver was late for work and she took it in stride. When they are angry some people:

1. Don't let things build up, speaks her mind at the time of the incident.
2. Take a look at what else is going on emotionally inside.
3. Over eat.
4. Lash out.

As these examples show there are many styles of working with anger. They may be positive and healthy or negative and unhealthy. It is even possible to exhibit a combination of positive and negative responses to coping with anger or to act passive aggressive.

There are times when anger can be a very positive motivating force in your life. Anger at oneself or others can be used as a base to make positive changes. It can be used as a positive motivation and even keep us sane at times.

HEALTHY WAYS TO EXPRESS ANGER

1. Make a responsible decision about what action, if any, you want to take. Figure out what the anger is telling you. Do you have some unmet needs? Are there some things going on

in your environment that you need to change? You may have to tell someone what you need. You can ask yourself, "Am I afraid of being left out? Am I afraid to do something by myself?" Sometimes you may get mad at a person who is late and did not call to tell you. If you get mad at this person, ask yourself what the anger is about. Are you afraid there has been a car accident or insulted that your feelings weren't taken into consideration? Once you know what is behind these feelings, you can ask the person for what you need to cope with these feelings.

2. Do not let anger control you. Screaming may help. You do not need to continue to scream. Sometimes other things are needed as well. It is best if you decide that for yourself. You may need time out, so go to a peaceful place away from the object of your anger and think about what you want.

3. Take responsibility for your anger. You are angry. Someone did not *make* you angry. What they did may have been the catalyst but you are responsible for your response. People often say, "He made me angry because he would not do what I told him." However, your emotional response is a result of your own interpretation and experience. No one can **make** you feel anything. When people say, "You made me do it, you made me lose control," they are saying, "I do not want to take responsibility for my own response and feelings."

4. Do not hit when feeling angry. Do not allow yourself to physically hit anyone or allow others to abuse you when you are angry. If abuse has occurred, seek professional help. Because the physical energy can be intense, hitting and throwing things is commonplace. Men are taught to express their feelings physically. Most would never consider crying. However, striking another person in order to express anger is an unacceptable way to burn off energy.

5. Get rid of the guilt. Do not hold on to guilt. Throw it all away. It does not help to feel like a victim. Whenever you feel guilt imagine that you put it in a shoebox, put the lid on the box, put the box in the closet and close the door. Whenever you feel guilty later, imagine doing this again. Do not carry guilt around with you. Leave it behind.

YOU HOLD THE KEY TO YOUR OWN ANGER MANAGEMENT

When you learn to change your self-talk (your internal dialogue) about yourself, others and the world around you, you can find anger relief. This is at the core of anger management. By gaining a true understanding of healthy thinking vs. unhealthy thinking you'll be able to work yourself out of anger or better still, keep your anger in check

We all know what anger is and we've all felt it whether as a fleeting annoyance or as full-fledged rage. It can help to complete an anger check at the end of the day. If you are still feeling a lot of anger try one or more of the following:

- Take a long hot leisurely bath.
- Talk to a neutral party.
- Listen to soothing music.
- Go for a brisk walk, jog or bike ride until you're calmer. NO DRIVING!!
- Clean house.
- Rake your yard.
- Count to 10 or 20.

Write down the feelings and then tear them up.
- Talk it out with yourself in private or seek out a friend.

Know the triggers that tend to make you angry. Have a plan ahead of time with things you can do to subdue the anger. Make notes and leave them in a conspicuous place

What are some of the triggers that make you angry?

_____

_____

_____

_____

What kind of plan do you have that can subdue your anger?

_____

_____

_____

_____

Don't carry around anger from the past. Letting go goes a long way to help put your anger into perspective.

WHAT IS ANGER?

Anger is a completely normal usually healthy human emotion. But when it gets out of control it turns destructive. It can lead to problems. You may have problems at work, in your personal relationships and in the overall quality of your life. In addition, it can make you feel as though you are at the mercy of an unpredictable and powerful emotion. Anger affects your body so "listen to your body talk" and you can be better in touch with your anger.

When you get angry, your body creates energy. Here's what happens:

- Adrenaline and other chemicals enter your bloodstream.
- Your heart pumps faster.
- Your blood flows more quickly.
- Your muscles tense.

Learning to recognize and express anger appropriately can make a big difference in your life. Destructive anger can destroy communication, relationships, property and mutual respect. It can accelerate out of control causing physical, verbal and/or psychological abuse. If not dealt with, anger may be expressed indirectly and be misinterpreted. Productive anger gives us energy to assert ourselves, open up communication and be goal oriented. It protects our self-esteem and sense of fairness while preventing long term frustration. Anger acts as a pressure valve. If conflict can be resolved as it occurs, tension is released in smaller doses and is more likely to be in proportion to the incident.

Productive anger can build stronger relationships by increasing trust, honesty and mutual respect. Handling your anger well and in a positive way can help you:

1. <u>Overcome problems</u>: anger is a sign that something is wrong. It may serve as a warning for you to think about your feelings and attitudes.
2. <u>Reach your goals</u>: trying to reach a goal can be frustrating. Frustration can lead to anger, which in turn can motivate you to work harder.
3. <u>Handle emergencies and protect yourself</u>: anger can cause an immediate burst of strength and energy. This allows you to react quickly if you are in danger.
4. <u>Communicate with others</u>: talking about your anger can help keep it from building up. You may release tension and enjoy better communication with family, friends and co-workers.

Too much anger or uncontrolled anger can cause problems such as:

1. Problems in your relationships with family and friends.
2. Problems at work.
3. Legal and financial troubles.
4. Physical and mental health problems.

Anger isn't good or bad. It's what you do with it that counts. You can find ways to help anger work for not against you.

Children and adolescents who cannot work out anger are prone to many disruptive behaviors: such as fighting, lying, steeling, cutting school and dropping out of school and drug abuse. Also research indicates that a child's inability to work out anger may lead to a personality prone to coronary and other health problems. It seems that parents who can help their children work out their anger will also help them live longer.

VALIDATE YOUR CHILDS FEELINGS OF ANGER BY ALLOWING THEM TO BE EXPRESSED

<u>Helping</u> parents investigate their children's anger. They use it as a cue that the child is hurting or experiencing some other distressful feeling. This requires that you be sensitive and aware of what's going on in their lives. The more you tune in to your children, the easier it becomes to recognize when they are stuffing their feelings or about to explode. Ask yourself:

- How do I know they're angry?
- What is making them angry?
- Why does it make them angry?

Tuning in to your children also helps them feel secure and provides them with the emotional climate that encourages the expression of their feelings. Investigating feelings validates them.

<u>Helping</u> parents also help them feel secure and provide them with the emotional element that encourages the expression of their feelings. Investigating feelings validates them.

<u>Helping</u> parents teach their children to express anger productively. Acknowledging and validating the right to get angry is one thing, expressing it productively is another. Two things parents can do to facilitate productive anger expression are setting limits and encouraging self-disclosure.

<u>Helping</u> parents teach their children not to hide their anger from their selves and others. Often unexpressed anger works its way to the surface and displays itself indirectly.

This check list is to help you determine if your children are hiding anger. Each item listed is a way anger may be disguised.

1. Procrastination is the completion of imposed tasks.
2. Perpetual or habitual lateness.
3. Sarcasm or liking for sadistic or ironic humor.
4. Frequent sighing.
5. Over-politeness, constant cheerfulness, smiling while hurting.
6. Over-controlled monotone speaking voice.
7. Frequent disturbing or frightening drama.
8. Difficulty getting to sleep or sleeping through the night.
9. Excessive irritability over trifles.
10. Boredom, apathy or loss of interest in activities about which you are usually enthusiastic.
11. Getting tired more easily than usual.
12. Slowing down of movements.
13. Waking up tired.
14. Chronic depression for extended periods of feeling down for no apparent reason.
15. Clenched jaws, especially while sleeping.
16. Facial tics, spasmodic foot swinging, etc.
17. Grinding of teeth, especially while sleeping.

ANGER AS A POSITIVE MOTIVATOR

There are times in which anger can be a very positive motivating force in your life. Anger at oneself or others can be used as a basis to make positive changes or accomplish personal goals or even great deeds in life. The following examples show how several people used anger as a positive motivation.

1. "I got real angry when I was passed over for a promotion," says John. "They promoted a guy who had more education than me, even though everyone knows I could do the job. Instead of letting this get me down, I decided to go back to school and work on my degree."
2. "My coach told me I probably wouldn't make the first team, says Linda. This made me so angry that it inspired me! I busted my butt and worked harder because I wanted to show coach that she was wrong about me. And guess what? I ended up making the first team."
3. "I got mad about getting a bad grade on my exam, says Lynn. I was angry at my teacher because I didn't feel like he prepared us enough for the exam. But I was mad at myself, too. So I put my nose to the grindstone and studied harder. I did much better on his next exam."
4. "When I'm angry at someone, I feel motivated to find out why," says Bert. "Understanding the problem first helps me figure out what I need to do to resolve it."
5. "My wife embarrassed me in front of my friends" says Ed. "So I confronted her in private with my anger and hurt feelings. We ended up talking about several similar incidences. Our open talk helped us work out some differences and made me feel closer to my wife."

The exercise below may help you find ways anger can work for you, not against you.

SELF-AWARENESS ACTIVITY

Describe how you have used (or can use) anger as a positive motivator.

_____
_____
_____
_____

How does your use of alcohol or other drugs impact on your anger or how you deal with it?

_____
_____
_____
_____

What do you think you need to change about the ways in which you deal with anger?

_____
_____
_____
_____

What would other people, who know you very well, say that you need to change about the way you handle anger?

_____
_____
_____
_____

EFFECTS OF ANGER

Mismanaged anger can affect your emotional health and well-being. In some instances, it may be a factor in mental-health problems, such as depressive illness, self-destructive or suicidal behavior or a personality disorder. Anger can complicate addictive disorders such as alcoholism, drug abuse, compulsive gambling or overeating. Difficulty in coping with anger has been intensified as a significant factor in relapse for people with addictive disorders.

Anger can affect your physical health; it can be a factor in headaches, ulcers, high blood pressure and anxiety problems, with sexual performance and other symptoms.

Problems may occur when anger is expressed too frequently or inappropriately. It can push people away or create very strong negative feelings towards you. Sometimes the other person is unable to forget or forgive you for things you have said or done while angry, especially if violence was involved. However, even passive forms of expressed anger (such as the silent treatment) can have a hurtful effect on other people.

Anger can be a factor in impulsive behaviors that are potentially harmful to you or others. For example, anger towards one's partner may be a factor in hurting yourself physically, seeking out others for sex, driving too fast, drug addiction or shopping too much.

You might also use anger as an excuse to justify failure in your life. You can blame others or society for bad breaks and let your anger get in the way of doing well in school or at work. If you grew up in poverty, for example, this experience could become the basis of an intense rage that is misdirected and ultimately hurts rather than helps you.

If you are a parent, your style of dealing with anger will be "modeled" by your children. They will learn much from you about what anger is and how it is expressed. Children will learn more from what you do, than what you say, about anger.

FAIR FIGHTING OR PRODUCTIVE ARGUING

Just like anger, fighting and arguing are just a part of our every day lives. They can be exhibited and expressed appropriately or non-appropriately. If we use fair fighting we can have our needs met more often. Below you will find a list, use it to learn how to fight fair:

1. Discuss what's fair and productive before you have an argument.
2. Take time to get control of your feelings and thoughts before you speak.
3. Ask yourself if this issue is worth arguing about.
4. Accept the fear factor of confrontation such as fear of rejection or loss of face. Others may respect your assertive communication and justified anger.
5. Describe your feelings and fears and own them so that you don't give your power away. Use "I" statements such as "I think," "I feel," "I'm afraid" etc . . .
6. Deal directly with the person or persons with whom you are angry rather than to bystanders.
7. If directness is too risky or inappropriate, find a friend to talk it out with.
8. Be specific when presenting the issue.
9. Do not just complain, ask for reasonable change.
10. Confine yourself to one issue at a time and stay in the present.
11. Ask for and give feedback during the argument. Try to understand the other's point of view.
12. Don't assume you know what the other person is thinking. Instead ask them.
13. Avoid words that blame such as: "you always," "you never," "you should," "you make me . . ."
14. Sarcasm, verbal abuse, name-calling and breech of trust only cause confusion, mistrust and bad feelings.
15. Take a look at what you are really angry about.

Arguing and fighting is never a single win/lose situation. Both parties ether win mutual understanding and respect or both loose mutual understanding and respect

ANGER TOOL KIT

Once you really understand that you are angry you can understand that your anger has an object and is really a specific feeling. To do this you must know how you are feeling right now.

_____ Anxious	_____ Grieving	_____ Obstinate	_____ Suspicious
_____ Aggressive	_____ Jealous	_____ Perplexed	_____ Bitchy
_____ Enraged	_____ Miserable	_____ Resentful	_____ Bitter
_____ Frustrated	_____ Negative	_____ Sad	_____ Sarcastic

What happened to make you angry?

_____

_____

_____

_____

If we can focus on the specific incident which triggered our anger, it then becomes more manageable:

Now let's take a look at who you are angry with;

_____ My own self	_____ My spouse	_____ My partner	_____ My boss
_____ Human race	_____ The kids	_____ God	_____ My Life

Once you really understand that you are angry and with whom you are angry you can understand that your anger has an object in the real world.

Anger will usually involve four general areas: 1) Our anger at others; 2) Other's anger at us; 3) Residual anger from the past or; 4) Abstract anger.

When you can understand your anger is real and normal, you can deal with it in an appropriate ways. It will be more manageable. To understand this will allow you to do it by answering the following questions.

How did the anger make me feel besides angry?

_____

_____

_____

_____

What about this angers me the most?

_____

_____

_____

_____

Some examples may be:

- There is nothing that I can do about.
- I feel so stupid.
- I feel guilty for allowing it to happen.
- I feel inadequate to cope with this situation.

We sometimes lose our self-respect and hold ourselves in contempt. We must understand that our anger consists of replacing these feelings of worthlessness. The only antidote for contempt is self respect.

SELF-AWARENESS ACTIVITY

Describe how your anger is affecting the following areas of your life in positive or negative ways.

Physical health.

_____
_____
_____
_____

Emotional health.

_____
_____
_____
_____

Satisfaction with life.

_____
_____
_____
_____

Relationship with family (parents, siblings, children).

_____
_____
_____
_____

Relationship with spouse or partner.

_____
_____
_____
_____

Relationship with others (friends, coworker, etc.)

_____
_____
_____
_____

Other negative effects of your anger (inability to finish school, hold a job, etc.)

_____

_____

_____

_____

Other positive effect of your anger

_____

_____

_____

SAMPLE ANGER LOG

Situation or Event	Degree of Anger (1-10)	Thoughts	Coping strategy
My boss criticized me.		What does he know? You can never please him. The hell with him.	Talked to my wife about the situation. Re-evaluated what my boss said and realized he was right. Told my self not to be so sensitive.
My son didn't clean up his room like I told him.		I'll show him. He's going to be grounded for a month. Why doesn't he listen to me?	Talked with son about expectations and consequences of not cleaning his room; reminded my-self that he is only nine years old and usually listens well. Why get so mad over this?
My wife rejected my sexual advances.		How could she do this to me? Doesn't she care about me or my needs?	She has a right to not want sex. I know she has not been feeling well lately. She has needs too.

HOW TEMPERAMENT AND SOCIETY AFFECT YOUR ANGER

You temperament determines how you respond to frustration. Some people appear to be more prone to feeling intensely agitated, upset, aggressive or acting on these feelings than others. It is possible that complex biological factors may contribute to such feelings.

Your parents or caretakers had a major role in shaping your personality and influencing how you deal with anger. Much of what you learned was through observing how they dealt with their anger or how they responded to you when you felt angry. Their personality and ethnic background influenced how they dealt with anger. In some families, for example, parents never get angry on the surface and consequently give subtle messages to their children that anger is a negative or unacceptable feeling and is not to be expressed in the family. Children of such families often learn to suppress and hold their anger inside because of the negative consequences of showing it.

In other families, children see parents outwardly express anger in very hostile or violent remarks or behaviors. These children may associate anger with violence and become violent when angered themselves. On the other hand, they may be so fearful of getting violent when angry that they deny feelings of anger and try to act as though they never get angry.

Other children see their parents deal quite openly and directly with anger in ways that are reasonable and lead to resolution of conflict and angry feelings. These parents do not lash out; hold grudges or exhibit hostility. Children learn from such parents that anger is one of many emotions experienced and that it can be worked through without great difficulty. Other people: besides your parents, can influence your beliefs and behaviors related to anger. These include relatives; brothers; sisters and other adults such as neighbors, friends, teachers or celebrities. Your beliefs and ways of coping with anger were shaped during the early years of your life.

Exposure to traumatic life experiences such as sexual or physical abuse or premature loss of an important person in your life can contribute to anger by making you feel cheated, violated or unfairly taken advantage of. Stress associated with repeated exposure to a serous parental problem such as alcoholism or mental illness can also contribute to angry feelings. For instance, if one of your parents was incapacitated because of serious mental illness, you may have felt cheated of a "normal" childhood or if your parent was an alcoholic or drug addicted you may have been subjected to the many inconsistencies at home. As a result of these or similar experiences, you may still harbor angry feelings inside.

Some people experience anger in relation to social, economic or political factors. Facing educational, economic barriers or getting sent to war can contribute to anger situations such as these. They tend to cause feelings of powerlessness (the individual has no control over his life) or feelings of deprivation.

SELF-AWARENESS ACTIVITY

Following are some questions to answer which will help you clarify your anger, as well as the specific influences on your ways of coping with anger.

Write down the words that you associate with anger.

_____
_____
_____
_____

What other emotions or feelings do you associate with anger?

_____

_____
_____
_____

What did you learn from the following people about anger and expressing anger?

Parents or caretakers:

_____
_____
_____
_____

Brothers or sisters:

_____
_____
_____
_____

Other relatives or friends:

_____
_____
_____
_____

What else has influenced your attitudes and beliefs regarding anger or how you cope with anger?

_____
_____
_____
_____

Describe your usual style (s) of displaying or coping with anger.

_____
_____
_____
_____

How does your use of alcohol or other drugs impact on your anger or how you deal with it?

_____
_____
_____
_____

What do you think you need to change about the ways in which you deal with anger?

_____
_____
_____

What would other people, who know you very well, say that you need to change about the way you handle anger?

_____
_____
_____
_____

Just remember, no matter what you learned as a child about anger, it is always possible to change how you deal with it today.

THE ANGRY STORY

Have you thought of some positive ways to deal with things that don't go your way? The following "story" might help.

When I get angry, I look like a/an (animal) _____ and I feel like (texture) _____. The way I sound when I am angry is like (sound)_____ or (music) _____.

If I could smell the anger that I feel, it would smell like (smell)_____. If I could taste my anger, it would taste like (taste) _____.

The people who make me angry are _____, and _____.

The situations that make me angry are _____, and _____ The things people expect of me that make me angry are _____, _____ , and _____.

The things people expect of me that make me angry: _____

When things do not go the way I want them to, I have learned to _____.

I deal with them this way because;_____

Some better ways to deal with things that do not go my way might be; to _____, _____ or _____.

WHEN TO EXPECT ANGER

Here are some ways in which expectations about ourselves and others make us more prone to experiencing anger:

- High expectations of ourselves that are not met cause us to get angry. Logic to the contrary, the message we give ourselves, is that we are a total failure because we did not achieve our goal. The result is destructive anger that lowers our self-esteem.
- Our high expectations of others cause us to get angry and lead to interpersonal conflict.

- High expectations that someone will continue to act in a way we have found objectionable in the past is likely to make our anger more intense and more frequent. This may lead to anticipatory anger (becoming angry before the other person does or says anything.)
- Low expectations that you can handle a particular situation will increase your chances of becoming angry. Telling yourself that you "can't do it" brings to life the self-fulfilling prophecy.

You can see how expectations may create problems for you. High or low, they can provoke your anger. Since it's impossible to avoid expectations, your best bet is to be realistic in your expectations.

GETTING TO KNOW YOUR ANGER

Anger is a normal human emotion. It is intense. Everyone gets angry and has a right to his/her anger. The trick is managing your anger effectively so that it will move you in positive not negative ways. The first step is getting to know your anger and its symptoms;

Do you . . .

Physical

___ grit your teeth
___ get a headache
___ get sweaty palms
___ get dizzy
___ get a stomachache

Emotional

___ feel like running away
___ get depressed
___ feel guilty
___ feel resentment
___ become anxious

Behavioral

___ cry/yell/scream
___ use substances
___ get sarcastic
___ become abusive
___ withdraw

Does your anger

___ last too long
___ become too intense
___ lead to aggression
___ interferes with major roles
___ creep out in mysterious ways
___ contribute to physical problems
___ come too frequently
___ flare up too quickly

ANGER INVENTORY (RATE 1-5) RANK YOUR ANGER IN THE FOLLOWING SITUATIONS

1—No annoyance 2—Little irritated 3—Upset 4—Quite angry 5—very angry

___ You have overheard people joking about you or your family.
___ When others do not treat you with respect or consideration.
___ When others single you out for corrections while the actions of others go unnoticed.

_____ A salesperson hounds you from the moment you walk into a store.

_____ You are trying to discuss something important with someone who is not giving you a chance to talk or express your feelings.

_____ Someone offers continual unsolicited advice.

_____ You are in a discussion with someone who persists in arguing about a topic he/she knows very little about.

_____ You have had a busy day and the person you live with greets you with complaints about what you have not finished.

_____ Someone is given special consideration because of his/her popularity, good looks, financial position or family statuses.

_____ Someone comments on your being overweight/underweight.

_____ TOTAL

The higher your score the more you need to learn how to keep your anger under control

ANGER CYCLE

1. An event/consequence occurs (trigger).
2. Cognitive awareness of threat, whether emotional or physical (thought).
3. Physiological stress response and build-up of anger energy (feeling).
4. Time to think and choose release of anger energy (behavioral reaction) expression can be adaptive or maladaptive.
5. Resolution equilibrium, withdrawal and forgiveness (honeymoon period) before the cycle will begin again.

EXAMPLE OF ANGER CYCLE

A Look Into Hell
The diary of an abused wife

Saturday, May 1, 2011

Dear Diary:

It happened again last night . . . the volcano blew!!

It has been almost a month since Jim hit me but last night I got it good. I've known for several days that it was coming (Phase 1 Tension building phase.) He would get mad at any little thing I did. "Dinner wasn't good, I hadn't washed the shirt he wanted to wear, I didn't park the car in the driveway like he liked, I went out to lunch with the girls, etc." Until last night the abuse was mostly verbal. He only hit me a few times and it wasn't really very hard. He usually just called me ugly names, threatened to leave me, threatened to take the checkbook away and said if I didn't "straighten up" he would see to it that I never saw the kids again. Stuff like that. I was so petrified but didn't say anything (ignored her feelings) because I figured that would just make it worse. What could I do anyway? Sometimes I felt mad and wished he would leave, and then I was scared to death that he would leave us. I tried (in vain) to do EVERYTHING right. I never talked back to him, I didn't talk to my sister on the phone, I stopped going to lunch with Janet (withdraws), I made sure I looked good when he got home, I cooked his favorite dinners. EVERYTHING! I walked on eggshells for two weeks. I felt like I was going to blow apart at the seams, but for the sake of the kids (psychological tension) I kept my mouth shut. I was at the point I just couldn't stand it anymore. I almost wished he would blow up and get it over with. Well, my wish came true. (End of stage one: Tension Building Phase.)

I had to work late last night but I thought it would be OK since Jim was paid and I knew he would go out with "the boys." The trouble was he needed something so he called me. When he didn't reach me I guess he really got mad. He sat around drinking with the guys for another couple of hours before coming home. When he got here I had just arrived so of course dinner wasn't ready. That was the beginning of the end. At first he didn't say anything to me but he made sure I knew he was mad by the dirty looks he gave me. I went ahead and made dinner. When he got to the table he started questioning me about where I had been. He didn't believe me when I told him I had had to work late.

Before I knew what was happening he was throwing the food at me and yelling and screaming. (Beginning of Phase 2: Acute Battering Incident.) I told the kids to go to their rooms and I tried to calm him down. He got more and more out of control. I told him I was sorry for working late and would never do it again but that didn't help. He just said that I "never learned" and that I had asked for it. He said I always had to learn everything the "hard way" and that he was going to "teach me a lesson."

I don't exactly remember everything that happened. It's kind of a blur. He hit me with a plate and I started crying. He said, "I'll give you something to cry about" and began to punch me. I fell to the floor and he began to kick me about my head and body. I could hear the kids back in their room crying but I knew they were too afraid to come out. He was saying terrible things about me being a slut and stupid and a terrible wife and mother. At one point I tried to call 911 but he hit me in the head and I guess it knocked me out. The next thing I knew I found myself on the kitchen floor just waking up in a daze. He was gone and I knew I had been "out" for a while because he had gone to the bedroom and taken some of his things before he left.

I was panicked. The first thing I thought about was his safety. I didn't know what to do. I tried to find him at some of his friend's homes but they said that they hadn't seen him. So I tried to clean up all the mess in the kitchen. I really didn't feel like cleaning but I knew if he came home and it was still there he would be mad again. After cleaning the mess I tried to clean myself up some and then I went to bed. I just don't know what I did wrong. (End of phase two: "Acute Battering Incident."

Sometime after midnight the phone rang. It was him. He was crying and said he was so sorry (Begin phase three: kindness/honeymoon phase.) He said that he just loves me so much that he can't stand to think I was with someone else. I told him I wasn't and he said he knew that now but I should have called him to let him know I had to work late. He is probably right. I guess I did mess up. He said that he wanted to come home and that he needed me. I tried to talk him into waiting until the morning so he wouldn't wake the kids but he said that he would kill himself if I didn't let him come home so I did.

He had a red rose for me when he got here. I don't know where he got it at that time of night. I guess he really does love me. He is such a good husband and father most of the time. It is just when I do things he doesn't like that he looses control. He said that if I was willing to try harder he was. He was just so sweet to me that I had to forgive him. Anyway he said he knew he was wrong to do this to me and he would never do it again. When I said he had said that before he said he really meant it this time and that he would even go to a marriage counselor if I wanted to. What could I do? I am his wife and he is the kid's father. I think he really means it this time!

May 2, 2011

Emotionally I feel better today than I have in a long time. I feel calm and happy. The worse part is that I am so bruised that I know I'll have to miss a few days of work and just when I am up for that promotion. Well, I don't think Jim wanted me to get it anyway because it would mean longer hours. I would think he would like the extra money but he said he made enough for our needs. He really is trying hard and we both want our relationship to work. I'll just have to try a little harder too. I know we can make it. (In stage three: "Kindness & Contrite Loving Behavior, BIG HOOK!)
Well, till tomorrow.

May 3, 2011

Jim's self talk!!!

Well, it looks like the house payment is going to have to be late again (feeling inept.) I just don't know where all my money goes (Phase one/tension build-up.) I work hard and I never waste money on myself but we never seem to have enough (feels bad.) I cannot make Caren understand that she cannot throw money away as she does (blames.) All those phone calls to her sister in California are unnecessary and she buys too many clothes. Who does she have to look good for? I will make her stop that right now (isolates her.) I am going to have to break her of her bad habits fast or we will go to the poor house. I try to be a good husband and father and give them everything they need but she just spends and spends. She is going to have to learn that I am the boss in this family and she had better start doing as I say (dehumanizes her.) I bet when she goes out to lunch with those friends of hers at work all the time she spends a bundle. Then they probably just sit around bad mouthing me and the other husbands. Who do these women think they are (dehumanizing)? They had better learn their place or this world is going to go to hell. I am going to make her take her lunch to work from now on so she will not go out with them (isolating her.)

May 4, 2011

Jim's Self Talk

(Phase 1 escalating)

I guess I shouldn't have been so hard on Caren last night but she just pushes me over the edge. I did not really hurt her though, just yelled a little. She always acts like its worse than it is. I think she just wants attention. It's like she WANTS to upset me. I told her not to buy any more clothes and then she turned around and bought that new dress. She said it was for a big meeting she has to go to next week but I don't know. I am beginning to wonder if she is having an affair and just wants to look good for her new boyfriend. You can't trust any woman as far as you can throw them. Of course I don't want her to leave. The guys would think I can't control my woman. Maybe I'll take her some flowers home tonight. That ought to hold her for awhile.

May 5, 2011

Jim's self talk at the bar after getting paycheck

(Phase one is escalating)

Where in the hell is she when I need her (he called her on the phone and she wasn't home)? She is probably out spending money. No wonder I cannot make the house payments on time she spends all my money. Or maybe she is out with some guy. I need to teach her that this kind of behavior must stop. I've tried talking to her but it doesn't work. I don't want to hurt her but she needs to learn. I'll have a couple more beers with the guys before going home just to relax me.

(Later that night at home)

Boy she is acting smug. She doesn't even apologize about being late and not having dinner ready. Oh, sure she had to work! I don't believe THAT! The guys were right tonight. You can't trust women. Even if her boss did want her to work late she should have said no. I should come first she's my wife. And she calls this slop dinner. I bet she doesn't cook like this for her boyfriend. (Escalates into Phase 2/physical violence).

(Later that night after leaving house) (Going into phase three/kindness & seduction)

God, Caren really made me lose control. I wish I wouldn't have hit her but I couldn't help myself. I know I probably shouldn't hit her but I love her so much that I can't stand it when I think she is cheating on me. I really did not hurt her bad but I better call and apologize before I go home (feels guilt not shame.) I will even take her some flowers (big hook.) That always works. I will just have to stay calm next time she upsets me. I want our relationship to be good like it was before she started working. I know I can change if she will.

WHAT CAUSES ANGER

The causes vary from person to person and from situation to situation

Some common causes of anger include:

- **Stress:** Stress related to work, family, health and money problems may make you feel anxious and irritable.
- **Frustration:** You may get angry if you fail to reach a goal or feel as if things are out of your control.
- **Fear:** Anger is a natural response to threats of violence or to physical or verbal abuse.
- **Annoyance:** You may react in anger to minor irritations and daily hassles.

- **Disappointment:** Anger often results when expectations and desires are not met.
- **Resentment:** You may feel angry when you have been hurt, rejected or offended

WHAT SETS YOU OFF

Different things trigger a person's anger. Some common triggers are listed below. Check the ones that trigger your anger. Use the blank spaces to fill in your own triggers

I feel angry when I:

___ think I am treated unfairly.

___ am embarrassed.

___ feel ignored.

___ don't get credit for something I have done.

___ have to follow orders.

___ fail at something or do not do something well.

___ feel helpless or out of control.

___ get jealous.

___ _____

___ _____

___ _____

___ _____

I feel angry when people:

___ insult me.

___ criticize my work or me.

___ don't listen to me.

___ disagree with me.

___ don't work as hard as I do.

___ lie to me.

___ tell me what to do.

___ are rude or inconsiderate.

___ are late.

___ don't act or feel the way I think they should.

___ _____

___ _____

___ _____

___ _____

I feel angry when faced with these events or situations

___ traffic jams and encounters with other drivers.

___ conflict at work.

___ family arguments.

___ child misbehavior or temper tantrums.

_____ waiting in line at the bank, store, etc.
_____ financial problems.
_____ yelling or loud noises.
_____ mistakes or error.
_____ wasted time.
_____ losing a game or a contest.
_____ name calling or teasing.
_____ child abuse.
_____ prejudice toward anyone.
_____ mistreatment of animals.

___ _____
___ _____
___ _____
___ _____

Once you're aware of things that set you off you can work to change.

RECOGNIZING YOUR BODY'S ANGER WARNING SIGNS

What are your warning signs?

Think about how you feel when you get angry. Check the warning signs you often have when you get angry. Write in signs that aren't listed. Listen to your body talk.

My warning signs are:

_____ tense muscles.
_____ tight fists.
_____ clenched jaw.
_____ sweaty palms.
_____ racing heartbeat.
_____ fast breathing.
_____ a feeling warm or flushed.
_____ upset stomach.
_____ loud or mean voice.

___ _____
___ _____
___ _____
___ _____

TAKE STEPS TO GET BACK IN CONTROL WHEN YOU'RE ANGRY

- Start by taking a "timeout."
- Stop what you are doing.
- When you feel your anger warning signs developing and you start thinking angry thoughts tell yourself to stop. This may help you calm down and think more clearly.

Try to relax

For example:

- Count from 10-100.
- Get a drink of water.
- Take a walk.
- Take several slow deep breaths.

Leave if necessary

If you are angry with another person, tell him/her that you need to take a timeout. Ask someone to watch a child or elderly or ill person for you if necessary. Then go to a safe place to calm down. Avoid driving.

Return when you're calm

Once you've got your anger under control, go back and talk with the person or face the situation that triggered your anger.

DEALING WITH ANGER

Taking time to get control of our thoughts and feelings before you speak can make or break communication. If you initially have so much angry energy to blow off before you can be in control of what you say or do, here are some active ways to let off stream and gather your thoughts.

- Go for a brisk walk, jog or bike ride until you are calmer, avoid car and motorized vehicles.
- House work.
- Yard work.
- Bounce a basketball or other sports activity.
- Count to 10, 20 or higher.
- Write down the feelings, then tear them up, burn them up, keep them or save them.
- Talk it out with yourself in private or seek out a friend.

When you have had time to stop, think and calm down return to the person and resolve the conflict assertively, productively and fairly.

HOW DO YOU TALK TO YOURSELF

You may say things silently to yourself every day that will affect your life. This is called self-talk. Whether your self-talk is positive or negative makes a big difference in how you handle anger. Below you will find some ways your self-talk can push you in the right direction in order to resist using inappropriate anger.

Avoid negative self-talk

This includes criticizing yourself and blaming yourself or others for your problems. Negative self-talk can add to your anger and make it harder to manage it effectively.

<u>Learn to use positive self-talk instead</u>

Try to stop negative self-talk as soon as it pops into your head. Replace the negative thought with a positive one. For example:

- Instead of saying, "I can't handle this traffic, I'm going to explode" you could say, "Relax. I can handle it. This happens to everyone sometimes. It won't last long."
- Instead of saying. "That jerk." She embarrassed me on purpose," you could say, "It's OK. She probably didn't mean anything by it. Maybe she's just having a bad day."

Learning to identify negative messages and change them to positive ones can help reduce the amount of anger you feel.

FIND HEALTHY WAYS TO EXPRESS YOUR ANGER

It is important to find healthy ways to express our anger so that it does not get out of control. Some ways to do this are:

1. Do not keep angry feelings locked inside you. Keep your composure and not hurt others, express angry feelings in an appropriate way.
2. Remember to calm down. Think carefully before you speak. Take a time out if necessary. You're less likely to say something you'll be sorry for later.
3. Name the problem. Calmly and clearly explain why you're angry or what the problem is. Don't yell, use insults or make threats. People will be less likely to consider your point.
4. Use "I" statements. After you describe the problem, use "I" statements to tell the person how you feel. These statements focus on you and your needs, wants and feelings. They also help the listener avoid feeling blamed or criticized.
5. Identify solution. Say what you would like to change or see happen in the future. If you are having conflicts with another person try to find a solution together.
6. Get help if you need it. Talk with a family member or friend if you're having trouble expressing your anger constructively. Or consider seeing a counselor or other mental health professional. He or she can help you learn ways to express your feelings through role-playing and other method.
7. Don't hold a grudge. After a disagreement, be willing to forgive the other person and yourself.

FOUR PROVEN TECHNIQUES FOR MANAGING ANGER

1. The first step towards managing anger is the identification of the mistaken attitudes and convictions that predispose us to being excessively angry in the first place. Once these mistakes have been corrected, you will be less likely to become extremely angry than you were in the past.
2. The second step is the identification of those factors from your childhood that prevent you from expressing your anger as appropriately as you otherwise might. These factors include fear, denial and ignorance and so on. These impediments to the effective and appropriate management of your anger towards others can be removed so that your suppressed anger will NOT compound itself inside of you, as it has been doing for years.

3. The third step is learning the appropriate modes of expressing your "legitimate" anger at others so that you can begin to cope more effectively with anger provoking situations as they arise in our personal relationships. When you are anxious or depressed in your relationships, you are often experiencing the consequences of your suppressed anger. The problem is that you have suppressed your anger so deeply that you succeeded in concealing it from your own self. All you are left with is the residual evidence of it; your anxiety or your depression. When you are depressed, very often you are also angry with your self without realizing it. The antidote too much of alcoholism and drug abuse is learning to appropriately manage your anger at yourself. About the management of your anger does not end in learning these new and more appropriate ways to express it. There remains one last step.

4. The fourth step in the anger management process is to bind up the wounds that may have been left by the potentially devastating emotional impact of anger. "Anger wounds" left in you against those who have wronged you. If you do not complete this moping up step, you will cling to the resentment of someone having done wrong and will carry the festering residue of your anger and rage in your heart forever.

One of the most effective means of giving ourselves immediate relief from anger in our personal relationships is to forgive others. Many of us can not forgive those who have trespassed against us. Something below the level of our conscious awareness prevents us from relieving our residual anger by forgiving the other person and we then carry a grudge in our hearts for thirty years. This unresolved anger poisons our relationship with our friends and loved ones. It even spoils our relationship with ourselves. We make our own life mean and miserable instead of happy and full. Very often this feeling is, "Why should I forgive them? What they did was wrong." However, is forgiveness for those who only do us right? Most people have a hard time forgiving others simply because they have a wrong understanding of what forgiveness is. When you forgive someone, it does not mean that you condone or are legitimizing their behavior toward you. To forgive them means that you refuse to carry painful and debilitating grudges around with you for the rest of your life. You are "refusing" to cling to the resentment of them having done you wrong. You are giving yourself some immediate relief from your OWN anger. To forgive them is an act that we do on our OWN behalf. It has nothing to do with "lifting" the other person's sin. You are not doing it for their sake. You are doing it for yourself. This is a choice you are making on your OWN terms in order to relieve your OWN pent-up emotions.

ANGER STYLES

There are three main ways we handle our anger. Sometimes one will lead to another. It is important to really find out our style of handling anger. The three styles are: 1) Stuffing; 2) Escalating; 3) Managing.

STUFFING

Do you "stuff" your anger? _____
Do you tend to avoid direct confrontation? _____

- "Stuffers" can deny anger . . . They may not admit to themselves or to others that they are angry.
- "Stuffers" may not be aware that they have the right to be angry.

Some reasons we "stuff" are: check the ones that apply to you:

1. Fear of hurting/offending someone. _____
2. Fear of being disliked or rejected._____
3. Fear of losing control._____
4. Feeling it's inappropriate (not ok) to be angry. _____
5. Feeling unable to cope with such a strong intense emotion. _____
6. Fear of damaging/losing a relationship. _____
7. It's a learned behavior but, it can be unlearned. _____
8. Trying to use a different style than the one I was raised with.

Consequences/Problems: You can add some others:

1. Anger comes out—regardless.
2. Impairs relationships.
3. Compromises physical and mental health.
4. _____
5. _____

ESCALATING

Do you "escalate" to rage? _____
Do you try to control, but lose control? _____

- "Escalators" blame and shame the "provoker."
- "Escalating" often leads to abusive situations.

MANAGEMENT I

Do you "manage" your anger? _____
Do you allow anger to mobilize you in positive directions? _____

OPEN HONEST AND DIRECT EXPRESSION is the most effective way of managing anger. Easier said then done, huh? When expressing anger directly keep these important skills in mind.

- Remind yourself that anger is a normal, human emotion—it's OK to feel angry!
- Before open, honest and direct expression, evaluate the following:

  1. What was the trigger event?
  2. Is this good timing for the listener?
  3. Set a specific time limit for anger discussion.
  4. Remember your body language.

     - Firm voice, moderate tone, direct eye contact, maintain personal "space," establish an even eye level with the listener.

5. Do not attack or blame the other person.
6. Focus on the specific behavior that triggered your anger.
7. Avoid black and white thinking, "You never . . ." Instead, say; "I'd prefer that . . . . Then I would feel . . . ."
8. Use "I" statements. "I feel angry when . . ." "I feel angry that . . ."
9. Avoid statements/actions that you'll regret later.
10. Don't drag in old issues now.
11. Check for possible compromises.
12. After open, honest and direct expression, close the discussion and then move on!

When it's over, pat yourself on the back for your assertiveness!

Say to yourself, "I (and perhaps the people around me) will be better off in the long run!"

NOW say to yourself, "By managing my anger I took an important step in improving my sense of well-being."

MANAGING II

Do you "manage" your anger? _____

Do you allow anger to mobilize you in positive directions? _____

OPEN, HONEST AND DIRECT EXPRESSION is the most affective way of managing anger (see Anger Styles, Managing I)

Additional effective anger management techniques

1. Choosing constructive (not destructive) methods, solutions and ideas.
2. Trying physical outlets such as; exercise, housework, crafts, etc.
3. Problem solving and coming up with action plans, such as, forming a neighborhood watch to combat vandalism.
4. Involving an objective third party. Ask someone you trust to be a sounding board. Who might this be? _____
5. Using the "empty chair" exercise. Pretend you're sitting across from the person you're angry with and say what's on your mind. Who is that person? _____
   _____
6. Writing a letter to the person you're angry with. You could describe your anger right now at the time of the anger event or both. You can destroy it, you can save it, you can mail it at a later date
7. Using relaxation techniques.

   • Guided imagery.
   • Self-help tapes.
   • Music.

8. Using positive self-talk

- "I am able to choose my anger style."
- "I am angry but I'm not going to let it _____"

9. Working towards anger resolution through acceptance (learning to live with the fact that certain people and situations, past, present & future, will not change.)

- Make realistic expectations.
- What is one of your frustrating anger situations? _____
  _____
  _____
  _____
  _____

- Can it really change as you'd like it to in the near future?
  _____ yes   _____ no

If not:

- Realize the powerlessness over the situation.
- Give yourself a time limit to be angry and then let it go!
- Constantly remind yourself, "I can not afford to stay angry. What is at stake here?"
- Recognize the need for forgiveness. "No painful event is allowed to contribute to my anger more than one time."
- Focus on the present.

Certain physical and mental health problems such as Alzheimer's disease or brain injury may increase your anger. And, handling anger poorly can lead to health problems. Talk to your health-care provider, if necessary, about your anger and how it affects you. Have regular checkups.

PHYSICAL ACTIVITY IS A GREAT OUTLET FOR ANGRY FEELINGS

Physical activity lets you quickly and safely let out strong feelings. And, regular activity can improve your overall health.

Here are some tips:

Talk with your health-care provider. Be sure to consult your health-care provider before stating an exercise program.

Choose moderate activities. Good choices include:

- Walking
- Swimming
- Tennis
- Dancing
- Yoga

<u>Don't overdo it</u>. Slowly increase the amount of activity you do. And be sure to warm up before you begin and cool down afterward.

What activities will you try to help manage your anger?

_____

_____

_____

MORE WAYS TO HELP GET A HANDLE ON ANGER

When things start heating up, try these methods to cool down:

<u>Have a sense of humor:</u> For many people having a good sense of humor helps them avoid getting angry. Try to find the humor in minor troubles and annoyances.

<u>Do a hobby:</u> For example, try gardening, learning a musical instrument or making crafts. A hobby can be a productive outlet for tension and energy. And, it can serve as a welcome distraction from angry feeling

<u>Write about your feelings.</u> Consider recording your thoughts and feelings in a journal or dairy. Write a letter (You do not have to send it.) Writing can help you work through situations and problems calmly and at your own pace.

<u>Get plenty of rest.</u> Most people need about 6-9 hours of sleep each night. When you're angry, you may have trouble falling asleep. In turn, this lack of sleep may leave you feeling more irritable. If you have trouble sleeping go to bed at the same time each night and avoid having caffeine in the evening. It can keep you awake.

LEARNING TO RELAX CAN HELP YOU STAY IN CONTROL

Using relaxation techniques regularly can help you reduce stress and stay calm. Try some of the following:

<u>MEDITATION</u>

This can help calm you and clear your mind of anger. Follow these steps.

1. Find a quiet place. Wear loose, comfortable clothing. Sit or lie down.
2. Close your eyes. Take slow deep breaths.
3. Concentrate on a single word, object or calming thought.
4. Don't worry if other thoughts or images enter your mind while you are doing this. Just relax and return to what you were focusing on.
5. Continue until you feel relaxed and refreshed.

DEEP-BREATHING EXERCISES

These can help keep anger from getting out of control. Follow these steps:

1. Sit comfortably or lie on your back.
2. Breathe in slowly and deeply for a count of five.
3. Hold your breath for a count of five.
4. Breathe out slowly for a count of five, pushing out all the air.
5. Repeat several times until you feel calm and relaxed.

PROGRESSIVE MUSCLE RELAXATION

In progressive muscle relaxation, you tense and relax each muscle group, starting at your head and working your way down to your toes. Here's how:

1. Wear loose, comfortable clothing. Sit in a comfortable chair or lie down.
2. Tense the muscles in your face for 5-10 seconds. Then relax them for about 20 seconds.
3. Tense the muscles in the back of your neck for 5-10 seconds. Then relax them for about 20 seconds. Notice the difference in how your muscles feel when relaxed.
4. Move down to your shoulders. Tense and relax the muscles the same way you did in step three
5. Repeat the same steps with the other muscle groups in your body; in your hands, arms, chest, stomach, lower back, buttocks, thighs, calves and feet one at a time

VISUALIZATION

This technique uses your imagination to help you relax and reduce your anger.

1. Sit in a comfortable chair or lie down.
2. Imagine a pleasant, peaceful scene, such as a lush forest or a sandy beach. Picture yourself in this setting
3. Focus on the scene. Continue until you feel refreshed and relaxed.

KEEP CONTROL OF ANGER

Don't keep angry feelings locked inside you. Express them in ways that help you keep control and won't hurt others.

1. <u>Remember to calm down.</u> Think carefully before you speak. You're less likely to say something you'll be sorry for later.
2. <u>Name the problem.</u> Calmly and clearly explain why you're angry or what the problem is. Don't yell, use insults or make threats. People will be less likely to consider your point.
3. <u>Use "I" statements.</u> After you describe the problem, use "I" statements to tell the person how you feel. These statements focus on you and your needs, wants and feelings. They also help the listener avoid feeling blamed or criticized.

4. <u>Identify solutions.</u> Say what you would like to change or see happen in the future. If you are having conflicts with another person try to find a solution together.

5. <u>Get help if you need it.</u> Talk with a family member or friend if you're having trouble expressing your anger constructively. Or consider seeing a counselor or other mental health professional. He or she can help you learn ways to express your feelings through role-playing and other methods.

6. <u>Don't hold a grudge.</u> After a disagreement, be willing to forgive the other person and yourself.

7. <u>Have more fun.</u>

- Make fun foremost.
- Demand more time for play.
- Invite child-like frolic into your life.
- Get inspired by connecting more with children.
- Don't be an "old fogy." Take more risks. Discover your freshly hatched "signs."
- Don't just focus on outcome-based activities. Do things just because it is fun.
- Laugh at yourself more often. Lighten up.
- Become a much more active listener. That's the best way to hear about new stuff.
- Go on "artist dates" with yourself. Get inspired by getting away.
- Fly in the face of "normal" often.
- Splurge on yourself.

MORE WAYS TO EXPRESS ANGER IN A HEALTHY WAY

<u>Feel the emotion.</u> Anger is emotional energy like any other emotion. It is just as valid as any other feeling. If it is there, feel it. When you get mad, you may need to move. You can feel the energy coursing through you and it feels like it is going to burst out. Your heart beats harder and you breathe faster.

<u>Look at the thinking that goes with the emotion.</u> Consider the thoughts that go along with your anger. See if you recognize any patterns. To get free of the anger, try to change your thinking. You may think, "If I am late everyone will think badly of me" but you can change that thought to, "If I am late, the meeting will start late, but it won't make that much difference."

<u>Make a responsible decision about what action, if any, you want to take.</u> Figure out what the anger is telling you. Do you have some unmet needs? Are there some things going on in your environment that you need to change? You may have to tell someone what you need. You can ask yourself, "Am I afraid of being left out?" "Am I afraid to do something by myself?" Sometimes you may get mad at a person who is late and did not call to tell you. If you get mad at this person, ask yourself what the anger is about. Are you afraid there has been a car accident or insulted that your feelings were not taken into consideration? Once you know what is behind these feelings, you can ask the person for what you need to cope with these feelings.

<u>Take responsibility for your anger.</u> You are angry. Someone did not <u>make</u> you angry. What they did may have been the catalyst but you are responsible for your response. People often say, "He made me angry because he would not do what I told him." However, your emotional response is a result of your own interpretation and experience. No one can make you feel anything. When

people say, "You made me do it, you made me lose control," they are saying, "I do not want to take responsibility for my own response and feelings."

<u>Do not hit when feeling angry</u>. Do not allow yourself to physically hit anyone or allow others to abuse you when you are angry. If abuse has occurred, seek professional help because the physical energy can be intense. Hitting and throwing things is common pace. Men are taught to express their feelings physically; most would never consider crying. However, striking another person in order to express anger is an unacceptable way to burn off energy.

FORGIVENESS: GIVING UP THE ANGER

Forgiveness may be one of the most difficult tasks we humans do. It may seem impossible to forgive at times or it might not be what we want to do, but it may be a wise choice.

The impact of NOT forgiving might be:

- Anger.
- Health issues.
- Impaired relationships.

In general, how do you see yourself as a forgiving or not forgiving person?

Not forgiving θ ———————————————— 10 Forgiving.
Put an x on the line above where you feel you fall.

What is one current "forgiveness issue" you have in your life right now? ———————————
———————————————————————————————————————

Where are you, on the continuum, in regards to this current forgiveness issue in your life?

Not forgiving θ ———————————————— 10 Forgiving

People who have forgiven (or reconciled) have reported feeling "not conquered by bitterness" and "not giving the person who hurt them the power." How might you feel if you move more towards the forgiving side? ———————————————————————————
———————————————————————————————————————

If you had the opportunity to say what you wanted to this person/persons, what would you say?
———————————————————————————————————————
———————————————————————————————————————

What steps can you take to see the person or persons who betrayed or hurt you as human beings, rather than "bad," "evil," or "monster-like?"
1. ———————————————————————————————————
2. ———————————————————————————————————
3. ———————————————————————————————————

ANGER—FRIEND OR FOE

Anger can sometimes be a very upsetting emotion to have. Often we are feeling shaky and flushed with our face locked in a scowl. More often than not, we may regret something we have said or done. Ben Franklin was quoted as saying, "Anger is never without reason, but seldom a good one." Much of human tragedy has been fueled by this powerful emotion. If it was unacceptable or unsafe to express anger when we were young we may find ourselves brooding silently or irritable. What is this feeling called anger and how can we make it work for us instead of against us? It's easy to see how anger could have been useful when we were living in more primitive times. Anger is kind of like a turbocharger in that it makes us stronger and faster. It is not too hard to see that it could help us to fight an enemy who was a physical threat to our family or us. One of the problems with anger is that when we get very angry our thinking gets very primitive and we start to see the other person as an enemy and suddenly the thought of hurting someone seems to make sense. Later, after we "cool down," we are more able to see the situation in a different way and the person seems more like us, with strengths and weaknesses.

What do you do when you get angry? Tom yells and criticizes others. Susan cries. Larry smiles and pretends he's not upset. Jake hits his younger sister. Linda tells people she's upset. And Tracy gets quiet and pouts. People show their anger in many different ways. Here are some ideas for making anger a friend and not a foe.

1. <u>Accept that you get angry</u>. All people experience anger in some form. It is not a bad emotion, although sometimes the way it gets expressed is negative. Unfortunately, some of you believe that you are bad, selfish and sinful or mean just for feeling angry. Instead, you should see anger as often trying to help you in some way. For example, maybe it's trying to help you stand up for yourself or to alert you to a problem. For those who think they never get angry, remember that feelings of irritation, frustration, disgust and annoyance fall in the family of angry feelings.

2. <u>Be in charge of how you express your anger</u>. Watch out for the dangers of either being out of control or over-controlled with your anger. Putting others down, name calling, hitting and breaking things may offer temporary relieve but it's destructive and often followed by guilt. The other extreme of always putting a lid on your anger leads to depression, surprise explosions or hard to control behavior or thoughts.

3. <u>Identify the issues, situations or relationships that tend to ignite your anger.</u> For instance, if drinking or being tired makes you more prone to anger, then don't discuss a touchy issue like finances, for example, with your spouse when you're tired or drinking. Pick another time when you have better control over your anger.

4. <u>Think when you're angry</u>. Make a partnership between your thoughts and feelings. Think with whom you're angry, what you're angry about and how you want to handle it. Sometimes thinking through your angry feelings resolves them. But avoid the tendency to rationalize your anger away so often that it never gets expressed.

5. <u>Talk about your anger</u>. While there truly are times it's best to bite your tongue, sometimes the healthiest thing to do is to express your irritation or anger directly. This is especially warranted with friends or close family members. For instance, you might say, "I feel angry with you when you . . ." To keep your anger to yourself too much tends to make the feeling get bigger than it needs to be.

6. <u>Realize that sometimes anger covers over vulnerable feelings of hurt, fear or insecurity.</u> At those times you'll get better results if you deal with those vulnerable feelings rather than getting stuck in the anger.

7. <u>If you are too hot under the collar, cool down before you talk about your anger.</u> Count to 10, go to the bathroom or walk down the hall to get a drink of water and then deal with the issue at hand. Too much anger sabotages good communication due to feelings of revenge or defensiveness.

8. <u>Work off the aggression that's underneath the anger.</u> Exercise can be helpful in reducing irritability.

9. <u>Realize that some people will not know how to deal with your anger even if you express it constructively.</u> They may be offended, defensive or hurt. If you need them to approve of your expression, you are in trouble.

10. <u>If you find yourself showing more angry feelings than loving feelings,</u> take a moment to look at what extra problems or pressures you are dealing with that may need to be addressed. You may need to talk to a friend or seek help from a professional.

11. <u>Forgiving yourself and others can help dissolve anger.</u> Identify the grudge you hold against yourself or others and then set a goal to release the grudge eventually. Remember that sometimes forgiveness takes time.

Anger is a common emotion that can interrupt clear thinking and good living. The more you deal openly and directly with your anger the sooner you can get on with thinking good thoughts and feeling loving feelings.

EIGHT WAYS TO DEAL WITH ANGER

1. Recognize and allow yourself to believe that anger is a natural healthy human feeling. Everyone feels it, we just do not all express it. You needn't fear your anger.

2. Remember that you are responsible for your own feelings. Don't give your power away. You got angry at what happened because of what you thought. The other person did not "make" you angry.

3. Remember that anger and aggression are not the same thing. Anger can be expressed assertively.

4. Get to know yourself so you recognize these events and behaviors that trigger your anger.

5. Find your own buttons so you'll know when they're pushed."

6. Learn to relax. If you have developed the skill of relaxing yourself, learn to apply this response when something triggers your anger.

7. Develop assertive methods for expressing your anger, following the principles described. Be spontaneous, do not wait and let it build up resentment. State it directly, avoid sarcasm and innuendo, use honest, expressive language; avoid name-calling, put-downs; and physical attacks.

8. Keep your life clear. Deal with the issues as they arise not after hours, days, weeks or stewing.

DEVELOP AN ANGER MANAGEMENT PLAN

Now that you've learned more about anger and how you respond to it you can develop your own plan for managing your anger.

Follow these steps:

1. <u>Set positive goals and a time frame</u>. Your goals should address both a specific behavior and your reaction. For example, over the next month your goal could be to communicate your feelings using "I" statements whenever you get angry at work. You can set different goals for yourself but don't try to meet too many at one time. You're less likely to reach them.
2. <u>Get support</u>. Tell family, friends and co-workers about your goals. They can offer encouragement and advice. Seek out their help if you're having trouble with your anger. Or, consider seeing a mental health professional.
3. <u>Track your progress</u>. Consider keeping a daily log or journal. Make note of times when you avoid getting angry or handle anger well. Seeing improvement over time can keep you from feeling discouraged.
4. <u>Reward yourself</u>. Treat yourself when you reach a goal or get halfway there. For example, go to a movie or enjoy a special meal.

What would your anger management plan look like?

You hold the key to your own anger management. When you learn about yourself, others and the world around you, you can find anger relief. This is at the core of anger management.

Write out your own management plan using the four steps above.

_____
_____
_____
_____
_____
_____

By gaining a true understanding of healthy thinking vs. unhealthy thinking you'll be able to work yourself out of anger or, better still, keep your anger in check

POSITIVE EFFECTIVE PARENTING
P.E.P.

CHAPTER NINE
Stress Management

CHAPTER NINE

Stress Management

REDUCING STRESS IN YOUR LIFE

I don't think anyone would disagree with me when I say that raising children can be very stressful. But, there are a number of things we can do to reduce stress and make parenting much more enjoyable. You can't eliminate stress altogether. However, you can "tame the beast" so you can live with it in peace. Help manage stress by taking time out from tension with relaxation techniques. Listen to how you communicate with yourself and others. Using social and physical buffers against stress can also help. The payoffs? Here are a few: a stronger immune system for fighting disease, lower risk of heart disease and other chronic illnesses and over-all better health. Other benefits include improved relationships and reduced burnout in both your work and personal life. First let's find out what stress is and what it does to us. Then we will go over some coping skills for reducing stress.

WHAT IS STRESS?

Stress is the way that we respond to change in our lives. It is the way our bodies react physically, emotionally, cognitively and behaviorally to any change in the status quo. These changes do not have to be only negative things, positive change can also be stressful. Even imagined change can cause stress. Stress is highly individual. A situation that one person may find stressful may not bother another person.

Stress occurs when something happens that we feel imposes a demand on us. When we perceive that we cannot cope or feel inadequate to meet the demand we begin to feel stress. Stress is not all bad. We need a certain amount of stress in our lives because it is stimulating and motivating. It gives us the energy to try harder and keeps us alert. When we find ourselves in a situation that challenges us too much we react with the "fight of flight" stress response. Stress actually begins in our brains and it is expressed in our body. Once we perceive a stress, our body sends out chemical messengers in the form of stress hormones to help our bodies handle the stress.

Too little stress may cause boredom and depression and too much stress, particularly bad stress (distress) is a killer. Stress is the body's physical, mental and chemical reaction to circumstances that frighten, excite, confuse, endanger or irritate you. Anxiety is a mental reaction and tension is a physical reaction.

CHRONIC STRESS

Stress hormones are important to help us meet the demands of stress occasionally but if they are repeatedly triggered disease will occur. Our body does signal us when we are experiencing the effects of chronic stress. There are many symptoms of stress. Some are:

Physical Symptom: Tension, fatigue, insomnia, muscle aches, digestive upset, appetite change, headaches and restlessness.

Mental Symptoms: Forgetfulness, low productivity, confusion, poor concentration, lethargy, negativity and busy mind.

Emotional Symptoms: Anxiety, mood swings, irritability, depression, resentment, anger, impatience, worrying and feeling pressured.

Social Symptoms: Lashing out, decreased sex drive, lack of intimacy, isolation, intolerance, loneliness, avoiding social situations, alcohol, tobacco and/or drug use.

Spiritual Symptoms: Apathy, loss of direction, emptiness, loss of life's meaning, unforgiving and no sense of purpose.

Managing Stress: Being able to manage stress is important in order to live healthy, happy and productive lives.

Negative Coping: Ignoring the problem, withdrawal, procrastination, alcohol/drug use, smoking, overeating, inactivity, being over-committed and buying things you do not need.

Positive Coping: Become aware of your reactions, maintain a healthy balanced diet, exercise regularly, balance work and play, practice relaxation techniques, meditate, develop a support system, pace yourself and simplify your life.

What are some or your stressors?

_____

_____

_____

_____

SELF-CARE TECHNIQUES

A daily choice to care for oneself helps instill feelings of worth and increases a sense of well-being. Try some of these things:

- Deep slow diaphragmatic breathing.

- Listen to relaxation tapes.
- Avoid caffeine.
- Use positive affirmations.
- Do something you love.
- Allow extra time for projects.
- Leave work at the office.
- Do not ruminate over the past.
- Try to live in the present.
- Take a brisk walk.
- Listen to your body's signals.
- Finish what you start.
- Do less, enjoy more!

SELF-OBSERVABLE SIGNS OF STRESS!!!!

1. General irritability, hyper excitation or depression.
2. Pounding of the heart and indication of high blood pressure.
3. Dryness of the throat and mouth.
4. Impulsive behavior, emotional instability.
5. The overpowering urge to die or run and hide.
6. Inability to concentrate, flight of thoughts and general disorientation.
7. Feelings of unreality, weakness or dizziness.
8. Predilection to become fatigued.
9. "Floating anxiety," that is to say, we are afraid although we do not know exactly what we are afraid of.
10. Emotional tension and alertness, feeling of being "keyed up."
11. Trembling, nervous tics.
12. Tendency to be easily startled by small sounds, etc.
13. High-pitched nervous laughter.
14. Stuttering and other speech difficulties.
15. Bruxism or grind of teeth.
16. Insomnia.
17. Hyper mobility. This is technically called "hyperkinesias," an increased tendency to move about without any reason, an inability to just take physically relaxed attitude, sitting quietly in a chair or lying on a sofa.
18. Sweating.
19. The frequent need to urinate.
20. Diarrhea, indigestion, queasiness in the stomach and sometimes vomiting.
21. Migraine headaches.
22. Premenstrual tension or missed menstrual cycles.
23. Pain in the neck or lower back.
24. Loss of or excessive appetite.
25. Increased smoking.
26. Increased use of legally prescribed drugs, such as tranquilizers or amphetamines.
27. Alcohol and drug addiction.
28. Nightmares.

29. Neurotic behavior.
30. Psychoses.
31. Accident proneness.

What are some signs of stress you experience at times?

_____
_____
_____
_____

DO ANY OF THESE STRESSORS HIT HOME?

Day-to-day life has countless stressors. Identifying even the smallest irritant, as well as major life stressors, assists us in recognizing the amount of stress we actually encounter and the VALUE of coping skills. Stressors have a cumulative effect and can have unhealthy consequences relating to personal health, relationships, child rearing and all other life areas.

Check below the stressors you've experienced in the last few months.

____ Your alarm clock not going off.

____ Your favorite sports team losing.

____ Recent illness.

____ Dealing with bureaucracy/red tape.

____ A divorce.

____ Losing a friends' phone number.

____ Working with incompetent people

____ Not being able to find a Kleenex.

____ Birth of a child.

____ Being late on a deadline.

____ In-law problems.

____ Spouse being under stress.

____ Recent death of someone close to you.

____ Having difficulty motivating yourself.

____ Anniversary of a beloved's death.

____ Not having enough money to pay bills.

____ Parents treating you like a child.

____ A new job.

____ Someone telling you how to feel.

____ Inability to conceive a child.

____ Having no money and not wanting to. borrow.

____ Arguing with a good friend or relative.

____ Out of town relatives staying with you.

____ Spouse being too dependent on you.

____ Unwanted pregnancy.

____ Not feeling well and not knowing why.

____ Best friend asking to borrow money.

____ Losing a game.

____ An appliance/machine not working.

____ Wanting to eat, but on a diet.

____ Too much to do not enough time.

____ Spouse late coming home

____ Moving to a new house or apartment.

____ Good friend feeling depressed.

These stressors may not change, however your ability to "cope" with them CAN change!!

15 PROVEN STRESS REDUCERS

1. Get up fifteen minutes earlier in the morning. The inevitable morning mishaps will be less stressful.
2. Prepare for the morning the evening before. Set the breakfast table, make lunches, etc.
3. Don't rely on your memory. Write down appointment times, when to pick up the laundry, when library books are due, etc. "The palest ink is better than the most retentive memory." Old Chinese Proverb.
4. Do nothing you have to lie about later.
5. Make copies of all keys. Bury a house key in a secret spot in the garden. Carry a duplicate car key in your wallet, apart from your key ring.
6. Practice preventive maintenance. Your car, appliances, home and relationships will be less likely to break down "at the worst possible moment."
7. Be prepared to wait. A paperback book can make a wait in a post office line almost pleasant.
8. Procrastination is stressful. Whenever you want to do tomorrow, do today; whatever you want to do today, do it now
9. Plan ahead. Don't let the gas tank get below one-quarter full, keep a well-stocked "emergency shelf" of home staples, don't wait until you're down to your last bus token or postage stamp to buy more
10. Don't put up with something that doesn't work right. If your alarm clock, wallet, shoelaces, windshield wipers, whatever, are a constant aggravation, get them fixed or get new ones.
11. Allow 15 minutes of extra time to get to appointments. Plan to arrive at an airport one or two hours before domestic departures.
12. Eliminate (or restrict) the amount of caffeine in your diet.
13. Always set up contingency plans, "just in case." "If for some reason either of us is delayed here's what we'll do . . ." On the other hand, "If we get split up in the shopping center, here's where we'll meet."
14. Relax your standards. The world will not end if the grass doesn't get mowed this weekend.
15. Pollyanna-Power! For every one thing that goes wrong, there are probably 10 or 50 or 100 blessings. Count them.

14 MORE STRESS REDUCING TIPS

1. Get to know your body. Shallow breathing and frequent fast pulse is an indication of your body's reaction to stress.

2. Learn to relax: Deep breathing is a natural relaxant. Try to take several deep breaths each hour.

3. Practice this simple exercise to help you relax. Tense all your muscles, hold for a count of five, and then let go. Do this 5 times a day and notice the difference.

4. At the end of the day, take a brisk walk or do a few minutes of fast dancing or body shaking. This stimulates the blood flow.

5. Smile. You will be surprised how good it makes you and others feel.

6. Practice unwinding everyday. Do not wait for your annual vacation. Your body is the only one you get, be good to it.

7. Have fun, learn to play a little. Plan frequent mini trips and outings. Sometimes all it takes is creative thinking.

8. Take a walk at lunchtime; get out of the office or house. Fresh air clears the brain and the changes of scenery helps you relax.

9. Be aware of your need for frequent relaxation times in your day. Try this simple exercise. Stand up and stretch like a cat, then close your eyes for 5 minutes and pretend you're walking on the beach or fishing in a cool brook. Teach yourself to relax.

10. Begin your day with some limbering up and simple stretching exercises, then jog in place or jump rope for a few minutes. This routing will help warm you up for the day. NOTE; after you loosen your muscles do something for your mind and soul. Take time to thank your Heavenly Father for a new day, a good mind and body and His love and grace that sees you through another day.

11. Keeping fit helps prevent stress. Vigorous exercise is a great way to get rid of uptight or stressed feeling.

12. Take your aggressions out on a racquetball court, golf court or swimming pool. Provide yourself with an outlet

13. Learn to make lists. Write down a daily list of priorities that helps you avoid too many deadlines and, at the end of the day, you can see your accomplishments.

14. Take control of your own life. Live up to your expectation not someone else's.

101 WAYS TO COPE WITH STRESS

Get up 15 minutes earlier * Prepare for the morning the night before * Avoid tight fitting clothes * Avoid relying on chemical aids * Set appointments ahead * Don't rely on your memory . . . write it down * Practice preventative maintenance * Make duplicate keys * Say "NO" more often * Set priorities in your life * Avoid negative people * Use time wisely * Repair anything that doesn't work properly * Ask for help with a job you dislike * Break large tasks into bite size portions * Look at problems as challenges * Look at challenges differently * Unclutter your life * SMILE * Be prepared for rain * tickle a baby * Pet a friendly dog/cat * Don't know all the answers * Look for the silver lining * Say something nice to someone * Teach a kid to fly a kite * Walk in the rain * Schedule play time into every day * Take a bubble bath * Be aware of the decisions you make * Believe in you * Stop saying negative things to yourself * Visualize yourself winning * Develop your sense of humor * Stop thinking tomorrow will be a better today * Have goals for yourself * Dance a jig * Say hello to a stranger * Ask a friend for a hug * Look up at the stars * Practice breathing slowly * Learn to whistle a tune * Read a poem * Listen to a symphony * Watch a ballet * Read a story curled up in bed * Do a brand new thing * Stop a bad habit * Buy yourself a flower * Take stock of your achievements * Find support from others * Ask someone to be your "vent-partner" * Do it today * Work at being cheerful and optimistic * Put safety first * Do everything in moderation * Pay attention to your appearance * Strive for excellence NOT perfection * Stretch your limits each day * Learn to meet your own needs * Become a better listener * Know your feelings * Know your limitations and let others know them too * Tell someone to have a good day in Pig Latin * Throw a paper airplane * Exercise every day * Learn the words to a new song * Get to work early * Clean out a closet * Play patty cake with a toddler * Go on a picnic * Take a different route to work * Leave work early (with permission) * Put air freshener in your car * Watch a movie and eat popcorn * Write a note to a far away friend * Go to a ball game and scream * Cook a meal and eat it by candlelight * Recognize the importance of unconditional love * Give yourself permission to get professional help if you need it * Keep a journal * Practice a monster smile * Remember you always have options * Have a support network of people, places and things * Quit trying to "fix" other people * Get enough sleep * Talk less and listen more * Freely praise other people *P.S. Relax, take each day one day at a time . . . you have the rest of your life to live.

WAYS TO RELIEVE STRESS

Blow bubbles	Watch a sunrise or sunset	Sing a new song
Meditate	Do deep breathing exercises	Use visual imagery
Go bowling	Luxuriate in a bath or shower	Lie back and watch clouds
Take pleasure in quiet-time	Listen to a relaxation tape	Give of yourself
Read a good book	Prioritize	Reflect on the positives
Fix yourself a cup of hot tea	Play an instrument	Enjoy the weather
Make an edible treat	Sing or whistle a song	Attend a free concert
Visit the library	Clean out a closet	Listen to music
Say hi to a stranger	Work on a jigsaw puzzle	Play your favorite game
Write a letter to a friend	Write creatively	Tear up an old newspaper
See a movie	Cuddle on the couch	Roller-blade
Join a support group	Draw or paint a picture	Have a good laugh
Window shop	Take a walk in the rain	Swim or splash in the water
Have fun with a pet	Put flowers in your home	Delight in your spirituality
Go to the park	Take a long ride	Light a candle
Nap for ten minutes	Weed a garden	Finish something
Plan your dream vacation	Catch-up with a family member	Reach out for support
Sit under a shady tree	Begin a new hobby or craft	Count your blessings

TWENTY-SIX SILLY WAYS TO DEAL WITH STRESS

Humor is a great stress reducer. These are not recommended to actually do; they are just good to think about for a laugh.

1. Jam miniature marshmallows up your nose and sneezes them out. See how many you can do at once.
2. Use your MasterCard to pay your Visa and vice-versa.

3. Pop some popcorn without putting the lid on.
4. When someone says "Have a nice day" tell them you have other plans.
5. Make a list of things to do that you've already done.
6. Dance naked in front of your pets.
7. Put your toddler's clothes on backwards and send them off to pre-school as if nothing is wrong.
8. Fill out your tax forms using Roman Numerals.
9. Tape pictures of your boss on watermelons and launch them from high places
10. Leaf through a "National Geographic" and draw underwear on the natives.
11. Tattoo "out to lunch" on your forehead.
12. Go shopping. Buy everything. Sweat in it. Return it the next day.
13. Buy a subscription of "Sleeziod Weekly" and send it to your boss's wife.
14. Pay your electric bill in pennies.
15. Drive to work in reverse.
16. Find out what a frog in a blender really looks like.
17. Tell your boss to "blow it out of your mule" and let him figure it out.
18. Sit naked on a shelled hard boiled egg.
19. Polish your car with ear wax.
20. Read the dictionary upside down and look for secret messages.
21. Start a nasty rumor and see if you recognize it when it comes back to you.
22. Braid the hairs in each nostril.
23. Write a short story using alphabet soup.
24. Stare at people trough the tines of a fork and pretend they're in jail.
25. Make up a language and ask people for directions.
26. Replace the filling of a Twinkie with ketchup and place it back in the wrapper.

SILLY STRESS STRATEGIES

What do these REALLY mean?

The answer key to these stilly stress strategies are at the end of this chapter. Try to find the hidden meaning in each of them.

1. Happy Birthday to me	2. Enroll in Turtle Academy	3. Put on rose-colored glasses
4. Proclaim yourself a hero	5. Become a vintage corvette	6. Retire from the Supreme Court
7. Dream on	8. Don't take the hinges off to walk through the door	9. Avoid leaping contests with leapfrogs

10. Go to a cave or lock yourself in the bathroom.	11. Don't take candy from babies	12. So, who cares:
13. Make lemonade	14. Plan for the downfall or Rome	15. Sorry, no way
16. Call out Sherlock Holmes	17. Use the gas in the tank	18. Fiddle while Rome burns, but keep one hand on the hose
19. Leave juggling to clowns	20. Take a vacation form your island	21. Let Michael row the boat ashore

STRESS REACTION

Stress is not a person, place or thing. It's a physical and emotional reaction to change—whether positive or negative. The fight or flight reaction kicks in, preparing your body. Your muscles may tense, your heart may race, you may breathe more rapidly and sugars and fats may be released into your bloodstream for quick energy. At the same time you may experience a wide range of feelings; from anxiety and worry to excitement and anticipation. Your actions may also reveal telltale sighs of stress, such as fidgeting, racing around, snapping at others or eating more than your body needs.

The two sides of stress: Not all stress is bad. In the short run, stress can help you be more alert, efficient and productive. How negative your stress reaction is depends on many things; how often it occurs, how intense it is, how long it lasts and perhaps most important of all, how you perceive the stressful event.

The bright side, the bleak side: Short surges of stress can add zest to your life, helping your body mobilize to meet specific demands. When you do not have the chance to recover from stress, your physical, emotional and mental resources can become depleted and lead to illness

The value of managing stress: You cannot eliminate stress altogether. But you can "tame the beast" so you can live with it in peace. Help manage stress by taking time out from tension with relaxation techniques. Listening to how you communicate with yourself and others and using social and physical buffers against stress can also help. So, what are the payoffs? Here are a few; a stronger immune system for fighting disease, lower risk of heat disease and other chronic illnesses and over all better health. Other benefits include improved relationships and reduced burnout in both your work and personal and family life.

How stress is unique: Public speaking may be thrilling for you, but for the next person the experience may be as terrifying as standing in front of a firing squad. The events that trigger your stress and your reaction to stressful situations are unique to you. The checklists on the next several pages may help you better understand your stress triggers and reactions. Simply being aware of them may lower your stress by helping you identify changes you can make.

Your stress triggers: Stress triggers come in many forms and differ from person to person. What are those seemingly insignificant daily hassles that don't last but cause you to fume? What major events have ushered big changes in your life? What ongoing small or big problems gnaw at you day in and day out? Check those below that have caused stress for you in the last six months.

Daily Hassles

- ☐ Misplacing or losing something
- ☐ Being caught in a traffic jam
- ☐ Waiting in line
- ☐ Oversleeping
- ☐ Disagreeing with coworker
- ☐ Running late
- ☐ Missing the bus
- ☐ Forgetting your umbrella or coat
- ☐ Coming home to a messy house
- ☐ Having your car break down
- ☐ Getting a traffic ticket
- ☐ Having an argument with your spouse of child

Major Events

- ☐ Marrying
- ☐ Being laid off or fired
- ☐ Experiencing the death of a friend, family member or coworker
- ☐ Moving
- ☐ Having a baby
- ☐ Going to war
- ☐ Having surgery
- ☐ Divorcing or breaking up
- ☐ Going to jail
- ☐ Changing jobs
- ☐ Starting school
- ☐ Receiving the diagnosis of a serious disease
- ☐ Having your children leave home or come back

Ongoing Problems

- ☐ Money or credit problems
- ☐ Noisy or nosy neighbors

- [ ] Chronic illness
- [ ] Disability
- [ ] Crime in the neighborhood
- [ ] Eating disorder
- [ ] Unsatisfying job
- [ ] Shaky economy
- [ ] Pore housing or poor living arrangement
- [ ] Alcoholism or drug addiction
- [ ] Poor relationships with a friend or family member
- [ ] Raising children through the adolescent years

IDENTIFY YOUR STRESS "SIGNATURE"

In the exercise above you gave some thought to your stress triggers. Now focus your attention on your unique reactions to stress, sometimes called a stress "signature". Since no two are completely alike, read the lists below checking off the physical, mental, emotional and behavioral reactions you typically experience when you are under stress. Check each that relate to you. Add any that are missing from these lists. Identifying your stress signature will give you a concrete gauge for measuring any future changes in your reactions to stress.

Your Physical Reactions:

- [ ] Headache
- [ ] Muscle tension
- [ ] Dry mouth
- [ ] Racing heartbeat
- [ ] Heartburn
- [ ] Colds
- [ ] Diarrhea
- [ ] Clammy hands
- [ ] Constipation
- [ ] Teeth grinding
- [ ] Skin rash
- [ ] Back pain
- [ ] Stomachache
- [ ] Chest pain
- [ ] Laryngitis
- [ ] Shaking hands
- [ ] Blurred vision
- [ ] Insomnia
- [ ] Fatigue

What have we missed that is on your list?

_____

_____

Your Thoughts and Feelings:

- ☐ Irritability
- ☐ Anxiety
- ☐ Forgetfulness
- ☐ Depression
- ☐ Apathy
- ☐ Nervousness
- ☐ Worry
- ☐ Confusion
- ☐ Excitement
- ☐ Hopelessness
- ☐ Cynicism
- ☐ Resentment
- ☐ Fearfulness
- ☐ Hostility
- ☐ Difficulty concentrating
- ☐ Racing or obsessive thoughts

What have we missed that is on your list?

_____

_____

Your Actions:

- ☐ Withdrawing from close relationships
- ☐ Snapping at others
- ☐ Overeating or under eating
- ☐ Being "accident-prone"
- ☐ Completing tasks with difficulty
- ☐ Trying to do several things at once
- ☐ Talking very fast
- ☐ Watching more television
- ☐ Smoking cigarettes
- ☐ Drinking alcoholic beverages
- ☐ Taking tranquilizers or other drugs
- ☐ Blaming others
- ☐ Crying easily
- ☐ Compulsively drumming your fingers or flicking your hair

What have we missed that is on your list?

_____

_____

THE STRESS CRUTCHES

Drugs, alcohol, cigarettes and food, all can become crutches used to stand up to stress. Because they may temporally calm your nerves, satisfy your urges or make you feel more relaxed, you may think they really do help.

However, crutches, whatever the type, may mask the deeper symptoms of stress. And when abused, they can lead to even more stress. They may make it more difficult for you to live up to your responsibilities, leading to physical burnout. Or, they may become an all-consuming addiction.

Identify whether or not you're propping yourself up with a crutch and find other means of support. Then you can learn to "walk" on solid ground without the faulty support of a stress crutch.

TIME OUT FROM TENSION

When you need to break the stress "strangle hold," you can use a variety of relaxation techniques that give your body time out. You don't have to use all the techniques on these pages. Try them for a week and find the ones that work best for you. Practice them once or twice a day or when you feel particularly stressed.

DEEP BREATHING

This might be a good technique to use if you respond to stress with fast shallow breathing. It's a good foundation for other techniques and you can do it anytime anywhere.

1. Sit or lie down in a comfortable position.
2. Place your hands on your stomach. Inhale slowly and deeply through your nose as though you're breathing into your stomach. Hold your breath for a few seconds.
3. Exhale all your air slowly through your mouth while pursing your lips. This helps control how fast you release the air.
4. Repeat these steps several times.

STRETCHING EXERCISES

Stretches are easy to learn and are one of the quickest ways to loosen "knots" in you muscles. Depending on where you "hold" your tension, try a variety of different exercises. The stretches below work on two common "hot spots," your shoulders and back.

SHOULDER STRETCH

1. Extend your arms in front of you at shoulder height and interlace your fingers.
2. Turn your palms outward. Lower your chin to your chest and extend your arms forward.
3. Hold for 10-20 seconds. Repeat 3 times.

Back Bend

1. Stand and place your palms on your lower back.
2. Slowly lean your upper body back without overarching your neck. Hold for 5 seconds.
3. Now slowly lean forward until you feel your low back muscles stretch. Hold for 5 seconds.
4. Repeat these steps 3 times.

MAKE LAUGHTER A HABIT

It's been called "the best medicine," a balm for the soul and a type of internal jogging. Laughter can satisfy these claims and many more, making it one of the best types of tension relief.

A good belly laugh works your lungs, heart and muscles, releasing pleasure-producing chemicals and relaxing your muscles.

Make laughter a daily habit. Buy a humorous desk calendar. Go see comedies or comedians. Watch the comic antics of your pet.

You don't have to have a belly laugh to gain some benefits. Even a smile can be enough to neutralize negative stress producing thoughts

WHEN YOUR MIND WANDERS

During relaxation techniques you may find that your mind keeps wandering. This drifting can interfere with your ability to relax. With practice though, you can learn to focus your mind. Accept that a certain amount of mind wandering is normal. Don't waste time punishing yourself for it.

Bring your mind back gently to a favorite image, a gently flickering flame, bubbles rising to the surface of a glass or your baby's face.

Whenever possible perform rhythmic activity like jogging before hand, which may help you focus on breathing and clear your mind.

LISTENING TO YOUR VOICES

You just learned how to use the power of your mind during relaxation techniques. Now consider the power of your mind's voices in your everyday life. Whether or not you realize it, your internal voices (your self-talk) and how you communicate with the rest of the world can affect your level of stress. Learn to identify, listen to and change the negative voices you hear.

Muttering Minds

Your mind has a continuous "tape" running. Is your tape playing negative self-talk or positive self-talk? The next time you catch yourself muttering about the incompetence of the driver ahead of you or your own interior IQ level put the thought on pause then rewind and erase. Next, put a new message on the tape. See if you recognize any of the voices bellow.

- It's a black and white life: This voice oversimplifies life. It says that situations are always black and white, either-or and yes or no, with nothing in between. This short-sighted vice traps you into thinking you have few options to choose from. It doesn't allow you to dream, to problem solve or to enjoy the richness of life

- Perfection and nothing less: Expecting perfection in yourself and others is a sure setup for failure. In fact perfectionism leads to procrastination, which leads to paralysis. These voices also often translate into "should" talk. "I should never make mistakes." "People should always treat me fairly." "Life should be easy for me."

- Molehills that are mountains: When you cannot separate the big stuff from and small stuff, molehills quickly turn into overwhelming mountains. Do not wait for a truly major event, such as a life threatening illness, to put things in perspective for you and make you downplay the insignificant problems in your life.

- The center of the universe: If you think things are always your fault, you may have put yourself at the "center of the universe." You may blame yourself for other's moods and feelings especially when it's someone you're very close to. Realize that you really don't have that much power. It may come as quite a relief.

- A view of the world that works: Stress-resistant people share a certain perspective that may make them healthier. They see change as a challenge and feel a sense of commitment to something and have a feeling of being in control of their lives. Take your cue from these people. Especially remember that even when you do not have control over events, you do have control over your reactions to those events, which can greatly lower your stress level.

EXERCISE EASES DEPRESSION AND ANXIETY

Exercise can improve symptoms of depression and anxiety. Even a little exercise helps. Use these realistic tips and goals to get started and stick with it.

If you have depression or anxiety, you might find your doctor or mental health provider prescribing a regular dose of exercise in addition to medication or psychotherapy. Exercise isn't a cure for depression or anxiety. But its psychological and physical benefits can improve your symptoms.

"It's not a magic bullet, but increasing physical activity is a positive and active strategy to help manage depression and anxiety," says Kristin Vickers-Douglas, Ph.D., a psychologist at the Mayo Clinic, Rochester, MN.

When you have depression or anxiety, exercising may be the last thing you think you can do. But you can overcome the inertia. See how exercise can ease depression symptoms and anxiety symptoms. Plus, get realistic tips to get started and stick with exercising.

How can exercise helps depression and anxiety? Exercise has long been touted as a way to maintain physical fitness and help prevent high blood pressure, diabetes and other diseases. A growing volume of research shows that exercise can also help improve symptoms of certain mental health conditions, including depression and anxiety. Exercise may also help prevent a relapse after treatment for depression or anxiety.

Research suggests that it may take at least 30 minutes of exercise a day for at least three to five days a week to significantly improve depression symptoms. But smaller amounts of activity—as little as 10 to 15 minutes at a time—can improve mood in the short term. "Small bouts of exercise may be a great way to get started if it's initially too hard to do more," Dr. Vickers-Douglas says.

Just how exercise reduces symptoms of depression and anxiety isn't fully understood. Some evidence suggests that exercise raises the levels of certain mood-enhancing neurotransmitters in the brain. Exercise may also boost feel-good endorphins, release muscle tension, help you sleep better and reduce levels of the stress hormone cortisol. It also increases body temperature, which may have calming effects. All of these changes in your mind and body can improve such symptoms as sadness, anxiety, irritability, stress, fatigue, anger, self-doubt and hopelessness.

If you exercise regularly but depression or anxiety symptoms still interfere with your daily living, seek professional help. Exercise isn't meant to replace medical treatment of depression or anxiety.

Exercise has many psychological and emotional benefits when you have depression or anxiety. These include:

1. Confidence: Being physically active gives you a sense of accomplishment. Meeting goals or challenges, no matter how small, can boost self-confidence at times when you need it most. Exercise can also make you feel better about your appearance and your self-worth.
2. Distraction: When you have depression or anxiety, it's easy to dwell on how badly you feel. But dwelling interferes with your ability to problem solve and cope in a healthy way. Dwelling can also make depression more severe and longer lasting. Exercise can shift the focus away from unpleasant thoughts to something more pleasant, such as your surroundings or the music you enjoy listening to while you exercise.
3. Interactions: Depression and anxiety can lead to isolation. That, in turn, can worsen your condition. Exercise may give you the chance to meet or socialize with others, even if it's just exchanging a friendly smile or greeting as you walk around your neighborhood.
4. Healthy coping: Doing something positive to manage depression or anxiety is a healthy coping strategy. Trying to feel better by drinking alcohol excessively, dwelling on how badly you feel or hoping depression and anxiety will go away on their own aren't helpful coping strategies.

Of course, knowing that something's good for you doesn't make it easier to actually do it. With depression or anxiety, you may have a hard enough time just doing the dishes, showering or going to work. How can you possibly consider getting in some exercise?

Here are some steps that can help you exercise when you have depression or anxiety. As always, check with your health care provider before starting a new exercise program to make sure it's safe for you.

1. Get your mental health provider's support. Some, but not all, mental health providers encourage exercise as a part of their treatment plan. Talk to your doctor or therapist for guidance and support. Discuss concerns about an exercise program and how it fits into your overall treatment plan.

2. <u>Identify what you enjoy doing.</u> Figure out what type of exercise or activities you're most likely to do. And think about when and how you'd be most likely to follow through. For instance, would you be more likely to do some gardening in the evening or go for a jog in the pre-dawn hours? Go for a walk in the woods or play basketball with your children after school? Do what you enjoy to help you stick with it.

3. <u>Set reasonable goals.</u> Your mission doesn't have to be walking for an hour five days a week. Think about what you may be able to do in reality. Twenty minutes? Ten minutes? Start there and build up. Tailor your plan to your own needs and abilities rather than trying to meet idealistic guidelines that could just add to your pressure.

4. <u>Don't think of exercise as a burden.</u> If exercise is just another "should" in your life that you don't think you're living up to, you'll associate it with failure. Rather, look at your exercise schedule the same way you look at your therapy sessions or antidepressant medication—as one of the tools to help you get better.

5. <u>Address your barriers.</u> Figure out what's stopping you from exercising. If you feel intimidated by others or are self-conscious, for instance, you may want to exercise in the privacy of your own home. If you stick to goals better with a partner, find a friend to work out with. If you don't have extra money to spend on exercise gear, do something that's virtually cost-free-walk. If you think about what's stopping you from exercising, you can probably find an alternative solution.

6. <u>Prepare for setbacks and obstacles.</u> Exercise isn't always easy or fun. And it's tempting to blame yourself for that. People with depression are especially likely to feel shame over perceived failures. Don't fall into that trap. Give yourself credit for every step in the right direction, no matter how small. If you skip exercise one day, that doesn't mean you're a failure and may as well quit entirely. Just try again the next day.

Stick with exercise when you have depression or anxiety. Launching an exercise program is hard. Sticking with it can be even harder. One key is problem solving your way through when it seems like you can't or don't want to exercise.

What would happen if you went out to your car and it wouldn't start? You'd probably be able to very quickly list several strategies for dealing with that barrier, such as calling an auto service, taking the bus or calling your partner or friend for help. You instantly start problem solving."

But most people don't approach exercise that way. What happens if you want to go for a walk but it's raining? Most people decide against the walk and don't even try to explore alternatives. With exercise, we often hit a barrier and say; "That's it. I can't do it, forget it." Instead, problem solve your way through the exercise barrier, just as you would other obstacles in your life. Figure out your options such as, walking in the rain, going to a gym, exercising indoors, for instance.

Some people think they need to wait until they somehow generate enough willpower to exercise. But, waiting for willpower or motivation to exercise is a passive approach and, when someone has depression and is unmotivated, waiting passively for change is unlikely to help at all. Focusing on a lack of motivation and willpower can make you feel like a failure. Instead, identify your strengths and skills and apply those to taking some first steps toward exercise.

SEEING YOUR CHOICES

Stressors you CAN control

Make a list of the stressors in your life that you have some control over. They might rarely be major events.

Example

    1. Car trouble
    2. _____
    3. _____
    4. _____
    5. _____

Action you can take

Take one or two of your stressors and generate as many options for action as you can. Write down whatever comes to mind. Don't edit, one idea may lead to another.

Examples:

    1. Get car fixed.

- Set up appointments for regular auto maintenance.
- Use public transit more regularly.
- Buy a more reliable car.
- Take auto maintenance class.

    2. _____
        _____
        _____
        _____
        _____

STRESSORS YOU CAN'T CONTROL

Now list the stressors in your live that you think you have no control over. You may find, however, that you can move some of these into the first category, stressors you can control. For example, you may feel helpless to do anything about a bad relationship but, in fact you can always end or change the relationship.

Example

    1. Being laid off

    _____

_____

_____

_____

Thoughts you can change

Generate new ways of looking at these problems. At first glance, the stressful event may have no redeeming qualities whatsoever. Think again. Is there anything to be gained from these experiences?

Examples:

1. Can take the opportunity to review my career path.
2. Can spend more time with my children before starting new job.
3. Can take a class during the daytime.

_____

_____

_____

SILLY STRESS STRATEGIES ANSWER KEY

1. Treat yourself special. Give yourself a treat or gift periodically for no reason at all.
2. Slow down. Unpack your schedule. Schedule more time than you think you need in order to avoid rushing and pressure.
3. Look for and appreciate beauty in the world around you. Smell the roses.
4. Reward yourself when you've worked hard or accomplished something. Don't wait for others to pat you on the back, do it yourself.
5. Take care of your body as well as you would an expensive sports car. Exercise, eat right, sleep well and avoid alcohol, caffeine and cigarettes.
6. Avoid making judgments about or taking responsibility for things that are beyond your control.
7. Have dreams and long-term goals to avoid getting stuck in mundane daily problems.
8. Simplify! Don't make big problems out of little ones.
9. Don't compare yourself to the best qualities of other people. Remember that everyone has both strengths and weaknesses. Don't make everything a competition.
10. Have some private time daily when you can relax, meditate, read or listen to music.
11. Be kind. Treat others with respect. It will come back to you.
12. Put things in perspective. Ask yourself how important will this be 100 years from now or even in 100 days.
13. Try to see stressful events as new challenges or opportunities for growth. If all else fails, try laughing at yourself.
14. Some stresses repeat themselves or can be anticipated. Recognize this and prepare for them.
15. Be open and politely assertive. Express yourself clearly and pleasantly without being defensive.
16. Investigate how realistic your worries are. Then forget your problems that are unlikely to materialize.

17. Regard stress, which you will have anyway, as motivators for positive change.
18. When in a crisis situation, do what you can but breathe deeply and remain calm.
19. Do one thing at a time. Delegate when possible.
20. Realize that you are not alone. Seek out support from people with similar problems.
21. Ask for and accept help whenever possible
22. Just know that every day is a blessing and, if things are not going well, there will always be tomorrow.

Sometimes we just have to say, "It is what it is." Perhaps we feel that there is nothing we can do about a problem right now. Just know that tomorrow is a new day, things will look differently and we can try something new. I have found that when I am at me lowest the serenity prayer helps me.

Grant me the serenity to accept the things I cannot change
The courage to change the things I can, and
The wisdom to know the difference.

POSITIVE EFFECTIVE PARENTING
P.E.P.

CHAPTER TEN
Feelings

CHAPTER TEN

Feelings

FEELINGS

Our lives are driven by our feelings. However, often we are really out of touch with our feelings at any given moment. Many times children must hide their feelings or put them away for a rainy day or until hell freezes over. We most likely have never learned how to really allow ourselves to feel. We were overwhelmed by our feelings in early childhood and are still living in fear of having our feelings.

What are some feelings you fear?

_____

_____

_____

_____

What are some feelings you believe your children fear?

_____

_____

_____

_____

Feelings originate in the body. It is becoming aware of them and making meaning out of them that is so difficult, especially for children. We are often unconscious of what is underneath the feeling. Our feelings can be triggered by our thoughts. Our thoughts are ruled by our false beliefs that we somehow acquired through growing up.

Once again, we far too often confuse the meaning of feelings and thinking. Thoughts are mental and feelings are emotional. We can't change our feelings, they just happen, because they are influenced by our thoughts. But, we must learn to identify them. This will help us understand what we are thinking about an event or consequence and learn to change the thought.

There are many great books and techniques for helping us to access our feelings. Becoming aware of our feelings and then taking responsibility for those feelings is part of becoming an adult. It is often very difficult to identify our feelings as we are not ever taught how to do this. While we are not psychotherapists, we do have to become aware of our own feelings to be able to better take care of ourselves.

First we must note that feelings are your own. They are always valid though not always justified. You have every right to them but don't give your power away by saying things like: "You make me mad." You can say something like, "When you do _____ I get mad."

Knowing that we are even having a feeling can be very difficult. The best thing we can do is to "listen to our body talk" since feelings "live" in our bodies. If our body is tense we may be feeling angry or scared. If our body is relaxed we may be feeling happy.

Sometimes when we analyze our feelings further we find that the underlying thought is not rational. We will talk about irrational thoughts later. To change feelings, and the behaviors that follow, all we need to do is change the thought. This will in turn change our behavior since behavior is the outward manifestation of feelings. The good news is that behavior is learned, it is not "hard wired," so it can be changed by changing our thoughts.

Most of our thoughts were formed as far back as childhood. One of the most important thoughts that we formed in childhood was about making mistakes. When we were young many of us were told things such as: "Mistakes are bad," or "You are stupid for always making mistakes." Actually these statements, and those like them, are incorrect. It is necessary for us to make mistakes so that we learn to do the right thing in various situations we find ourselves in throughout our lifetime. Good judgment comes from experience and experience comes from poor judgment. It is ludicrous to think that people don't make mistakes. We learn more from our mistakes that from the things we do right.

What are some mistakes your child has made recently?

_____

_____

_____

_____

What are some mistakes you have made recently?

_____

_____

_____

_____

Making a mistake is not as important as what we do about it. This is why it is important to teach children that they are not a bad person for making a mistake it is what they decide to do about it that counts.

The first thing to do is to be accountable for the mistake. Once this is done, amends can be made. If it is not possible to make amends then an apology is in order. The three R's of recovery are a way to help children make amends.

1. Recognize the mistake with a feeling of responsibility instead of blame.
2. Reconcile by apologizing to the person or people.
3. Resolve the problem when possible by working together on a solution.

You must be careful with the timing of the 3 R's because sometimes right after a mistake a person needs a short "cooling down" period. I do not suggest making anybody apologize before they truly feel they are sorry.

You may also use the 3 R's when you feel you have made a mistake. Don't hesitate to let your children know that grown-ups make mistakes too. Approaching mistakes in this manner will actually help children develop a strong self image.

Yes, feelings are natural. Like I said earlier, they can save our lives. The trouble comes when we are unable or unwilling to acknowledge and then express our feelings in an appropriate way.

Identifying how you feel can sometimes be confusing. You know that you're feeling something but may not know exactly what. Feelings give us valuable information. They can tell us we are in harm or trouble. They can tell us when good things are happening. They tell us if we should fight or flight. More than we know, being in touch with our feelings has saved our lives.

We can't change our feelings until we have changed our thoughts. Something must intervene in the thought process. Since our behavior is the outward manifestation of our thoughts and feelings, behavior can only be changed by changing our thoughts and feelings.

The trouble comes when we are unable or unwilling to acknowledge and then express our feelings in an appropriate way. We so often want to deny them, cover them up or lash out in an unacceptable way. One way to express and own our feelings is by using "I" statements.

Use "I" statements such as: "I feel hurt when you don't do your chores," or "I feel happy when or because . . . ."

Have the kids' think of times when they could have used "I" statements. Write out an example for them to fill in the blanks.

_____

_____

_____

_____

You can also use some "I" statements with them. Write some of your own "I" statements.

_____

_____

_____

_____

PRIMARY AND SECONDARY FEELINGS

It can be useful to distinguish between primary and secondary feelings. Primary feelings are mad, sad, glad, and fear. There are many secondary feelings that fall under these primary feelings. I will have a chart of these later. Other feelings, emotions and experiences are combinations of these primary emotions. For example, guilt is a combination of fear and anger in different proportions. You may feel primarily scared and a little angry or primarily angry and a little scared. Shame is a combination of sadness and fear. And, jealousy is a combination of sadness and anger.

Some people think anger is a secondary emotion; a combination of fear and sadness. I suggest anger can be a primary or secondary emotion. When anger becomes routine or the one emotion that someone feels comfortable expressing, it is a secondary emotion. When anger is a secondary emotion, it helps to go deeper and become aware of other feelings that are present.

Next, is the connection between our emotions and our body. Each primary emotion creates body sensations. We feel our feelings in our bodies. Tuning into your body sensations or, "listening to your body talk," can help you to identify how you're feeling on a deeper level and to stay with your feelings. For instance, when you are angry you could feel tension, sweaty palms, faster heartbeat, etc. When we are glad or happy we can smile, laugh, etc.

People ask what they should do with their emotions or feelings. The best thing you can do with your feelings is to identify the primary emotions and to feel them. Staying aware of your body sensations helps you to do that and to remain grounded.

To identify your primary emotions, notice what you're feeling then see if you can identify between, mad, sad, glad and fear. This will help clarify how you are feeling.

There may be other secondary feelings you experience which underlie these primary feelings. When you are feeling an emotion not listed, take a moment to tune into yourself and spend time considering the primary emotions to see if you are feeling any of them. We often feel more than one feeling at a time and it can get quite complicated trying to sort it all out. Focusing on the primary emotions or feelings helps to simplify the process and to go deeper.

BECOMING AWARE OF YOUR FEELINGS

Becoming aware of our feelings and then taking responsibility for those feelings is part of becoming an adult. It is often very difficult as we are not ever really taught how to do this. We do have to become aware of our own feelings to be able to change our thoughts and provocations, to better our relationships and take better care of ourselves. We can begin to train our children to do the same and take care of themselves. We will see our children be able to become better behaved and grow into self sufficient adults. Then they will teach their children to do the same and the circle will be broken.

HELPING CHILDREN IDENTIFY AND DEAL WITH THEIR FEELINGS

I wrote this poem to show children ways to deal with their feelings and work them out in a constructive manner. When reading this to your children it would be helpful to ask them to remember times when they have experienced some of these feelings in their own lives. And think of ways they could work them out in a constructive manner that will make them feel good about themselves.

HOW AM I FEELING TODAY

Today I feel SORRY
I did something you see
That I am not proud of
It wasn't like me

But we all make mistakes
Every child, woman, man
But we must keep on trying
To do the best that we can

Today I feel FRIGHTENED
There are things all around
They all seem to scare me
So I'm feeling quite down

But mom says these things
Can not hurt me
For they are not real
They just seem to be

Today I'm DETERMINED
To do many things right
I'll try very hard
I'll use all of my might

Yes this may not be easy
But I can do it I know
And I'll learn better ways
As I continue to grow

Today I feel PROUD
Of myself for I know
I'm a good and kind person
Getting better as I grow

Tomorrow will bring many
Good things to me
For I'm a fine person
Striving always to be

Today I feel LONELY
No one seems to be here
For me when I need them
To comfort and cheer

I'm not really alone though
There are others around
Who can soothe me and hold me
When I'm feeling down

Today I feel HAPPY
I'm jumping for joy
I'm playing with my friends
Every girl, every boy

I'm turning cartwheels
All across the floor
I do love this feeling
I just want some more

Today I feel ANGRY
I'm mad as can be
Someone hurt my feelings
But my mom made me see

It's OK to be mad
I'll get over it
I just can't hit someone
I can't throw a fit

Today I feel CURIOUS
I want to know why
The grass is so green
Why there are stars in the sky

I could ask someone
Why these things are so
Then I'd know more every day
As I continues to grow

Today I feel LOVED
And it feels very good
I feel very happy
I feel like I should

Sometimes I don't feel loved
But I know that I am
So I just go on doing
The best that I can

Today I feel SAD
I do not know why
The sky's filled with clouds
There's a tear in my eye

But I know that tomorrow
The sun will shine again
I'll laugh with my family
And I'll play with my friends

Today I feel STUBBORN
I just want my way
I won't listen to anyone
Can't hear what they say

But if I open my ears
My mind and my heart
I'll feel I belong
I won't feel apart

Today I feel GUILTY
For I took my brother's toy
I accidentally broke it
And he's not a happy boy

In order to repay him
I gave him one of mine
Both my mother and my father
Said that was quite kind

Today I feel EMBARRASSED
For I fell down and skinned my knee
At first I just could not get up
And my friends all laughed at me

Soon one of them reached out his hand
To help my up you see
I know the others seem unkind
But they didn't really mean to be

Today I feel SHY
I'm hiding from all my friends
I want to go outside and play
But don't know where to begin

My sister told me to
Take one step at a time
Put a smile on my face
Then I'll feel really fine

Today I feel DISAPPOINTED
For it is my birthday
I didn't get what I asked for
I didn't get my way

But when I stop and think of it
The things I really want
Are not those that I can see
But those sent from above

Today I feel ANXIOUS
I can't seem to calm down
Things just keep on spinning
Around and around

So I'll take some deep breaths
And just close my eyes
I bet this will help
I won't be surprised

Today I feel CONFIDENT
I can do nothing wrong
I will try almost anything
I'm feeling very strong

I'm facing every task ahead
While holding my head high
For I am not afraid today
I feel like I can fly

This poem is dedicated to my beautiful and intelligent granddaughter Bryanna Lynne Bradshaw
May she grow up with integrity, dignity and grace.

THE CIRCLE OF THOUGHTS, FEELINGS AND BEHAVIOR

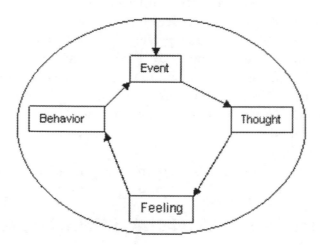

Our thoughts are based on how we see the world and our place in it. They stem from the things we learned from birth. Our feelings are triggered by our thoughts and we have very little control over them. If our thoughts are pleasant ones and they are meeting our needs, our feelings will also be pleasant. Our behavior will mirror our feelings. Our behavior will then produce another event or consequence. If we can begin to identify our feelings we can better identify our thoughts and will be able to change our thoughts and our behavior will follow. When our behavior is adaptive it will lead to pleasant events or consequences which follow. And the process will begin again. We will also be able to be more effective parents.

IRRATIONAL THOUGHTS

When our thoughts are irrational it is very difficult to make sense of them. The following is a list of irrational thoughts:

1. <u>Overgeneralization</u>: a general conclusion is made from one or two situations. Example: you have cleaned your apartment and it looks better than it did before you moved in. You did this so that your landlord would refund your deposit. However, your landlord doesn't refund your deposit to you. From this, you believe that all landlords are out to rip you off.
2. <u>Global labeling</u>: you make an illogical leap from one characteristic to a general category that includes many characteristics. Example: "My neighbor is a real redneck. He had only an eighth grade education."
3. <u>Mind reading</u>: assuming that you know the way someone was thinking, feeling and why he or she is behaving the way they are. Example: your friend walks by without saying "Hi." He acts like he doesn't see you. You assume that he is mad at you. In reality he was absorbed in his own problems.
4. <u>Filtering the negative</u>: negative details are magnified, and positive aspects of the situation are ignored. Example: you plan to go on a picnic in the park, it's poring down rain, and will be raining all weekend. You get depressed because your plans are ruined, instead of making other plans or rescheduling the event.

5. <u>Catastrophizing</u>: the reality of the present situation is ignored and replaced with fantasies about disaster. Example: your boyfriend/girlfriend hasn't called you for a week. You think he/she hates you and that you'll never see him/her again.

6. <u>Blaming</u>: external events and people are perceived as responsible for the person's happiness. Example: saying to or about someone, "You made me angry."

7. <u>Fallacy of fairness</u>: the assumption that life must be fair and people must agree on the standards for fairness. Example: you think it's not fair that someone else received a merit scholarship because your grades are better than his/hers.

8. <u>Polarized thinking</u>: things are black or white. There is no middle ground. Example: you either like me or you don't.

9. <u>Should</u>: rigid rules and expectations are imposed on all conditions. Example: people should always be on time.

HOW FEELINGS, THOUGHTS AND BEHAVIOR INFLUENCE EACH OTHER

Thoughts Influence Feelings: After studying hard, but doing poorly on a test, you <u>think</u>, "I never succeed at anything," which leads to <u>feeling</u> bad about your abilities as a student and feeling hopeless about the future

Feelings Influence Behavior: You <u>feel</u> hopeless about studying for the next exam and dwell on your sad feelings. You then procrastinate studying <u>(behavior)</u> and do not study hard because you still feel so discouraged about your last exam.

Behavior Influences Thoughts: Your lack of studying <u>(behavior)</u> for the next exam results in another poor grade. You <u>think</u>, "Here we go again. I don't know why I even keep trying. It's useless. I'm a failure."

Feelings Influence Thoughts: A friend has to cancel their plans with you because they have a family obligation. You <u>feel </u>disappointed, which prompts you to <u>think</u>, "Maybe they just made up that excuse because they don't want to hang out with me."

Thoughts Influence Behavior: You begin to <u>think</u> badly of your friend and recall times in the past when you haven't gotten along. When your friend calls to make plans, you get even <u>(behavior)</u> by telling them that you have other plans when you really don't.

Behavior Influences Feelings: Your friend accepts your excuse and doesn't appear to feel bad. You spend the day alone <u>(behavior)</u> and convince yourself that your friend is probably having more fun without you. You <u>feel </u>lonely, sad, and disappointed.

FEELINGS INVENTORIES

Our feelings are our guide to life. When we have so called negative feelings, it means that we also have unmet needs that go with them. It is often unconscious. When we experience positive feelings such as being hopeful, engaged, present, confident and affectionate it indicates that our needs are being met. The book, "Non-violent Communication" by Marshal Rosenberg, addresses the issues of feelings and their meanings. You can find a list of feelings at one of his associated websites.

The following are words we use when we want to express a combination of emotional states and physical sensations. If we can learn to identify our feelings, by listening to our body talk, we can identify the underlying thought. If we have "good" feelings then our thought about an event was usually "good" and we will be able to change our thoughts, feelings and behavior as well as that of our children. This list is neither exhaustive nor definitive. It is meant as a starting place to support anyone who wishes to engage in a process of deepening self-discovery and to facilitate greater understanding and connection between people.

There are two parts to this list: feelings we may have when our needs ARE being met and feelings we may have when our needs are NOT being met.

FEELINGS WHEN YOUR NEEDS ARE SATISFIED

AFFECTIONATE	EXCITED	JOYFUL
Compassionate	Amazed	Amused
Friendly	Animated	Delighted
Loving	Ardent	Glad
Open hearted	Aroused	Happy jubilant
Sympathetic	Astonished	Pleased
Tender	Dazzled	Tickled
Warm	Eager	
	Energetic	
	Enthusiastic	
	Giddy	
	Invigorated	
	Lively	
	Passionate	
	Surprised	
	Vibrant	
CONFIDENT	**EXHILARATED**	**PEACEFUL**
Empowered	Blissful	Calm
Open	Ecstatic	Clear headed
Proud	Elated	Comfortable
Safe	Enthralled	Centered
Secure	Exuberant	Content
	Radiant	Fulfilled
	Rapturous	Mellow
	Thrilled	Quiet
		Relaxed
		Relieved
		Satisfied
		Serene

		Still Tranquil Trusting
ENGAGED Absorbed Alert Curious Engrossed Enchanted Entranced Fascinated Interested Intrigued Involved Spellbound Stimulated	**GRATEFUL** Appreciative Moved Thankful Touched **Hopeful** Expectant Encouraged Optimistic	**REFRESHED** Enlivened Rejuvenated Renewed Rested Restored Revived
INSPIRED Amazed Awed WONDER		

FEELINGS WHEN YOUR NEEDS ARE NOT SATISFIED

AFRAID Apprehensive Dread Foreboding Frightened Mistrustful Panicked Petrified Scared Suspicious Terrified Wary Worried	**DISCONNECTED** Alienated Aloof Apathetic Bored Cold Detached Distant Distracted Indifferent Numb Removed Uninterested Withdrawn	**PAIN** Agony Anguished Bereaved Devastated Grief Heartbroken Hurt Lonely Miserable Regretful Remorseful
ANNOYED Aggravated Dismayed Disgruntled Displeased	**DISQUIET** Agitated Alarmed Discombobulated Disconcerted	**SAD** Despair Despondent Disappointed Discouraged

Exasperated	Disturbed	Disheartened
Frustrated	Perturbed	Forlorn
Impatient	Rattled	Gloomy
Irritated	Restless	Heavy hearted
Irked	Shocked	Hopeless
	Startled	Melancholy
ANGRY	Surprised	Unhappy
Enraged	Troubled	Wretched
Furious	Turbulent	
Incensed	Turmoil	**TENSE**
Indignant	Uncomfortable	Anxious
Irate	Uneasy	Cranky
Livid	Unnerved	Distressed
Outraged	Unsettled	Distraught
Resentful	Upset	Edgy
		Fidgety
		Frazzled
		Irritable
		Jitter
		Nervous
		Overwhelmed
		Restless
		Stressed out
AVERSION	**EMBARRASSED**	**VULNERABLE**
Animosity	Ashamed	Fragile
Appalled	Chagrined	Guarded
Contempt	Flustered	Helpless
Disgusted	Guilty	Insecure
Dislike	Mortified	Leery
Hate	Self-conscious	Reserved
Horrified		Sensitive
Hostile		Shaky
Repulsed		
Enraged		
CONFUSED	**FATIGUE**	**YEARNING**
Ambivalent	Beat	Envious
Baffled	Burnt out	Jealous
Bewildered	Depleted	Longing
Dazed	Exhausted	Nostalgic
Hesitant	Lethargic	Pining
Lost	Listless	Wistful
Mystified	Sleepy	
Perplexed	Tired	
Puzzled	Weary	
Torn	Worn out	

199

EMOTIONS

Usually when we think of emotions we consider them to be single entities. Anger is different from happiness, which is different from boredom but it doesn't seem like there are parts to anger or sadness. Appearances can be deceiving though. When thinking about emotions, and our awareness of them, it becomes apparent that what we call emotions consists of two parts, the feeling and the mood.

The mood, in broad terms, is the changes in our awareness of the world that characterize the emotion or a thought. By changes in awareness I don't mean that when we are angry one object visually looks different than when we are sad, but that how we conceptualize the world changes. When we are afraid, things that normally seem indifferent seem threatening, when we are angry these same things are likely to seem annoying, etc. So, while the information that represents the physical properties of the world, in our experience remains unchanged, the additional "interpretive" information that our mind incorporates into our perceptual experiences is altered. In one sense moods are necessarily conscious, since their effect is to alter conscious experiences. On the other hand there is no reason that the person who the mood is affecting will necessarily be aware of its effects, it is possible that they will, but if is also possible that they won't.

In contrast to moods, a feeling is a part of experience that reflects some aspect of mental activity or thought, not necessarily correctly. Just as perception fills experience with information derived from the outside world, a feeling fills experience with information derived from mood. Since the effects of a mood (although perception altering) are not themselves part of perception in the sense that the information one perceives is being altered. Unlike a mood a feeling is necessarily conscious, since it is defined as being part of an experience. And, unlike a mood, a feeling has little direct effect on action or perceptions. At most it allows us to react to our own moods appropriately, so that we can compensate for the effects of the mood if we wish, but the actual act of compensating is not performed by the feeling.

Together, being in a mood and feeling that one is in a mood, is what we call an emotion or a thought. So why break emotion into these two parts? Well for starters it shows how emotion is part of consciousness. We explain such effects by saying that the person is in a certain mood but that the appropriate feeling is missing or misrepresenting the mood. And, when the actual moods we are in is brought to our attention, either by others or by observation of ones own actions, the appropriate feeing manifests as a result of this realization.

PLEASANT FEELINGS

OPEN	HAPPY	POSITIVE	GOOD
Understanding	Great	Eager	Calm
Confident	Gay	Keen	Peaceful
Reliable	Joyous	Earnest	At ease
Easy	Lucky	Intent	Comfortable
Amazed	Fortunate	Anxious	Pleased
Sympathetic	Delighted	Intent	Encouraged
Interested	Overjoyed	Anxious	Clever
Satisfied	Gleeful	Inspired	Surprised
Receptive	Thankful	Determined	Content
Accepting	Important	Excited	Quiet
Kind	Festive	Enthusiastic	Relaxed
	Ecstatic	Bold	Serene
	Satisfied	Brave	Bright
	Glad	Daring	Blessed
	Cheerful	Challenged	Reassured
	Sunny	Optimistic	
	Merry	Confident	
	Elated jubilant	Hopeful	

LOVE	INTERESTED	STRONG	
Loving	Concerned	Impulsive certain	
Considerate	Affected	rebellious	
Affectionate	Fascinated	Unique	
Sensitive	Intrigued	Free	
Tender	Absorbed	Dynamic	
Devoted	Inquisitive	Tenacious	
Attracted	Nosy	Hardy	
Passionate	Snoopy	Secure	
Admiration	Engrossed		
Touched	Curious		
Sympathy			
Close			
Comforted			
Drawn toward			

DIFFICULT/UNPLEASANT FEELINGS

MAD	AFRAID	HURT	SAD
Livid	Falling	Crushed	Tearful
Angry	Loud noise	Tormented	Depressed
Frustrated	Anxious	Deprived	Suicidal
Pissed off	Tense	Pained	Forsaken
Rage	Hopeless	Tortured	Sullen
Furious	Afraid	Dejected	Weepy
Upset	Lost	Rejected	Empty
Vengeful	Scared	Injured	Loss
Annoyed	Helpless	Offended	Sorrow
Mean	Alone	Afflicted	Hopeless
Hateful	Dark	Aching	Grief
Irritated	Vulnerable	Victimized	Guilty
Wronged	Shaken	Heartbroken	Blamed
Bothered	Uneasy	Agonized	Shame
Agitated	Worried	Appalled	Regretful
Volatile	Confused	Humiliated	Blue
Homicidal	Caution	Wronged	Isolated
Ill	Phobic	Alienated	Lonely
Resentment	Unsafe		Gloomy
Hostile	Paranoid		Inferior
Insulting	Alone		Inadequate
Sore	Dark		Unwanted
Annoyed	Petrified		Unsatisfied
Upset	Terrified		Tearful
Unpleasant	Suspicious		Pained
Offensive	Alarmed		Anguish
Bitter	Frightened		Desolate
Inflamed	Timid		Desperate
Provoked	Shaky		Pessimistic
Incensed	Restless		Unhappy
Infuriated	Doubtful		Lonely
Cross	Cowardly		Mournful
Boiling	Quaking		Dismayed
Fuming	Menaced		

INDIFFERENT	DEPRESSED	CONFUSED	HELPLESS
Insensitive	Lousy	Upset	Incapable
Dull	Disappointed	Doubtful	Alone
Nonchalant	Discouraged	Uncertain	Paralyzed
Neutral	Ashamed	Indecisive	Fatigued
Reserved	Powerless	Perplexed	Unless
Weary	Diminished	Embarrassed	Inferior
Bored	Guilty	Hesitant	Vulnerable

Preoccupied	Dissatisfied	Shy	Empty
Cold	Miserable	Stupefied	Forced
Disinterested	Detestable	Unbelieving	Hesitant
Lifeless	Repugnant	Skeptical	Despair
	Despicable	Distrustful.	Frustrated
	Disgusting	Misgiving	Distressed
	Abominable	Lost	Woeful
	Terrible	Unsure	Pathetic
	In despair	Uneasy	Tragic
	Sulky	Pessimistic	In a stew
	Bad	Tense	Dominated

There may be other feelings you experience which aren't listed above. When you're feeling an emotion that's not listed, take a moment to tune into yourself, and spend time considering each primary emotion and whether or not you are feeling any of them. We often feel more than one feeling at a time and it can get quite complicated trying to sort it all out. Focusing on the primary emotions helps to simplify the process and to go deeper.

POSITIVE EFFECTIVE PARENTING
P.E.P.

CHAPTER ELEVEN
Children of Divorce

CHAPTER ELEVEN

Parenting children of divorce

PARENTING CHILDREN OF DIVORCE

Generally parents who are getting a divorce are concerned with the effect it will have on their children. Divorce brings with it special challenges. Both mother and father face the challenge of parenting outside the typical family framework. It is important for each parent to keep in mind that, although the spousal role is being severed, the parental role remains in tact. Of course the way each parent "parents" does change. Often the non-custodial parent will feel constrained by a new unrehearsed setting within which they carry on their parenting role. Developing a strong healthy relationship between the "visiting" parent and children plays a crucial role in maintaining the child's positive self-esteem.

While parents may feel angry and confused by the divorce, children are frightened by the threat to their security. Divorce may be misinterpreted by the children. They may feel that they are to blame for the breakup of the family. Often they interpret the parent's leaving as a sign of punishment or that they are not loved anymore. Positive visitation and honest communication can help alleviate many of these fears. Visitation helps to maintain a sense of family life and reassures the child of both parents' love

However, if not handled appropriately, visitation can take a heavy toll on children and parents alike. In many cases, the parents now have two different sets of expectations. They have different ways of running their households. Children can get confused, not having the maturity to express themselves with words, and begin to act out and displace their feelings. Often when children return from their visitation with the other parent they are rowdy, cranky, whining or even aggressive. Parents can help reduce this by listening to the children without judging, by providing positive suggestions to correct inappropriate behavior and by following the visitation dos and don'ts included here.

While it is true that both parents can experience feelings of anxiety at the time, the visiting parent may feel especially jarred. Fearing rejection by the child, they may respond in extremes by staying away or by giving too much materially. It is easy for both the child and the custodial parent to misinterpret these responses. Open communication between all parties is necessary to alleviate misunderstandings.

In successful visiting relationships each parent provides for the children in a primary way and satisfies the desire to protect the parent-child relationship outside the marriage. This effort may be compromised if parents fail to recognize that every member of the family experiences intense emotional feelings during a divorce. During this transition, both parents must be prepared to respond not only to their children's increased need for attention but to their own emotional needs as well. The special needs of everyone involved should be given equal consideration.

Parents' ongoing commitment to the child's well-being is vital. Children need to know that their mother and father will continue to be their parent even though they won't be living together. One of the best ways to support children involved in a separation or divorce is to assure the child frequent, meaningful and continuing contact with both parents and the extended family the child normally saw before. If both parents put the kids' interests first, they will be in the best possible position to ensure that visitation arrangements make sense and serve the children well as they grow to adulthood.

What are some things you do to help alleviate fear and confusion in your children at this time?

_____
_____
_____
_____

How have you been successful in providing for the children that satisfied the desire to protect the parent-child relationship?

_____
_____
_____
_____

SEVEN IMPORTANT THINGS TO FOLLOW FOR THE FAMILY OF DIVORCE

1. Minimize conflict.
2. Identify your needs and concerns.
3. Identify your child's needs and concerns.
4. Compile the components of your agreement using worksheets and checklists.
5. Use strategies that will help you negotiate effectively.
6. Make decisions in the best interest of your children.
7. Take advantage of practical solutions to the 40 most common issues parents face, including: medical, dental, vision and psychiatric care.

TEN TIPS FOR THE FAMILY OF DIVORCE

1. Answer any questions simply and directly, it is not necessary to give them more information then requested. If they ask embarrassing or inappropriate questions let them know and refuse to answer.
2. Let them know you both will always be their parents and you will always love them. Don't be long distance parents, physically or emotionally. If you must live in another town stay

in touch with frequent letters and telephone calls. You may also use the computer. Make sure your child has your address and telephone number so they will always have easy access to you.

3. Show your love in actions, not just words. Don't make promises you cannot keep. Promises not kept are worse then not making plans at all. Don't attempt to substitute your love with money or gifts. Kids know when they are being bought off.

4. Remember birthdays, holidays and all other important events. These times are important to children and indicate to them that you are there and that you care. It may be difficult to remember these dates in your busy life so use a calendar and mark them down.

5. Do not badmouth your spouse or anyone else in your family. Hold children to this rule as well. Children will not love you more if you attempt too make your spouse the bad guy in their eyes. This only makes it difficult for them and at some point, they will more than likely resent you for your attacks. Children need to feel it is okay to love both parents without making anyone unhappy.

6. When you are angry at one another do not take it out on the children. For example, "You are just like your father . . . your mother . . ."

7. Don't compete for your children's love and time. They need and want to have a healthy relationship with both of their parents. The more you work for this, the better adjusted they will be.

8. Do not put your children in the middle. Do not make your children the mediators for you and your spouse. Put your feelings aside for the sake of your children and handle, in an adult fashion, all practical matters that must be decided directly with your spouse.

9. Expect that your children may have sad, angry, depressed feelings following the divorce and allow them to tell these feelings to you without criticism. Just be able to talk about what they are feeling will go a long way in helping your child adjust to the changes in his/her life.

10. Accept that your marriage is over and proceed with your own life. Don't try to obtain information about your ex-spouse's private life through your children. The best thing you can do for yourself and your children is to move ahead with your life and find happiness in a new relationship.

P.S. Don't forget to take some time for yourself to rest and heal during this stressful period in your life. Also patience will go a long way.

Just remember that if what you are doing is not serving you as well and you wish it would, just do something different.

SHARED PARENTING AFTER DIVORCE

After observing women's rights and responsibilities for more than a quarter century of feminist activism, Karen Crow says that, "Shared parenting is the best option for women."

Shared parenting is an egalitarian approach which allows each fit parent substantial time with the child. Because both parents remain involved, the children do not lose their relationship with either parent. This eliminates many "single parent" issues. Shared parenting makes sense now because the old model of a "stay-at-home mom" has been replaced by the reality that most kids have two parents who work, both before and after divorce.

SHARED PARENTING AFTER DIVORCE BENEFITS MOTHERS

By dividing the parental time commitment, shared parenting gives Mom time off to pursue her education, work late to advance in her career or to enjoy some leisure. Moms with shared parenting are less stressed, and therefore better parents and workers.

Shared parenting is the best solution for children after divorce. Kids enjoy continued love and interaction with both parents and the extended families of both parents, lessening the emotional trauma of divorce. Kids in shared parenting spend more time with a parent and less time with a paid baby-sitter. Kids in shared parenting arrangements have egalitarian (equal) role models. Kids also benefit from geographic stability because the divorced parents do not move away. The children are more likely to remain in one school and to maintain their circle of friends. When neither parent is lost to a child, relationships with stepparents are enhanced. The stepparent is not expected to take the place of a parent.

Presumptive shared parenting laws, the basis for such laws is simple, divorcing parents may agree to any schedule of physical time with the children. However, if the parents do not agree and if both are fit the court will order 50-50 placement.

Can divorcing parents really work out shared parenting agreements? Yes, with education in co-parenting and access to mediation services.

SPARE THE CUSTODY FIGHT & SAVE THE CHILDREN

by Mimi E. Lyster

This article originally appeared in the Summer 1995 issue of Nolo News. Mimi E. Lyster is a mediator and the author of "Child Custody: Building Agreements That Work," new from Nolo Press.

Every year, a million children see their parents divorce. And often, the most pressing concern of those two million parents is: "Who gets the kids?"

Angry, hurt and overwhelmed with both the divorce or separation process and their own feelings, parents may try to gain the upper hand by demanding full custody of the children. Their anxiety is fueled by well-meaning but disastrous partisanship of friends and relatives, who frequently urge them to fight for the kids in court. Before long, the family has slipped into a long, expensive and emotionally draining journey through the world of child custody litigation, the result of which is likely to please no one.

WHY TO AVOID COURT

It's true that courts are responsible for preserving and protecting children's "best interests" when their parents divorce. All but a few states have laws that spell out what factors a court should consider when determining what best interests are. So why not let an impartial judge resolve your sticky custody and visitation disagreements?

The answer to this is simply because laws set standards for children in general not your children in particular. A judge or court-appointed evaluator must try to understand the family's situation and each parent's position within a few minutes or hours and then to make wise decisions with the children's best interests in mind.

Although state laws set guidelines for custody decisions, judges have considerable discretion in interpreting them and imposing their own views of what constitutes a good environment for children. The chance that a judge's decision will be ideal for your specific situation is slim.

With rare exceptions, you can do a whole lot better crafting your own decisions, which fit your unique situation, rather than hiring lawyers and turning the ultimate decisions over to a judge. You and the other parent can negotiate a parenting plan with the other parent that reflects the needs and best interests of their children and assures them the maximum possible contact with both parents.

Only if the children's safety or well-being is at risk and their parents cannot agree on a way to reduce that risk can court intervention be crucial.

What would your parenting plan look like?

_____

_____

_____

_____

MAKING A BAD SITUATION WORSE

Even if your separation or divorce will be better for your children in the long run, for the short term, most children feel that things couldn't be worse. Divorce can shake a child's confidence that he or she will continue to be loved, cared for and safe, even when the child understands the reasons behind the decision.

A custody battle only makes things harder. Most researchers who study the effects of divorce on children believe passionately that using the court to resolve custody issues is a mistake in all but a few cases. It is far better, in their opinion, for parents to negotiate their own parenting agreement, with help from mediators, counselors and lawyers as needed.

No matter how much you may believe that your life would improve if you won and the other parent lost a custody battle, the fact remains that children need both their parents. That means that part of being a good parent after separation or divorce is finding a way to work with the other parent, at least as far as the children are concerned, rather than fighting over custody in court.

NEGOTIATE? YOU MUST BE KIDDING

Not surprisingly, most divorcing parents panic at the prospect of working together. Fortunately, even couples with a painful bitter past or ones going through an intensely acrimonious divorce, can devise a successful custody and visitation agreement that favors the best interests of the children. Even if the other parent is inflexible or both parents want something mutually exclusive, for example sole custody of the children, the process is not doomed. If parents can describe their concerns, goals and perceptions of the situation in some detail, they will at least have a good list of issues to address and resolve. And there's plenty of help available.

To improve your ability to work with the other parent, you may want to improve your negotiation skills, try to find ways to set aside your feelings regarding the separation or divorce, and get some outside help from a mediator or counselor. The real key to success is to focus on your children, not a potential outcome in court. Think about your children's needs and wishes, your goals for them and concerns you have about their health, education and their relationships with parents, siblings or other important people.

If both you and the other parent put your kids' interests first, you will probably find that you can adjust your positions enough to produce a good agreement. Both of you will be in the best possible position to ensure that your custody and visitation arrangements make sense and serve your children well as they grow to adulthood, and work for you as well.

Name some things you can do to improve your negotiation skills?

_____
_____
_____
_____

What can you do to devise a successful custody and visitation agreement?

_____
_____
_____
_____

WHAT I WISH MY PARENTS KNEW

Have you ever wished you could get inside the mind of your child? Have you had problems with communication and yearned to understand his or her thinking? Youth across the country desire to have their opinions known. Yet, out of fear, embarrassment or lack of opportunity, their thoughts go unheard. Here, youth take the spotlight, speaking openly and honestly about the concerns of today's children.

WHAT WOULD YOU LIKE THE PARENT YOU LIVE WITH TO KNOW?

"Most of all, I hope my Dad knows how much I appreciate him. I know raising kids on your own is not easy. I don't say as often as I could how much I love him but he means the world to me, as a role model, dad and buddy."
-David, Age 17

"Sometimes I feel guilty for visiting my Dad. I come home and my Mom wants to know everything. If he buys me something, she will say 'Oh like that makes up for him not being there for 4 years."

I know they had their problems and don't get along but I don't think that should mean that I can't like my Dad."
-Jennifer, Age 13

"Ever since my Dad left my Mom has a lot less time. When the weekend comes, she makes a big production out of making sure we go somewhere and do something special. We go to an amusement park or shopping. At first it was fun but now I would rather just have 20 minutes a day where we could just hang out and talk."
-Todd, Age 15

"My Mom will cry and it makes me sad."
-Elsa, Age 4

"I don't like it when they fight about money. I hear them on the phone and it makes me feel like I just want to get away."
-Tony, Age 10

"She needs to get a life. She always wants to talk to me, go out for dinner, do shopping together and talk to my friends. It is like I'm my Dad. I was going to send in one of those personal letters like in Sleepless in Seattle! She needs to go out and meet people because what happens when I move out? I don't plan on living here forever."
-Sam, Age 16

"I don't think she realizes that she uses the divorce as an excuse for everything. I will ask if we can go to the zoo and she will say 'We don't have money, we could have if your dad hadn't left." Somebody will ask her to do something and she will say "I can't I am going through a divorce." I don't use it as an excuse, why should she?"
-Jane, Age 12

"My Mom always wants to talk to me about the divorce and how it makes me feel. I don't want to talk about it, maybe later when I'm ready."
-Frederick, Age 8

"That it is hard on me. I need time to understand it. I have a lot of questions and I am going to need a lot of answers."
-Samantha, Age 11

"She is a good Mom, she does a good job. I wish she would do a little more for herself instead of always focusing on us. I told her that once and she just laughed. I guess she didn't think I was serious."
-Rick, Age 13

"I want my Dad to know I am here for him. He tries to be so strong but I know this hurts him, I can see it. I want him to know he can talk to me."
-Jose, Age 15

"He doesn't have to be SUPER DAD. He goes to work and then comes home, does laundry, cooks—he wants to do everything. I try to help and he'll say "Oh no, I can get that." I wish he knew it is okay to ask for help, I mean, we are a family."
-Cynthia, Age 10

WHAT WOULD YOU LIKE THE PARENT YOU DON'T LIVE WITH TO KNOW?

"When I visit my Dad he has his friends over and stuff. I think that time should be just for me. There is so much I need to tell him and I don't get the chance."
-Charles, Age 14

"I miss her. I wish she would want to see me."
-Julia, Age 7

"We will stay close throughout this. A divorce can't separate us. He will always be as important to me as he was when he lived at home. Nothing anyone can say will ever change that."
-Kent, Age 17

"I know he tried everything he could to make the marriage work. I respect him and I miss him so much."
—Danielle, Age 12

"My Dad seems to think since he lives across the country he doesn't need to visit us regularly. It's not right, we are still his kids. If he wanted to move that far away then he should have the money to fly us there. If you ask me he is running away from it all. But then he will call once a month and want to be all love and I'm like "Who is this?""
-Rose, Age 16

"On the weekends I spend with my Mom she always buys me a ton of stuff. Those things aren't important to me, only she is."
-Jeanette, Age 14

"I wish he knew that I want to spend time with him too. When we visit, he spends all his time with my brother and that is not fair. They always got along better than we did when we all lived together but I still need him to."
-Karen, Age 15

"Our visiting time should be spent visiting, not talking about Mom."
-Troy, Age 11

"I love him."
-Elsa, Age 4

CHILDREN AND DIVORCE

Josh, age 10, is behaving in ways he never did before. He appears angry, deliberately disobeys and refuses to listen. He can't fall asleep at night, and when he finally does, he is often awakened by frightening nightmares. Most of his afternoons are spent sitting alone in his room repetitively playing with his computer. His teacher has complained that he is not turning in his homework and that he is withdrawn and isolates himself from his classmates. His mother is worried about him and upset over his behavior, but is not sure how to help. Her situation with Josh is not atypical. In fact it is a situation experienced each year by parents of over one million children in this country. The explanation for Josh's behavior lies in the fact that his parents have recently separated and are getting divorced.

Divorce is now an experienced fact of life for almost one out of every two children in the United States. Research shows that few children survive their parents' divorce without exhibiting some sort of symptom. The symptoms range all the way from difficulty in school and trouble with peers, to depression and running away from home. With some children, the emotional scars from parental divorce can last a lifetime and unresolved issues can affect their adult relationships.

So what can divorced or separated parents do to help their children get through this life transition more easily? How can parents help a child sort out his or her complex feelings surrounding the divorce?

Experts say the key to helping a child weather a divorce is to understand what the child feels and needs during this time. Just being able to know, from the child's viewpoint, how divorce feels, can be a big step in helping the child manage. According to D.M. Young, a psychotherapist who specializes in working with children of divorce, there are common reactions that most children experience when their parents separate or divorce. These reactions include: sadness, disappointment in parents, shame, fear that parents will stop loving them, anger, self blame and guilt.

Unfortunately, most children aren't aware of the depth of their feelings and don't know how to talk about them. Often parents are not aware of the extent of their children's emotional turmoil; they only see hostile behavior or the tendency to isolate themselves. Therapists agree that, once the children are told of the divorce decision, it is important that parents be alert and sensitive to symptoms indicating underlying feelings. For example: if your child suddenly seems to withdraw from other children, is overly self-critical and appears to be furious with you a lot of the time, he could really be feeling shame over the divorce, confusion over why it occurred and fear that he will be abandoned.

Too often the participants of the breakup of their family have nowhere to turn for help with these feelings. While parents may mean well they are often so immersed in their own pain or anger that they are of limited aid to their children. In addition, because of the tendency in children of divorce to keep "secret" their family's situation and their pain, many children do not have the resource of friends to express and resolve the issues they face. So these children are left to fend for themselves in terms of their emotional pain and confusion.

Talking about the divorce, especially with people who are understanding and sensitive, may be the most beneficial way of dealing with feelings associated with it. Additionally, parents' willingness to share that they are sad too, and that they understand and encourage their child's expression of feelings, gives the child the sense that angry and sad and afraid feelings are okay and nothing to be ashamed of. Expression of these feelings helps the child to resolve them, and move on to feeling better.

What do you do to help your children get through this life transition more easily?

_____

_____

_____

_____

Divorce can be a difficult time for children (as well as for adults)! It is important that parents be aware of the stresses on their children at this time, and take steps to help them cope. Time does heal, but the healing is more complete, and the scars not as long-lasting, when the wounds are recognized and dealt with as they are occurring.

Summary

"Positive Effective Parenting's" primary purpose is to inspire positive changes in children's attitudes and behaviors, decrease conflicts, stimulate communication and cooperation, raise self-esteem and enhance what is already working, establish and maintain respect by changing the quality of adult-child relationships through specialized training geared to all who are responsible for the care and well-being of children

All families face problems. It is how we deal with these problems that make a healthy or unhealthy family. We need to look for all the good within our family dynamics. With a little work you can put some PEP in your family experience with "Positive Effecting Parenting."

Perfection is not the goal. The goal is to gain understanding, compassion and wisdom that will help you enjoy your child, yourself and parenting. It is time to act now. So what can YOU do? First of all, make raising your children to become self regulating adults, raise their self-esteem as well as your own, a priority in your life. Most people do what they do because that is all they know and they are eager to learn other principles that work better. Once you see that doing something new and different works, you will do it more often. It begins to feel good and its fun. So take a risk now. Make a change. Good luck to you all on your new journey

Quotes, Mottos & Poetry

1. Good judgment comes from experience and experience comes from poor judgment.
2. No matter how messy things are, you can always clean them up.
3. I am FINE: Freaked out, Insecure, Neurotic, Emotional.
4. Between great and nothing I would take great.
5. Behavior is learned and can always be redirected.
6. Children are like wet cement. What ever falls on them sticks.
7. The best anger style is Assertive.
8. Use only fair fighting.
9. The best thing to spend on your children is your time.
10. You instill fear, you earn respect.
11. Anger is the only thing you can't get rid of by losing it.
12. It is a wise parent who knows their own child.
13. Love all, Trust a few, Do wrong to none.
14. Always kiss your children goodnight even if they're already asleep.
15. An angry man opens his mouth and shuts his eyes.
16. Let anger not lead your thoughts.
17. An angering one does not have clear thoughts.
18. Let today and tomorrow be where you are going.
19. Free yourself and others from anger.
20. FEAR . . . False, Evidence, Appearing, Real

You Can Love Me, But Only I . . .

You can love me but only I can make me happy
You can teach me, but only I can do the learning
You can lead me, but only I can walk the path
You can coach me, but only I can win the game
You can even pity me, but only I can bear the sorrow
For the Gift of Love is not a food that feeds me
It is the sunshine that nourishes that which I must finally harvest for myself.
So, if you love me, don't just sing me your song . . .

Teach me to sing, for when I am alone, I will need the melody

Only as high as I reach can I grow, only as far as I seek can I go, only as deep as I can look can I see, only as much as I dream can I be.

You remember the things you want to remember.

"Be like a postage stamp. Stick to one thing until you get there."—Josh Billings

"Arriving at one goal is the starting point to another."—John Dewey

"There is no such thing as a self-made man. You will reach your goals only with the help of others,"—George Shinn

"The indispensable first step to getting the things you want out of life is this: decide what you want."—Ben Stein

"If you don't know where you are going, how can you expect to get there?"—Basil S. Walsh

"People with goals succeed because they know where they're going."—Earl Nightingale

"The most important thing about goals is having one."—Geoffrey F. Albert

"The world has the habit of making room for the man whose words and actions show that he knows where he is going."—Napoleon Hill

"There is no achievement without goals."—Robert J. McKain

"The tragedy in life doesn't lie in not reaching your goal. The tragedy lies in having no goal to reach."—Benjamin Mays

Anger creates anger
Love creates love
Respect creates respect

Suggested Reading

"Redirecting Children's Behavior"
    Kathryn J Kvols

"Please Understand Me II"
    David Keirsey

"Anger Work Out Book"
    Dr. Weisinger

"Raising Kids O.K."
    Dorothy E Babcock, R.N., M.S.
    Terry D. Keepers, Ph.D.

"Children"
    John W. Santrock

"P.E.T. Parent Effectiveness Training"
    Dr. Thomas Gordon

"How to Parent"
    Fitzhugh Dobson

"Positive Discipline"
    Jane Nelsen, Lynn Lott, & Stephen Glen